KT-368-784

The Spotted Deer

BY

J. H. WILLIAMS

AUTHOR OF

ELEPHANT BILL

ILLUSTRATED BY
STUART TRESILIAN

RUPERT HART-DAVIS
SOHO SQUARE LONDON
1957

Printed in Great Britain by Richard Clay and Company Ltd.,
Bungay, Suffolk

FOREWORD

THE trust that can be built up between man and the other animals is something of which I have written before—how delicate it is, how quickly an animal will detect in a human being the failure of confidence, the smell of fear. In the animal world, man loses his domination only when he loses his conviction that he is the dominant.

There are many animals in this book, but it is more concerned with the relationship of human beings to one another, the question of mutual trust.

I am trustful by nature. But if I were not so, I should have become trustful by conviction. If you trust a man, you can never be certain that he will not deceive you; but if you don't trust him, you give him every excuse to deceive you at the earliest chance. If you trust, you may live in a fool's paradise. If you don't trust, you live in a hell which you have created for yourself. You are far more likely to provoke an attack by being prepared for it than if you are unready and unsuspicious. Forewarned, forearmed, the saying is; but how frequently its corollary is Forearmed, forlorn. It is the man, terrified of being stabbed in the back, who is punched in the face.

CHAPTER I

DURING the Burmese rebellion it was impossible for any of us to retain that spirit of mutual confidence which is the basis of civilised life. Suspicion crept in and poisoned human relationships. The old pattern of life had been simple enough. The European population had been divided up between Government and Trade, rather suspicious of one another, even in quiet times. The Burmese population with which we as forest men were concerned consisted of our own people, the elephant oozies and their camp-followers; of jungle villagers such as fire-watchers, fellers, rice traders and bazaar vendors; of elephant contractors, who might equally well be Indian, Karen or Siamese as Burman; and dacoits —men who, for one reason or another, had put themselves beyond the law and who existed by robbery and, on occasion, murder.

The 'rebellion' did not entirely change this old pattern, but it mixed with it the struggle for Burmese national independence—

something not very fully thought out, a hazy vision of future glory combining the past grandeur of the Burmese kings with all the advantages which had accrued from union with India under British rule. Exactly what Burmese nationalism wanted was not very certain; but it existed, dangerous, sporadic, a mixture of idealism and roguery, a force capable of suppressing the feelings of common humanity in the interest of those 'greater ideals', which appear so brilliant from a distance but vanish like a mirage when you approach.

The distinction between a dacoit and a patriot was difficult to make. Not all dacoits were nationalists, nor all nationalists dacoits; but there was a hard core who found the struggle for independence gave a cloak of respectability to practices of which their fellow Burmans had disapproved.

Most of our oozies continued loyal throughout the troubles, but even then you could never be certain whether the oozie merely remained with his elephant after it had been commandeered by rebels, or if he took it over to the rebels of his own accord.

The bad feelings between Government and Trade were exacerbated by the rebellion. "Of course," said the Government people, "this would never have happened if those wretched timber people hadn't come in to exploit the teak forests. They've taken millions out of the country."

Our reply was that the teak-extraction companies had been operating under a Royal Charter granted by the King of Burma in 1862, twenty-five years before the British had annexed Upper Burma. During the time of our operation we had built up excellent relations with the Burmese peasants, with whom we worked in far closer contact than did Government officials. We had seen the rebellion coming, but our reports had been treated as alarmist by most Government officials. When we warned them that the Burmans were opposed to Government but not to Trade, they laughed at us. After all, Government officials devoted their lives to the good of the Burmans; the teak wallahs were in Burma for money, capitalist exploiters (who incidentally were just taking a whacking because of the slump in teak following the Wall Street crash of 1929).

Of course we put on a gallant united European front in face of the Burmans themselves. There was no public criticism of Government. We knew that we had got to hang together. But that trust between man and man had disappeared and there were plenty of private recriminations. Cooped up in our respective country stations, unable to continue teak extraction while the troubles lasted, getting on one another's nerves as we came to the end of our jokes and our tempers, we blamed the Government for having got us into this mess.

But at last it was over. The up-country stations emptied as the jails filled. My six forest assistants left for tours of their respective districts, while I remained in headquarters to receive their reports.

During the 'rebellion' there had been a black-out of information, and the news that did come through was so coloured with passion that it did not really make much sense to me. 'The rebels', after all, had consisted of numbers of individuals who for different reasons had decided to take up arms against the Government; but they still remained individuals. I could not believe that they had all suddenly become monsters.

It was heartening to read the reports as they came in. They restored my faith. In one district sixteen elephants had been begged, borrowed or stolen during the rebellion. The assistant reported that the last of them had just been returned. Inside the hollow bell suspended from its neck was fixed a document with the official rebel stamp of the 'Galon'.[1]

The assistant said that the document hidden in the elephant's bell was an apology to the Thûthé for any inconvenience caused by the borrowing of the elephants.

[1] The 'Galon' was a mythical bird, a sort of phoenix, who was the emblem of the unconquerable. The Galon in Burmese legend had killed the Naga, or dragon. And the Government had been taken by the rebels as the Naga of the day, the dragon who in taxes and footling permits had robbed the peasants of the money they had earned from the teak traders, or Thûthé. The Galon was tattooed on the wrists of the rebels.

The Burman storekeeper in another district reported that over two hundred baskets of rice had been taken by rebels from the go-downs. Each basket had been accounted for by 'Galon' receipts, and there was a written undertaking that the accounts would be settled, after the Government had been overthrown!

It was good to know that the highly coloured accounts of the Burmans transformed into brutalised thugs with which we had been regaled during the rebellion were the inventions of alarmist officials. The Burmese sense of humour had survived this out-break of nationalism. They were still the delightful people with whom I had worked for the last twelve years.

I was glad to be reassured of this, because I was expecting a new forest assistant out from England—the first it had ever been my responsibility as a forest manager to induct into his job. This in-duction was something which I had dreamed of doing many, many times since I had received my own at the hands of that jungly eccentric, Willie.

Of that shattering introduction to life in the Burmese teak forests I have said all I want to say in *Elephant Bill* and *Bandoola*. It was quite certainly one of the most obvious ways of how not to receive a young recruit. But how should one do it? I was soon to be put to the test.

The ideal thing, I decided, would be for me to make a complete and thorough tour of my whole forest area, taking the young recruit with me, rather than attach him to another assistant. His name, by the way, was Archie—which of course was not his fault, but his parents'. I would not hammer anything into Archie: just en-courage him to ask questions, and answer them as fully as I could. In that way I could teach him the elements of the job without his even realising it. Of course, success or failure would ultimately depend on Archie himself. It wasn't everybody's job, this lonely life in the forests. Of the eight recruits who had joined the Com-pany with me, only one other, besides myself, had stayed on. A seventy-five percent wastage of man-power seemed too high to me.

My dreams of man-management were interrupted by an S.O.S. from Ronnie Andrewes, one of my forest assistants, who had recently returned to his District. It was a long-winded full official report of an emergency which had arisen. Also enclosed was a private note, putting it in a nutshell. It read:

DEAR BILLY,

Sorry to bother you with all the enclosed but I am in trouble. First I have paid out 5,000 rupees in wages in 10 rupee notes having first stamped them all with my personal buffalo receipt stamp No. 1., but like an ass that I am, not counter-stamped them with my elephant issue stamp. I have only one excuse for it. I have had thrust upon me an emergency beyond my coping capacity. Believe it or not a chap with the name of Ferdinand Stipplewether—he is a type from the Frontier Force, only been out a year, and as far as I know never yet seen an elephant, let alone the Frontier—he mistrusts everything. Perhaps with musket and blowpipe he is just the chap to keep the frontier clean, but not here. As you know in the early days of the rebellion, I supplied him a detachment of Military Police here, as a jungle outpost, and my chaps moved them without a hitch.

Now Stipplewether arrives to supervise the withdrawal! A march of sixty-five miles to be done in three stages, with fifteen elephants to transport the stores, mostly ammo; boxes and boxes of it. Up to three nights ago all was well. No trouble about the elephants or the oozies. Then when he heard I wasn't coming with them he got almighty wind up that an elephant might bolt, carrying the precious ammo. Believe it or not he demanded the right to shoot any elephant. I told him to shoot himself, 'cos he was getting no elephants from me. We didn't lose an elephant during the rebellion and now this ass arrives here for some shooting practice. That's how we stand Bill. I've got my elephants here, and over the stream he has his ammo. He won't go away. What's the form—you give permission to shoot, or come out and shoot him yourself.

Yours,

RONNIE.

P.S.—Bring some more whisky. He's drunk all mine but with no success. I believe he thinks all my oozies are all dacoits in disguise and will go charging off with the ammo.

Ronnie Andrewes was always in some sort of trouble. He had a genius for making things go wrong which might have made his fortune if he had been a clown. The offence which he had committed was one of his own invention. It was Ronnie who had thought up the scheme for stamping each note with a buffalo receipt stamp and then counter-stamping it on issue with an elephant issue stamp. Unless the note had the two stamps, it was to be assumed as stolen; and to encourage traders to report these thefts, I had promised to double the value of all such notes which traders could produce.

By forgetting to counter-stamp, Ronnie had sabotaged his own anti-dacoity scheme and presented a sum to the traders equal to that which he had paid out. Meanwhile it seemed he was far too busy having a private quarrel with Ferdinand Stipplewether to do any useful work. There was nothing for it but to visit Ronnie. With communications so disrupted, I decided that it would be as quick to go via Rangoon. On arrival there I called on the Chief Secretary. The Chief Secretary smiled as I explained the situation. "Of course young Stipplewether has his qualities—very definite qualities," he said. "On the other hand, one has to recognise that the elephants could transport the ammunition without Stipplewether, whereas Stipplewether could not transport the ammunition without the elephants."

"I think the sooner he returns to the frontier, the sooner the forests will return to normal," I said.

"You mean some work more suited to Stipplewether's undoubted talents? Exactly what occurred to me. Perhaps you would take the letter, an immediate transfer. I'll give you a copy for your records."

If all Government officials in Burma had had the humanity and tolerance of that Chief Secretary, there would probably have been no rebellion, and certainly little cause for irritation on the part of Trade.

It was very different when I reached Ronnie Andrewes' head-quarters.

The two young men had not spoken to one another for days. That did not mean that the quarrel had lapsed. It was conducted even more vigorously in silence than it had been in speech. It had descended now to the deeper cat-and-dog levels.

They were both ready, and indeed eager, to speak to me; nor did they object to sharing the whisky which came out of my bottles. But neither would go beyond that.

I tried to thaw Stipplewether out by using his Christian name. But it was not a success. Ferdinand sounded pompous, and Ferdy absurd.

At last I said, "What is all this nonsense?"

Immediately both of them started to talk at once, repeating the arguments which they had had together *ad nauseam*.

"I think your objection to Ferdinand shooting your elephants is absurd, Ronnie," I said.

"Why?" they both asked.

"Because it's quite obvious he wouldn't hit one."

Ronnie thought this was funny, and it put him in a good humour. I had not thought it possible for Ferdy to be more supercilious than he already was. But he bristled with hauteur.

"Do you really expect that the Secretariat is going to support you in this idiocy?" I asked.

"I trust they have every confidence in me," he answered.

"I can't see any reason why they should." I handed him my carbon copy of the Chief Secretary's letter. Then I poured Ronnie and myself another whisky.

"I don't think this is a very funny joke," said Ferdinand Stipple-wether. "If this were genuine, I would surely have received the original."

I handed him the original, sealed and stamped.

"I expect you'd like to do your packing to-night," I said. "I'll bring those Military Police in myself."

I felt that I could understand that blind fury which had goaded

13

the Burmese peasants to revolt against the meddlesome interference of the Ferdinand Stipplewethers of this world. They could
not appeal, as I had done, to the wisdom of the Chief Secretary.
There were only two ways of dealing with people like Ferdy: the
rocket from above or the bullet from below.

CHAPTER II

I HAD always visualised myself welcoming a young recruit at my
forest headquarters; replaying, in fact, my own introduction as it
should have been, with myself in the rôle of Willie. But when I
returned to Rangoon, I found that Archie had arrived on the
Warwickshire, and had already made himself conspicuous by the
two enormous Great Danes he had brought with him.

Before I met him, I was invited to dine with my General
Manager, a bachelor who was known by everyone as P. N. C., the
use of his initials somehow combining affection and respect in
whatever proportions one wanted.

With me the proportions were equal. I was much younger than
he was and I respected the years of experience he had earned in
the forests before he took his position in Plush Chair Number One
at the Rangoon office. He knew what he was talking about, and I
owed him respect and gratitude for the way he had steered me
through and out of many escapades in my younger days.

He always got the best out of me, because he trusted me. During

15

the rebellion he had thrown a great responsibility on my shoulders. What had made it easier to bear was that he had never tried to bear it for me. He was not the man to interfere.

This was the first time I had seen him since the rebellion, and during dinner we talked about what had happened. There were just the two of us. P. N. C. never dealt exhaustively with a subject. It was as if he pulled back a series of curtains and one saw one view after another and then passed on. He said something—I have forgotten what it was—about the way I had acted during the rebellion. It was very gratifying to know that P. N. C. thought I had acted in that way, even though I hadn't. It was an admirable way to behave; and even if I hadn't done so in the past, there was no reason why I should not try to do so in the future. And perhaps that was what P. N. C. had intended all the time— not to praise me for anything I had done, but to suggest what I might do.

I told him what had happened with Ronnie Andrewes and Ferdinand Stipplewether, and he laughed. Then he said, "It was a very good thing you didn't let him go with the elephants. Something would have gone wrong, if he felt like that."

But he was not interested in the rebellion or in Ferdinand Stipplewether. P. N. C. was one of the most thrifty men with his time that I have ever met. He did not spend it on the past, when there was so much to concern him in the present and future.

After dinner we sat on the large open veranda and he said, "Bill, I know you're not due for home leave till the middle of next year; but you ought to have a change. It's been a strain—probably bigger than you realise. You ought to get away from Burma for a while. Australia's too far. But what about Ceylon? A short sea-trip each way, a week in the hills, talking tea instead of teak. How d'you feel?"

"I don't feel like that at all, P. N. C.," I said. "Here have I been cooped up for a year. The change I need is to get back on the job. I'm perfectly fit, and the further I keep from the fleshpots, the more I can save for the home leave."

16

He looked at me quizzically. "Perhaps there's more to it than that?"

"There's this young fellow Archie," I said. "I'd like to initiate him in the way he should go. Make a tour of the whole forest with him and avoid his getting a wrong impression of the rebellion."

He nodded approval. "The best fertiliser, a farmer's boots on his own land. A lot to be said for that."

We sat smoking for a time. I knew P. N. C. hadn't finished with me. He would waste no time when he had. "There is something else," he said. "Not a vacation work. Take you out of Burma for about three months. Might appeal to you. Certainly you've been the person we thought of right from the beginning."

I said nothing. We seemed to be coming to the reason why I had been given such a good dinner.

"It's been on the *tapis* quite a time," P. N. C. said, "only of course one doesn't shout these things from the house-tops. And then the rebellion put the kibosh on everything."

This was certainly the true reason for our meeting. P. N. C. was naturally rather formal in his speech. But I had noticed before that he spoke colloquially whenever he thought something was important.

"One of the reasons why we've slumped in teak," he said, "is because the Yankees in the Philippines are rapidly developing the methods of extracting hardwoods."

"You mean I might do a trip to the Philippines to study high-line skidding?"

"No, no. Nothing like that," said P. N. C. "What we would want is a report on the unexplored forests of the North Andaman Islands: what's there and whether we could open them up as a normal elephant extraction project. We'd hardly choose you if we were thinking of a purely mechanised operation, would we, Bill?"

I was glad. Though I should have liked to visit the Philippines and study American logging methods, I knew in my heart of hearts that it was animal management, and not timber extraction, which was my true love.

"Of course, the snag is labour," P. N. C. said. "There just isn't any local native labour, as far as anyone knows. And even if there were, there's apparently nothing they're good at, except cannibalism."

"But there are quite a lot of convicts down in the South Andamans," I said.

"That's true," said P. N. C., as though the thought had only just occurred to him. "But, then, you wouldn't want to work with convicts on parole. Of course there would be a great many Burmans among them. There wouldn't be any difficulty about the lingo. But after the rebellion, to tumble into this. . . . I mean, when we were talking about a holiday away from it all. . . . I mean, it's out of the frying-pan, isn't it?"

"If only I can have them away from any Ferdinand Stipplewethers," I said—"just the plain dacoits and murderers and opium addicts—I don't mind. But not, please, any government officials. That would be the end."

"I think that might be—er—wangled," P. N. C. said. "Of course the whole thing is very much under your hat at the moment. Not a word to anyone. And you'll want to do that tour of your forest first. With this new recruit, Archie." He gave me a smile, which began very delightfully but ended with a surprise remark as he helped me to a drink. "I've asked Mac to drop in for a drink on his way to the Gymkhana Club."

Mac was the Chief Engineer of Bombine, a hell of a good chap when confined to the sawmills or a bar, but with the usual engineer's ambition to extend his domain to the forest itself. He couldn't see an elephant without thinking how much better it would be if fitted with an internal-combustion engine instead of a heart.

"Is he on this?" I asked.

"Don't you worry, Bill," P. N. C. said soothingly. "If it comes off, you'll be in charge"—he leant forward—"and I warn you that if you report favourably and convince the Board, you may very well spend the rest of your working life in the Andaman Islands."

"It'll be nice to see Mac again," I said. I liked Mac as a man. He had a dare-devil quality I admired. It was only as an engineer I distrusted him.

He arrived at that very moment under the porch in a powerful sports car. He revved up the engine to an ear-splitting roar before he cut off. Then he strode over, a giant of six foot four. "Well, P. N. C., how's things? When are you off, Bill?"

"Off where?"

"The Andamans. I heard they'd given you three months."

"P. N. C.'s only just mentioned it."

"That's because he doesn't know any more than that." Mac poured himself a four-finger peg of whisky from the decanter.

"And what do you know that he doesn't?" I asked.

"You'll have to learn a different timber lingo, Bill," he said. "Before you leave the Andamans, you'll be talking in millions of board feet, instead of round tons."

It was all very jolly, but there was a serious undercurrent. Mac was as good as saying, "It may be all right for an elephant wallah to make the report; but if we decide to open up the Andamans, the big job, the boss job, should go to an engineer."

"That'll work itself out, you two," P. N. C. said. "The point is, Mac, do you want to send an engineer with Bill?"

"You bet I do," Mac said. "Bill will have quite enough on his plate without his bothering with our stuff. I think I might be able to spare Jeff."

I couldn't have chosen a better colleague. Mac was perfectly right. I was an Elephant Forester; I knew about elephant management, about timber extraction using elephants and the general business of getting the logs launched to float down-river to the sawmills. Jeff was a brilliant Forest Engineer, more specialised than Mac, but, within his speciality, the best man in Bombine.

Our Mac finished off his whisky and announced that he was going down to the Gymkhana Club to review the 'fishing fleet' that had come in on the *Warwickshire*. 'Fishing fleet' was an irreverent term used to describe the young ladies who came annually to

Rangoon from home as spinsters and in many cases remained there as matrons. "It's dance night," Mac said. "I can give you a lift, Bill. But it must be now, as I've got a date."

I looked at P. N. C. He shook his head. "There *was* another little thing I wanted to mention," he said.

We waited until Mac had roared off. "It's probably nothing," said P. N. C. "You know what a gossip Geeson is. But I thought you ought to hear it, all the same. So I asked him round."

Geeson was the Captain of the *Warwickshire*, and he used to take a fatherly interest in all the young men he brought out to Burma for Bombine. He brought out so many of them and took such a large percentage of them back again for good that it was not unnatural that he had got into the habit of estimating the likelihood of each one making the grade. It was also not unnatural that P. N. C. had come to rely on Geeson's unofficial estimates of character. One could tell quite a lot more about a young man by how he had behaved on the journey out than by a sticky interview in the Rangoon Office.

When Geeson arrived, P. N. C. explained that I was the Forest Manager who would be looking after Archie. "I thought perhaps it might interest him if he knew what you told me at tiffin," P. N. C. said.

Geeson flushed. "I don't want you to make too much of what I said."

"That's why I want you to tell Bill yourself," P. N. C. said.

"Perhaps I'm making too much out of it," Geeson said. "He was quite normal as far as Suez. He danced and flirted with the 'fishing fleet'. Very nice—nothing very serious. But from there other trouble usually starts; anyway, he fair ate up an Anglo-Malayan girl who got on at Marseilles. I remember taking her home from Penang, years ago. Even as a kid she was very pretty. Now she has finished at the Sorbonne or somewhere in Paris, and she really is quite ravishing."

"So young Archie was ravished?" I said.

"I don't blame him. Nor do I blame her. Because Archie is a

very handsome and lusty young man. But I had to speak to him. There are ways of doing these things, you know. He flew off the handle, and thought it was colour prejudice on my part. Couldn't see what makes the scandal is not what you do, but how openly you do it."

"I don't quite see what you're complaining of," I said—"that he fell in love with this girl or that he didn't?"

"You're quibbling, Bill," P. N. C. said. "Either of those things could be awkward."

"You're quite right," I agreed grudgingly, because I thought it was part of my job to sum up Archie. What he had done on the boat was no concern of mine. But if he fell down on the job, I'd tell him soon enough.

Geeson and I left P. N. C.'s house together and drove to the Gymkhana Club. We found Mac had kept his date by joining the proppers of the bar. I handed Geeson over to him and went to watch the dancing.

The 'fishing fleet' were in full sail, hoist with 'arrival frocks'.

Geeson joined me, holding a drink in his hand. 'More gossip', I thought. I did not want his company. I was enjoying the spectacle. I had seen nothing like it for a year, though it had continued throughout the rebellion.

Geeson nudged me as a particularly fine-looking young man passed partnering a striking girl.

"That's Archie," said Geeson.

"Who's the girl?" I asked. " 'Fishing fleet'?"

"I didn't bring her out," he said. So Archie had at least forgotten shipmates soon enough.

Later I saw him at the bar and introduced myself. I arranged that Archie should be my guest at the Rangoon Sailing Club at 6 p.m. the next evening, as I was going to be more than busy throughout the day.

I was late. It was half-past six before I reached the Sailing Club. It was over a year since I had been there last, but the view was as lovely as ever looking from the long, raised veranda across the

Kokine Lake, gay with sailing-craft tacking this way and that in the light evening breeze.

I stood a moment, watching. Then people at various tables, thinking I was alone, called me to join them for a drink. "Thank you, I'm looking for someone." As I waved the invitations away, I saw Archie. He was standing at one of the centre tables, waving to me and attracting what seemed to me a disproportionate amount of attention for so harmless a gesture. As I walked across to his table, friends of mine greeted me and then did a double-take as they saw whom I was going to greet.

It was not until I was quite close that I understood what had happened. Without my inviting her, Archie had brought his Anglo-Malayan girl friend along, not realising that the Rangoon Sailing Club was one of the stickiest Europeans Only clubs in Burma. I could not believe that Archie would deliberately have exposed the girl to the embarrassment. I was astonished that she should have accepted. She was a most beautiful girl, and in Paris, London or Rome she might have passed for a Spaniard. But in Rangoon there was no doubt what her parentage was.

Archie introduced me to her, and I could feel the looks of all my friends and so-called friends. They were waiting to see what I was going to do.

It had not seemed possible to me that the girl would not have known about the colour bar in the Sailing Club. But then I remembered what Geeson had said about her being sent to Europe as a young girl. In Paris she had been treated like anyone else, except with greater deference in homage to her beauty. She hadn't realised that she was coming to a part of the world where beauty, intelligence and charm were rated lower than pigmentation. I felt very sorry for her and would have liked to say, "My dear, why don't you sail back to Europe on the *Warwickshire*?" But instead I asked her what she would like to drink. After all, they were both my guests.

"What does one drink in *this* Yacht Club?" she asked, as though she knew what one drank in every other Yacht Club in the world and wanted the information to complete her knowledge.

22

"The only drink the club is famous for," I said, "is its Rabbit Cocktail."

"What's in it?" Archie asked.

"That's the barman's secret," I said, "but it seems effective."

They both ordered Rabbit Cocktails, and I stuck to whisky. I wondered if I was being rather mean to the Eurasian girl. These Rabbit Cocktails were dynamite, and the joke about them was that they were called Rabbit Cocktails because after drinking three of them no woman could write the word 'rabbit' on the order chit. I could imagine the club gossips: "Not only did he invite this half-caste girl, but he made her blotto, *blottissimo*!"

I wished we had been anywhere else than at the Sailing Club. The girl was as intelligent as she was lovely. She had trained as a pianist. She wanted to become a professional, but her parents had recalled her to Penang. I could imagine the shocks ahead of her.

"Why do they call it a Rabbit Cocktail?" she asked, after she had finished the third.

"Just write me a chit for another round and I'll tell you," I answered.

She took a pencil and wrote it out without hesitation or mistake. "Well, why?" she asked again.

"Because . . ." I said, unable for the moment to think of any reason why the wretched drink should have been given such a silly name, "because . . . well, it eliminates the rabbits. The fact that you were able to write it without difficulty after drinking three shows that you are a 'seeded' drinker. You could probably drink a dozen without turning a hair."

"I don't know about *that*." As she said this slowly, a dangerous, dotty gleam came into her eye. "Shall we see, Archie, shall we?"

My future assistant gave me a look of pain as my toecap caught him on the ankle. "Didn't you tell me you were both going out to dinner?" I said. "You oughtn't to leave it too late."

"I have never taken so painful a hint," Archie said to me next day, after I had read him a little homily on the colour bar in Sailing

Clubs. "Next time if I seem to be slow in getting your drift, just fill me with a load of buckshot, and I'll understand."

I always find irony rather a heavy form of humour, and it seems to me especially out of place when a young assistant is being instructed in his duties by his immediate superior. Things were certainly working out very differently from the way they had when I had reported for duty to old Willie. I wasn't making Willie's mistakes. But as I looked at Archie, cheerful and unperturbed, I wondered whether, instead of repeating Willie's howlers, I was not committing far more shocking howlers of my own.

When I saw P. N. C. at Head Office next morning, he said, "You seem to have had quite an evening."

"You could have knocked me down with a feather," I answered. "Obviously, I had no idea . . ."

"Nor, it appears, has this young man, Archie."

"Of course, I'm going to put him wise."

"I'm not sure that wisdom is necessary. Common sense'd be enough," he said. "We all have our different methods, I suppose." He did not say any more. But there was something mocking in his smile which made me suspect that he did not share my views on how to introduce a new assistant manager to his job.

"It'll all be different when we get out in the jungle," I said.

CHAPTER III

ARCHIE had a rich uncle who was a City of London expert on Burma. This uncle had given him the Great Danes, Cæsar and Brutus. "Aren't they a bit big?" Archie asked.

"Nonsense, my boy," the rich uncle said. "No better camp dog than a Great Dane. When they are hungry you just go out and shoot a stag."

There weren't any stags in Rangoon, but the two dogs took a sizeable steak out of the rump of a night-watchman. "The sooner we get in that stag country, the better I shall be pleased," Archie said.

"I'm sorry to shatter your faith in your rich uncle," I said, "but the truth is, if you see half a dozen samba stag in the course of a year, you'll be lucky."

"Well, I can't feed them on night-watchmen. It's too expensive," Archie said. "They'll have to turn vegetarian."

The dogs created a sensation at every riverine station at which the steamer stopped. People were used to my Alsatian bitch Molly Mia, but when they saw the Great Danes they cried, "Thim baw Quai" (dogs which have come by steamer from overseas), and the pariah dogs yelped and were off, tails well down between their legs.

Over and over again I was asked what sort of creatures Cæsar and Brutus were.

"You might," I answered, "call them a kind of tiger with spots instead of stripes."

When we reached my headquarters, there was another S.O.S. The headquarters of a nearby Forest District needed specie to pay out as advances to contractors. There was no time to get Archie equipped, so I went ahead alone, leaving him with the English-speaking Burmese clerks to arrange his stores, his tentage, his servants and all that goes with organised touring with elephant transport.

I arranged for him to meet me a week later at the Ngamo rapids on the Sihaung River. Part of his journey was by launch, and the last day was in country canoe-boats, using poles.

Archie joined me on the afternoon appointed. He had undergone a week's acclimatisation. His skin was tanned. A Burmese cheroot stuck out of his chubby cheeks, and he had learnt to smoke it without removing it from his mouth.

"You're certainly right about those stags," he said, patting his rifle. "I didn't even see a sparrow all the way up."

He asked what 'ngamo' meant, and when I told him 'bearded fish'—the name they give to the mahseer—he immediately wanted to go fishing with his new rod and Devon spinners. Sure enough, it wasn't long before he landed a mahseer. Beginner's luck.

I decided that I was going to enjoy Archie, and Archie was going to enjoy Burma. He tried to feed the mahseer to the Great Danes, but they wouldn't even sniff it.

"I wish my uncle wasn't so rich," he said; "then I could write and tell him what I think about old men who send youngsters into the jungle to feed Great Danes."

Later that evening came the most familiar call of the Burmese jungle, the call of the muntjac or barking deer: three successive barks up-stream from our camp. It came perhaps from a hundred yards away, perhaps from half a mile. The Great Danes leapt up and gave tongue, filled with excitement. Archie called them to heel, but when he turned to me, he was as excited as they were. "I'd like to stalk that," he said.

"Why not?" I answered. It was all good experience for him, and as he ran to his tent for his rifle, I called Maung Tin, one of my camp boys, and told him to go with the Thakin Galay to shoot that 'gyi'. "Stick to the river-bank," I warned, "and get back before dark."

Cæsar and Brutus had to be chained to the pole of Archie's tent, and they strained to follow their master. Archie was terribly in earnest, and took no notice when I shouted, "Don't shoot my elephants by mistake." But Maung Tin glanced back and grinned. It wasn't as easy to bag barking deer in Burma as rabbits in Devon.

I settled down to my paper work, but after a little time Archie's head servant, Lok Taw, passed by my table. He stopped and asked me if I were well—as it was customary for a servant to do, if he had not seen one for some time.

I liked Lok Taw. He was elderly and efficient, and I asked him the customary question—how he liked his new Thakin Galay— with a genuine interest. I wanted Archie and Lok Taw to get on with one another.

"'Thabaw too bah thee," he said, meaning that Archie was 'most agreeable and of a cheerful temper'.

It was true, I thought. But were these necessarily the qualities which made a good forest man? Old Willie had been pretty good, and nobody could have said that he was either agreeable or of a cheerful temper.

I finished my paper work and started to read, watching out of the tail of my eye a couple of elephant men piling a huge log fire in preparation for the night. About one of them there was something familiar. Yet I could not place him. He was not a man whom I had employed before. And yet I had seen him several times. He had an attractive personality, that sort of personal magnetism that draws the attention—not always a very useful quality, unless it is accompanied by others more solid.

Suddenly I remembered who he was. His name was Tun Gyaw, and he was a 'black-list' Burman, a man who should never have been employed as one of Archie's camp followers. He had served more Europeans than any servant I ever knew: Deputy Commissioners, British Superintendents of Police, rice-traders, Irrawaddy launch skippers and Forest Assistants in every teak-extracting company in every Forest District in Burma. There was something irresistible about him, a sort of recurrent freshness. He was the New Year's Resolution, bright, fervent but not lasting.

I knew he could speak a little English and understand quite a lot. He had the reputation of being a first-class 'follower', while he lasted. But there was something unstable about him. He never lasted anywhere for long, and he had the habit of quitting at the most awkward times. There was very little positively against him, except that though he had worked here, there and everywhere, he had never stayed anywhere long enough to earn a reference. When an employer asked him for his credentials, Tun Gyaw would produce a greasy old wallet in which he kept visiting-cards of everyone he had ever served. "I did not ask for references," he said with a fine contempt; "for me the card is enough." He made it sound as if it ought to be enough for you too.

Tun Gyaw had never served me personally, but I had toured with another Forest Officer who had him as a camp follower. I had admired him at work. Pitch a tent, strike a tent, systematically stack, load and unload kit from elephants in record time, find his way in the jungle—he was good at all these things. But what was uncanny was his knowledge of the trees, shrubs, creepers and grasses of the forest. He knew not only their names but also the purposes for which they had been created by 'Buddha Pyiah'. The wood of this tree was good for this or that. That shrub had leaves of certain medicinal value. That creeper was good elephant fodder; that one was dangerous. That grass the tiger ate as an emetic when he had indigestion. This fruit provided a cleansing purge for the after-birth of elephants. He could keep one interested and absorbed with his information for mile after mile on the march. On arrival in camp his Shan bag—a highly decorated, coarse silk haversack hung over one shoulder—was always full of various mushrooms and fungoid growths from trees, of ferns and leaves of shrubs which helped to enliven the flavour of the camp curry.

He was not pure Burman in appearance: he had a 'Delta' look about him—a splash of Talaing or Indian blood. His skin was dark, and he was taller than the average Burman: he must have stood about five feet ten inches. He moved freely, with the legs and arms of an athlete.

As far as I was concerned, Tun Gyaw's good qualities outweighed his weaknesses; and he was well worth employing, while he lasted. But for some reason he had been placed on the Black List. This was not compiled by the police; it was a list of 'undesirable elements' made by the firm. Copies were kept at every Forest District Headquarters, and periodically new names would be circulated from the Rangoon Office.

The Black List was useful in some ways. It enabled a forest man to avoid employing any man who was coming in merely to make trouble, or someone wanted by the police, or a man so addicted to opium that he could not be relied on any more. But there was a danger of abuse. When a man's name was placed on the Black List, no reason was given. He might have murdered his wife, been guilty of dacoity or he might just be unreliable. In very rare cases there might be an element of spite on the part of his employer, in others a genuine miscarriage of justice. But there was no appeal against the Black List, because the man himself was not informed of the reason why he was on it. Nor were we allowed to exercise our own judgment. We might think that a man had been unfairly placed upon it, but that did not authorise us to employ him. My duty was to sack Tun Gyaw; and I was very annoyed at whoever it was who had put me in such a false position by employing him in the first place. Perhaps the Burman who engaged him was a relation.

Tun Gyaw knew himself that he was on the Black List, and he could no doubt have tried to keep in the background, hoping that I would not notice him. Instead he was going out of his way to draw attention to himself by heaving far heavier branches on to the fire than any of his companions, and so demonstrating what a keen worker he was.

I called him over. "Who engaged you for Thakin Galay?"

He sat on his haunches with his hands in the shiko position before his face. "The head clerk in Mawku, after you had left."

"Let's have a look at your wrists," I said, rather in fun.

I insinuated that he had been with the rebels, but there was no 'Galon' tattooed on him.

"I've got nothing against you," I said, "but you're blacklisted for any camp in this forest, and that means I can't employ you. I'll pay you off, and you must go away to-morrow."

He pleaded that he had already been given a month's pay in advance. He had to work that off, anyway. And wouldn't I give him a chance? He had a plausible story about having been ill and out of work; and he swore that if I gave him a chance, I'd never regret it.

I warned him severely and agreed to give him a second chance. By the time he's worked off his month's wages, I thought, he'll probably be ready to move. Tun Gyaw was profuse in his thanks and went back to his work.

By the time that I had bathed in my tin tub and taken a sun-down peg of whisky it was dark. The camp-fire was burning and the camp lamps had been produced, when out of the shadows appeared Tun Gyaw. He was worried that Thakin Galay had not returned.

Aware that this show of solicitude was merely to impress me, I said, "That's my concern, not yours." Then I added, as a joke, "Your concern is to keep Thakin Galay's bath-water hot."

I myself was rather worried at Archie's absence, after my strict instructions to Maung Tin to be back by sundown. A little later, Archie's head servant, Lok Taw, came along. We were discussing what could have happened, when we heard two rifle-shots, followed by two more and then, after two minutes' interval, by a third pair. This was Maung Tin's signal that they were lost, or in some kind of trouble. I fetched out my own revolver and fired two returning shots in reply.

I could not leave camp myself, as I had a lot of specie there. But it did not take long to organise a search-party of elephant men, with bamboo torches. I picked Tun Gyaw to go with them, and in a very loud voice, so that I could hear, he shouted to another servant to keep the Thakin Galay's bath-water warm.

I could not help laughing, and Lok Taw, who was with me, laughed too.

"What do you think of Tun Gyaw?" I asked him.

"All right," said Lok Taw. "Too much swank, but all right."

"He wasn't put on the Black List just for swank," I said.

"But don't you know?" asked Lok Taw, as though it was a joke. "He tried to poison T'Myoo Thee Thakin. It was during the rebellion. In Pyinmana. I was head servant."

"Really!" I said. "So he tried to poison T'Myoo Thee Thakin."

Though everything appeared rather tragic to T'Myoo Thee Thakin himself, to everyone else he and his exploits seemed comic. His Burmese nickname meant 'Something different'. He was something different from the other Thakins. He did not shoot or fish or play games. He didn't laugh. Nor did he bath: the tin bath in the chummery, the bucket and tipper in camp he viewed with distaste and abhorrence. This the Burmans regarded as the most richly comic of all his qualities. He was as suspicious of cleanliness as he was of his fellow creatures. God had created the universe, one gathered, expressly for the torment of T'Myoo Thee Thakin.

His misery in Burma culminated in his contracting an internal complaint which Lok Taw aptly described as "An thee ane thee yaugah"—the disease of both ends. This was probably brought about by his own dirty habits. He was convinced that someone else must be to blame, and he summoned the cook.

"It wasn't the curry," said the cook. "All the servants have eaten the curry and none of them is affected. What about the savoury of mushrooms?"

"Where did you get them?" asked T'Myoo Thee.

"Tun Gyaw brought them," said the cook, "but no one knows more about mushrooms, good or bad, than Tun Gyaw."

Tun Gyaw, on the other hand, had just drawn his wages and moved on, as was his habit; and in that T'Myoo Thee saw the most sinister significance. "Of course, I see. It was deliberate. He gave you the poisonous mushrooms, drew his pay and vanished."

Nobody could convince T'Myoo Thee that this explanation was pure fantasy. Nor could any doctor cure his illness. No sooner was it stopped at one end, than it started again at the other. In desperation T'Myoo Thee resigned and took the next boat to London. But before he did so, he put Tun Gyaw's name on the Black List. "It was the last thing he did in Burma, and the worst," Lok Taw said.

Here was one of the cases where the Black List had apparently worked with gross injustice. I was prepared to take the responsibility of employing Tun Gyaw. But if anything went wrong—as it quite likely might, with a man as irresponsible as he was—the fault would be mine. It was a case of 'give a dog a bad name'. Once a man's name was on the Black List, there was no means of removing it.

I decided that in fairness to Archie I would have to warn him, as soon as he came back.

I did not have very long to wait. We could hear the search-party signalling to Archie with rifle-shots, and their answers. Then there was silence, and about half an hour later torch-lights could be seen coming down the river bank.

"What happened?" I shouted, as they came close.

While Archie tried to tell me in English, Maung Tin poured

forth in rapid Burmese the story of how they had met a bear and
shot it. But they hadn't killed it, and to prevent themselves being
mauled, they had to climb a tree.

As they were talking, with Archie swearing because he didn't
know the Burmese language, I saw another group of servants and
elephant men, in the centre of which Tun Gyaw was standing,
waving Archie's rifle in the air, and explaining with a wealth of
detail how, apparently single-handed, he had rescued his new
master.

Archie looked across at Tun Gyaw and smiled. "Tun Gyaw's a
bright boy, isn't he?" he asked.

I did not reply.

CHAPTER IV

Just before midnight I awoke from a deep sleep. Somewhere a voice was shouting. I recognised it as the voice of Joseph, my old cook, as I swung my legs out of bed. Then there was a great squawking of chickens.

As I grasped my shot-gun, I heard the other servants beginning to yell. I ran out of the tent and, coming to the crowd, I saw what they were shouting about. A leopard cat had got among the chickens, and there it was, crouched with a bird in its mouth, caught in the light of Joseph's torch as if it was a trap.

I gave it both barrels; and the leopard cat fell. So did a dozen more of the chickens.

By this time Archie had arrived, and he was thrilled to see his first leopard cat. He thought nothing of the dead chicken, until I explained that before we set out on our first jungle tour from this camp on the Sihaung River, we should have to get some more village chickens. For fresh meat we could not rely on shooting enough pigeons and barking deer.

This meant sending a couple of men back down-river to the villages we had left behind. If they bought small birds, each of them ought to be able to carry between twenty and thirty in light open-work baskets slung from either end of a pole across their shoulders.

From my followers I picked San Ba and from Archie's Tun Gyaw. I was getting bored with Tun Gyaw's obtrusive acts of service, and a mission which would take him out of my sight for eight days seemed an excellent idea. To each man I gave fifteen rupees and explained in Burmese what they were to do, emphasising that they must be back punctually on the eighth day.

San Ba was back within the week, bringing with him thirty-two chickens and two dozen eggs, lime-coated for preservation. Joseph, to whom he accounted, asked him if he had news of Tun Gyaw. But San Ba said they'd agreed to go to different villages and he had seen nothing of Tun Gyaw from the day they had left us.

"If this means he's had another attack of *wanderlust*," I said, "he's through as far as I am concerned."

Archie was convinced he would return. "He knows it's his last chance," he said. "Something's gone wrong. But he'll be back."

We waited for a couple of days longer. There was plenty for us to do. I was involved in sheets of figures, working out a fifteen-year teak-extraction plan. Archie was somewhere out of sight, busy struggling with his first Burmese grammar.

In the middle of an abstruse calculation I looked up and saw Joseph. How long he had been standing there I don't know. "What is it?" I said. "I'm busy."

"Tun Gyaw's come back," Joseph said. "No money. No chicken. No eggs. No explanation."

"Leave it," I said, "don't worry."

I returned to my calculations without having lost my thread and for another couple of hours wrestled with figures of trees, logs and elephant power, till my graph of working plans was finished. It was five o'clock—too early for a drink. So I called for a pot of tea.

My servant placed the tray on my table, and as he was going

away I said to him casually, "Tell Tun Gyaw to come. I want to speak to him."

I was checking my figures when I saw him arrive. I did not look up. He squatted a few yards away from me on the other side of my camp table.

After a minute, he cleared his throat to draw my attention to his presence.

I looked up. "How many chicken did you get?"

"None."

"How much money have you got left?"

"None."

"Then why have you come back?"

He looked at the ground in front of him in shame and muttered something that was inaudible. We both knew why he had come back. It was his only chance of a job in this forest.

I cursed him softly in idiomatic Burmese. I said I knew he had spent the money on wine, women and song. He could try that with my money, if he was willing to take the consequences. But I wouldn't have him trying it with Thakin Galay's money, just because he was inexperienced.

He did not try to excuse himself. I could see what I had said hurt, because the expression on his face grew sullen.

"All right," I said at last. "*Go* and I will deduct the fifteen rupees from your pay." I repeated the word 'go', adding to it a Burmese affix which is seldom used because it implies on the part of the speaker such disgust with the person spoken to. It was more wounding to the pride of any Burman, good or bad, than outright dismissal from his job.

It made me almost ashamed to have insulted Tun Gyaw so deeply, and I looked down at my papers so that he could go away without any further humiliation.

But Tun Gyaw did not go.

I pretended to be immersed in my figures, but I knew that Tun Gyaw was still sitting there. Unless he obeyed my order, the insult would rebound on me.

It was a situation which I had never had to face before—a private rebellion. The atmosphere grew electric between us, with me willing him to go and Tun Gyaw squatting there, adamant in his refusal. It occurred to me that I had made a mistake in beginning the interview in hard anger. A little humour would have found out what had happened and I could always have turned cold with anger later. But such reflections were no use to me now. Every moment of successful defiance I was losing a little more face.

I slammed down my Eversharp pencil on the table with a crack and stood up glaring at him.

"Didn't I tell you to *go*?"

Very slowly Tun Gyaw rose to his feet. But it was not in order to go. He drew himself to his full height, and with equal slowness his right hand moved to behind his back. There he held it, gripping the handle of the dagger the sheath of which was tucked into his *lungyi* shirt, hidden by his linen coat.

I moved to one side so that there was no longer a table between us. I wanted liberty of manœuvre. If I had been wise, I would have said in quite a different tone of voice, "Don't be foolish. Sit down." It wouldn't have mattered much what I had said, provided that I broke the dramatic tension. But I was its victim, as much as Tun Gyaw. "How dare you threaten me, when you know that you are in the wrong?"

Tun Gyaw drew his dagger. It was a dahmyoung, with a handle of ivory and a single-edged blade of gleaming steel eight inches long.

It was a challenge, but there was no need to accept it. I could have called to Aung Net, my personal servant, or to Archie, who, though out of sight, was in easy hearing distance. It would have been better for us both if I had.

But all I thought was that I was not going to be threatened, and if anyone tried it, I needed no help in defending myself. I moved in towards him, and he raised the dagger to strike.

With my left well inside the dagger I parried and gave him a right hook to the jaw. It spun him completely round, and as he spun, he switched the dagger from his right hand to his left. I thought he would go down, but instead he lunged at me left-handed.

This time I parried with my right and caught him with my left fist a blow on the cheek which sent him staggering back, but still did not knock him down. He switched the dagger to his right hand and we were back where we had started. Blood started to trickle from his right nostril, and he came forward crouching like an animal and holding the dagger low. He was going for my belly.

I did not wait for him. I took a flying tackle at his knees, getting below his guard by surprise. I lifted him bodily to throw him. For a moment I felt the warmth of his body against mine. Then, as I threw him, there was a stabbing pain in my arm and a grating thud against my left ribs.

His dagger had caught me; but there he was spread-eagled, and I leapt forward, digging my knee in his belly and holding his wrists flat against the earth. As I called "Aung Net! Murder!" I saw that blood—my blood—was flowing up Tun Gyaw's dagger to the hilt.

Our faces were close together, and I noticed that his, which I had always thought so dark, was a sort of ashy green with fear. He thought I was going to kill him, because if our positions had been reversed he would have killed me. I was trembling with excitement and relief, and I remember hissing at him in Burmese, "If you move an inch, I'll bury that dagger in your belly."

As I said it, I wondered whether the words sounded as hollow to him as they did to me. I could hear Aung Net shouting as he ran towards us, and I thanked God, because there was a humming in my head and I knew that if I had to kneel on Tun Gyaw very much longer, I should keel over.

Then Aung Net took the dagger out of Tun Gyaw's limp grasp and I stood up, feeling rather strange and seeing round specks revolving before my eyes.

As Tun Gyaw got to his feet, Archie came running up. "What's happened, Bill?"

"He stabbed me," I said.

Archie made for his servant. "You bastard!" he said in English. "You bloody bastard!"

Tun Gyaw backed away, making deprecating gestures with his empty hands. He was backing towards the river-bank, which here fell in a cliff of about twenty-five feet. He was aiming to make a get-away. I could see that, but I was too dazed to shout to Archie or Aung Net.

As it was, Archie helped him. With a straight left he lifted Tun Gyaw in the air and he disappeared over the edge. There was a cry and a crash from the momakah bushes in the creek-bed.

I wasn't so interested in Tun Gyaw as in the extent of the damage he had done to me. The cut behind my arm caused by the edge of the dagger was bleeding freely. But it wasn't much to worry about. In my ribs there was acute pain, and from the wound, covered by my shirt, blood was running down my hip into my shorts and reappeared again at the knee as a little rivulet before disappearing into the top of my stocking.

I ripped off my shirt and saw the hole.

"How deep is it?" Archie asked, with asinine curiosity.

I felt no impulse to put my finger in and tell him. I was losing blood fast and knew that I should black out at any moment. I took out my keys and handed them to Archie. "There's twenty thousand rupees in the cash-box," I said. "If I've had it, make straight for the main river and headquarters."

I shall never forget the expressions that came over his face as he looked first at the keys and then at me. I thought, 'Well, you swore you wouldn't initiate Archie the way Willie initiated you. And you certainly haven't. But God knows whether this way was any better.' I staggered and caught hold of Archie's arm, and he helped me into the tent.

"Lie down," he said, "lie down."

I collapsed on the camp bed and everything was going round and I thought I was going to pass out, but I was determined to hang on to the daylight. Then my head steadied and the pain in my ribs reasserted itself and I thought, 'O God! I pray it hasn't punctured my lung!'

I sat up and looked round, and there was a group of gaping Burmans, servants, cooks and elephant men, in the tent and outside. I wanted to tell them to go away, but at the moment I could not remember a word of Burmese. But there, thank God, was Archie, who spoke English. "Medicine chest," I said, pointing with my good arm to where it was.

He found the medicine chest and opened it. He didn't know anything about first aid. But I told him to fill an elephant irrigation syringe with a solution of Friar's Balsam and syringe out the stab-wound. Then he lightly plugged it with cotton-wool. The wound in the arm he dressed, using Friar's Balsam again, and bound up.

I asked for a cup of tea, and with it Aung Net handed me a lighted cigarette. I inhaled it deeply, catching my breath with the stabbing pain.

Aung Net removed the plug and watched the bleeding hole intently. But not the faintest wisp of smoke came from it. I coughed, and he replaced the plug. He at least was convinced that there was no deep penetration of the lung!

That night every elephant man went out with a lighted bamboo, searching for Tun Gyaw. We knew that he would not dare to enter the jungle alone. By dawn he had not been found. But a dug-out canoe was missing. He had clearly made a get-away to the main river by night.

Archie wanted me to be taken to the main river as quickly as possible. The sooner I had an anti-tetanus injection, the better. But for five days there was nothing I could do but rest in a camp-chair, trying to keep as still as possible. The risk of tetanus had to be taken.

On the sixth day I felt it was safe to move. Four days later I arrived by country boat at Headquarters. Tun Gyaw was already there, in the police lock-up.

He had made for a village where he had a girl friend. He told her what had happened—that he had either killed or wounded me. Then he gave himself up to the Headman in grief and remorse and the Headman had brought him in to the police station.

Archie had to return to Headquarters with me. Gone were my dreams of taking him through the Forest Area to learn the job. It would be some time before my wounds had healed, and after that there would be the trial of Tun Gyaw. I decided that the best way to further Archie's education was to send him to a small District Headquarters at Sinthé on the Sittang River, under the care of an English-speaking logging clerk. I impressed on both of them the importance of Archie's learning to read, write and speak Burmese.

At Headquarters I was examined by a sub-assistant surgeon. There was no X-ray apparatus within hundreds of miles, so I had to take his word about my wound. He said that a number of nerves had been severed, and that I should have a painful time while they were joining. No ribs had cracked, providentially. If they had, Tun Gyaw would have been facing a murder charge.

Within three weeks the wound had healed, though the pains in my ribs persisted. As luck would have it, I did not have long to wait for the District Sessions, at which so grave a case had to be heard. Tun Gyaw was accused of attempted murder, of causing grievous bodily harm and appearing before a European with a hidden and pointed dagger.

Before the trial I did my best to prevent anybody reading a political significance into the attack. I was afraid that the Ferdinand Stipplewethers would try to prove that this was a continuation of the rebellion. Even the Deputy Commissioner of my District considered recalling all officers from tour.

As the trial approached, I was more concerned with my own responsibility. Tun Gyaw's attack was clearly going to be treated very gravely. Yet I was conscious that I myself had provoked it by the way I had behaved.

When I went into court, my sympathies were with Tun Gyaw. When he saw me alive and well, his face was wreathed in smiles.

'Now he knows that at any rate he won't be hanged,' I thought cynically. But of course it could not have been that, because his lawyers had told him so before.

I realised with a shock that it was something quite different. Tun Gyaw and I had more in common with one another than with anyone else in the court. We had very nearly committed a murder together—the murder of me. I was thoroughly ashamed of my own part in that affair, and I thought Tun Gyaw was ashamed of his. If only the judge could have ordered him to say that he was sorry, I felt that justice would have been done, and Tun Gyaw and I would have left the court friends for life. As it was, I was afraid that Tun Gyaw would have to pay the penalty alone for what was in some measure my crime.

He wore a red jacket of light cotton as a sign that he was a danger-ous criminal under charge of attempted murder. There were three Burmans for the defence. One of them was a third-rate advocate who had been briefed by a political party from Mandalay to make as much capital out of the trial as he could. Apart from them there seemed nobody on Tun Gyaw's side. The Burmans who filled the little court-house were all on the European side: English-speaking clerks from the offices of Government or Bombine. I looked at them and then at the aged and respected Judge Carrapiet, and I felt there was only one person in that court who could really represent Tun Gyaw, and that was I. And I was the chief witness for the Prosecution.

I was handed a tattered copy of the Holy Bible, and I held it up in my right hand and promised to tell the truth, the whole truth and nothing but the truth.

Tun Gyaw did not follow what I had said. He looked first at me and then at Judge Carrapiet, who, in default of a clerk of the court, took down everything himself on a battered old portable typewriter. In Burmese I asked the Judge if I might also swear on the *Kyeinsa*, the Burman Book of the Oath.

"As the witness pleases," said the Judge, "but all evidence and proceedings will be taken in English."

43

I was passed what looked like a long, flat ruler, about four inches wide. Inside the flat length, which was bound and sewn up in red cloth, was an abbreviated copy of the Book of the Oath, written on palm leaf. Its frayed edges could be seen through the loose stitching. I held it while the Judge mumbled something in Burmese. Nobody stirred in the court. I held it above my head and kissed the *Kyeinsa*. It was a solemn moment. As all Burmans know, the most terrible torments await those who abuse the Book of the Oath. Disasters are ready to assail not only the perjurer but all his family. On him and them is turned the fury of the spirits that guard the sacred relics of Buddha. The anger of the Nats who dwell in waters is turned upon him, the spirits of rivers and streams, of still lakes and roaring torrents and eddying whirlpools. On him and them turns the wrath of the forests and the beasts that dwell therein, the elephant, the tiger and the snake. Against them that bear false witness turn also the monsters of supernature, the dragons breathing fire and the invincible galons, malign ogres and demons of a malevolent essence. The winds and the clouds are against the perjurer; and the sun turns away from his people. He is outcast from the moon and the stars.

The *Kyeinsa* was filthy and evil-smelling, more used, if possible, than the dog-eared Bible on which I had sworn. But my oath was a solemn promise to Tun Gyaw that I would tell the truth.

I gave my evidence, and Tun Gyaw's advocate in cross-examination asked me only one question: "Do you think this man came to see you with the intention of murdering you?"

"No," I replied.

The advocate, who had grown fat apparently from political defences, turned and smiled greasily at the Judge, as though he had gained a reluctant admission from me.

Then Tun Gyaw took the oath. He looked terrified, and I soon understood why. Perhaps my oath upon the *Kyeinsa* made it worse for him. If his own spirits judged between the two of us, Tun Gyaw stood to suffer damnation. His evidence was that I had pointed at him not a pencil, but a revolver, ordering him to raise his arms above his head.

He was so frightened, he said, that he drew his dagger. Then I attacked him and tore off his shirt. In the struggle that followed I fell on his naked knife and he ran away, because he was afraid of what I had done to myself.

When he was cross-examined by the Prosecution, Tun Gyaw looked at his greasy advocate every time, in the hope that he would give him the answer. In a very short time he had tied himself up in such a tangle of contradictions that he broke down and asked if he might be allowed to tell the truth instead. This was addressed almost as an apology to his advocate.

His story was a confirmation of mine, with one damning addition. He said that he had armed himself because he intended that night to murder the cook for having told tales to me about him. This caused laughter in court. His face lit up, and he looked more cheerful. He had, after all, told the truth, and whatever the Judge could do to him was less awful than the vengeance of the outraged spirits.

The trial should have been over in a couple of hours. But the old Judge was not very good at typing, and it took two days for him to bang down the evidence.

The charge of attempted murder was withdrawn. But the confession that he intended to murder the cook told against him, and he was found guilty on the two other charges. He was sentenced to a long term of imprisonment, which, as far as I could gather, would mean that he would be deported to the Andaman Islands— the Black Isles, as they were known to the Burmese, the Islands of No Return.

I had done my best for him during the trial; but I could not rid myself of the conviction that it had taken two to make this quarrel, and that if I had shown Tun Gyaw the sympathy and understanding that I prided myself on having for elephants, he would now be devotedly serving Archie and teaching him the lore of the jungle.

45

CHAPTER V

DURING my convalescence and the trial, I heard continually from Archie, "I am getting down to the language," he wrote; "I shall soon be talking it in my sleep."

When I rejoined him, I was astonished at the progress which he had made in the spoken language. His reading and writing were disappointing. I said to the English-speaking logging clerk, "Thakin Galay says that he will soon be talking Burmese in his sleep."

The clerk laughed uproariously, "I think so," he said, and laughed again.

Archie had settled down and made himself very comfortable. He had made friends with everyone in the neighbouring village of Mehaw, which was about half a mile from the forest bungalow, rice and store go-downs, where he was camped. He had done a lot of fishing and shot a young bull bison, which had been put to good use, for he had sun-dried and cured large quantities of biltong for Cæsar and Brutus. The veranda rail of the small bungalow was hung with strings of the stuff. Twice daily half a dozen village girls carried water from the river to his camp, first to the cook-house and then to fill his tin tub and large pegu jars, kept as water receptacles.

There was something wrong with any new Assistant to Burma who did not find this delightful daily scene worth watching. I saw him looking at them in the distance, all in Indian file with water-bowls balanced on their heads, putting on an excellent show of the 'elephant wobble' from the hips, which every Burmese girl practises from the age of ten.

When they arrived at the bungalow, Archie tried his colloquial Burmese on them, much to their tittering delight. I could imagine Archie talking Burmese in his sleep to any one of them, and I could hear P. N. C.'s warning. "What did I tell you, Bill? First Anglo-Malaya and now a harem of village water-carriers—watch it."

I had known these girls since their childhood. Among them was Ma Kywai, by far the prettiest, and she was dolled up more than the others. I watched Archie talking and laughing with her. It made me feel a bit old, but I found this flirtation charming and really harmless. It was difficult to be firm, and even more difficult to take up the melodramatic attitude which Willie had taken up with me as a young assistant. "In this country there is the choice of two evils—women or the bottle. Choose which you like, but don't mix 'em." It was all very well talking of being firm. I had been firm with Tun Gyaw, and where had it got either of us?

That night, over a drink, I said, "What do you think of these Burmese girls?"

Archie looked at me wickedly. "Jolly attractive, I think."

I cleared my throat. "One doesn't want to take them too seriously. They are all like that when you first come out: each trying to out-do the other. They'd go to any ends to be the chosen one."

"I can believe that," said Archie—"definitely."

"I think you're making too much of a fuss of Ma Kywai," I said.

"Are you angry?" he queried.

"There's nothing to be angry about. They are all eighteen."

"Ma Kywai is very attractive," he said. "And she's teaching me very good colloquial Burmese."

"I know," I agreed, "but . . ."

"Besides, I'm sorry for her," he said. "She's got some sort of swelling on the front of her neck. That's really how I first noticed her, especially. She pinched a tin of shaving talcum-power from me, and then begged some iodine for the swelling. But it doesn't seem to have done any good."

"Sounds like goitre," I said. "But she wouldn't know how to treat herself. For all you know, she'll drink it. Never hand out medicines unless you see how they are used."

"But I did—we smeared it on, then powdered it. That's what she's been doing every day," he said. "But she seems to be getting worse, and I'm worried."

"So am I," I said. "You mustn't see her any more."

"What do you mean?" he asked. "What do you think it is?"

"It might be highly contagious." I did not intend to read him a moral lecture, but there was no harm in scaring him medically.

Next morning there was no girlish laughter. Archie remained in his room. When the girls came up, I called Ma Kywai to me. She was flushed and had a fever. I examined her neck. The goitre was in a very early stage; just a fullness in the throat, not a disfigure-ment. What was strange was that it was hot to the touch, red and inflamed at one point, as if the core of an abscess was forming.

"What have you been doing, Ma Kywai?" I asked.

She blushed. "I smeared on 'Sey Nee' which Thakin Galay gave me," she said.

"And what else? This soreness is not from smearing on iodine."

After a pause she said, "Nothing else."

She was lying. And when I told her so, she burst into tears.

48

"Is it bad, Thakin Gyee?" she asked.

"I am going to poultice it," I said. "If I don't you may die."

She was frightened, but when I called Archie, she cheered up. I showed him how to mix a paste of Epsom salts. "You'll have to do it on elephants eventually," I said, "so you might as well practise on her."

He laughed and winked at Ma Kywai over my shoulder. He was relieved that I was in the know and felt that now there was nothing to worry about.

But I was still worried. Somebody else was trying to practise medicine in the village. Until I could find out who it was, no amount of poulticing would prevent these swellings recurring.

An hour later the Headman of the village came to pay his respects. He was the same Headman to whom Tun Gyaw had given himself up. It seemed to have added to his stature. All over the world association with crime seems to confer a sort of glamour. He was a charming old man, but he did not congratulate me on having recovered from Tun Gyaw's murderous attack, "How lucky it is for Tun Gyaw that you are still alive!" was the way he put it. It was one way of looking at it, I suppose.

As he squatted before me, the old man counted out a little pile of silver rupees. He passed it over to me. "Fifteen," he said.

I counted them. There were fifteen. "But what are they for?"

"For the chicken Tun Gyaw never bought," the old man said. "When he gave himself up to me, he asked me to pay you back; or if you died, then to the new Thakin Galay."

I did not understand. "But if Tun Gyaw had the money all the time," I said, "why didn't he buy the chickens?"

"He didn't have the money when he stabbed you," the Headman said. "He had used it to bet on the Thone sey chauk Gaung lottery, and the draw took place that day. He did not know that he had won."

The Thone sey chauk Gaung is the Thirty-six Animal Lottery. Six months before the draw a blind girl from the village had chosen one of the thirty-six animal symbols and placed it in a box, which was sealed and handed over to the safe keeping of the Headman, who swore that he would not let anyone open it until the day of the draw. Villagers had probably come from miles round to place their bets as to the symbol it contained.

"Tun Gyaw was the only one to back the bear," said the old man. "He won five hundred rupees."

"I thought the bear was unlucky," I said.

"Tun Gyaw said it was the new Thakin Galay's lucky animal."

"I still don't understand why he came back empty-handed," I said. "Why didn't he wait till the draw?"

"He was afraid you would be gone. He did not want to lose the job, because you had taken him in spite of his being on the Black List."

Now I knew all the details of the wretched affair I felt even more uncertain that I had been wise in taking the firm line. But the affair of Tun Gyaw was ended. I thanked him and changed the subject. What concerned me was Ma Kywai. "You have a lot of goitre in Mehaw, I hear."

"There has always been goitre in the village," he said. "Especially with young girls, when they first reach puberty. The neck swells, and they do not like it. But when they marry, then the neck stops swelling."

Some years ago a young Indian doctor had come to the village giving 'Sey Nee' injections. But the Government stopped him, and the trouble had started again. There were a dozen young girls with it, some with abscesses. "I beg you come to the village and see for yourself," he said. "If you cannot cure them, can you ask for the doctor to come again?"

I went with him to the village, and there I was appalled by what I saw. There were some girls who had used the iodine liniment which Ma Kywai had said she had used. Their delicate skins were not in the least sore. But on others the abscesses, which threatened on Ma Kywai's neck, were open and festering. The dressings were foul and putrid.

I spent the whole afternoon cleaning the wounds and redressing them, but none of the girls would tell me what or who was the cause of the trouble.

When I got back to camp in the evening, Archie's main anxiety seemed to be whether the Headman suspected anything between him and Ma Kywai. I said that it was quite possible that the Headman had advised Ma Kywai to go to see Archie about her goitre in the first place and had connived throughout. "How was he to know that you didn't know the first thing about goitre?"

"But that isn't true," Archie said. "Ma Kywai explained that it's caused by lack of iodine in the water. That's why I gave her the bottle of iodine."

"What bottle?" I asked, filled with a sudden awful suspicion.

"That big one," he said. "It must hold about a quart."

"But damn it, man! That's the elephant iodine. Heaven knows what they may have done with it!"

Archie apologised feebly.

"Ma Kywai isn't just that sweet little girl you think she is," I said. "She's been doing something with that iodine which she wouldn't tell me about. You've got to get her over here to-night and impress on her that if she doesn't tell me what she's been up to, something awful will happen. Tell her she'll die; which she might."

"I thought she wasn't to come to the bungalow?"

"I don't mind what you do," I said, "provided only that you can make her talk. I'd say get her to tell you, but I don't think your Burmese is good enough."

I did not expect to be woken up in the early hours of the morning; but that is what happened. I opened my eyes, and there she was in the dim light by my camp-bed.

I turned my lamp to the full, and she showed me her neck again. The swab of Epsom salts which I had applied the day before had worked a miracle. If the others in the village reacted as well, some good would have been done.

"It's a lot better, Ma Kywai," I said. "But tell me the truth. What happened? I am not angry with you."

She explained, as the Headman had done, how some years ago the Indian doctor had come to the village and injected the girls with iodine. So when she had got the bottle of elephant iodine from Archie, she had given it to the Sey Sayah, or quack doctor, from Singon. He had learnt a little about the treatment from the Indian doctor, and for a silver rupee he inoculated each of the girls affected with an injection of iodine into the swelling.

Light dawned in my mind. The quack had not sterilised his equipment. "What sort of needle did he use?"

"He used a big thorn from the wild lime-tree," she said.

From the top of the tamain skirt which she wore drawn across from armpit to armpit she took a finely-pointed thorn three inches in length. It had been fire-smoked until it was as hard and polished as steel. She was using it as a pin, but she showed me how it had been finely grooved from the base to the point. Its purpose was to act as a channel down which the iodine could flow into the swelling of the goitre after the thorn had been stabbed in.

"He punctured you with this?" I said. "It must have been agony."

"It was," she answered, "it was torment. And it took so long. About an hour." She begged me to tell no one that it was she who had told me of the quack. "Because some of the girls were quite cured," she said.

There were so many who weren't that I was determined to track down the quack in Singon, to recover the bottle of iodine and threaten him with the consequences of earning more silver rupees in this way. But I was careful not to mention the name of Ma Kywai.

We stayed in this little headquarters for another week, during which time I passed on to Archie the job of taking the daily goitre parade. I said nothing about him and Ma Kywai. I reckoned that if I tried to squash the affair it might merely strengthen Archie's feelings. By the end of the week I don't think he was terribly sorry to wave her good-bye. It had been good while it lasted; because it hadn't lasted too long. And there would be no harm done, because these Burmese girls did not take such affairs too seriously.

Archie was eager to start on the tour at last; a tour I was determined should differ from my own lonely beginning with four elephants, one of whom died immediately of old age.

All the village turned out to see us off. Our twelve travelling elephants were laden, and Ma Kywai and a dozen of her friends stood watching. Archie had given all of them long pastel-coloured voile scarves, which were around their necks and hung down in front of their neatly starched white coats and different-coloured tamains. Everyone was happy. The new Thakin Galay had healed goitres and there was no sadness in the parting as we waved goodbye and struck into the jungle.

The elephant-riders banged their hand-gongs as the leader elephant led off. As the animals got into line on the move, their large wooden bells, each of a different note, set up a sound like the laughter of running water. Cæsar and Brutus followed us at heel, with Molly Mia, my Alsatian bitch.

We toured for a month. By then Archie knew a great deal about elephants and teak, where the elephant camps were, how they were managed, how to put in forest returns, and so on. He had met all the other Forest Assistants in their own areas and was accepted as one of us. In the natural course of the tour he gathered a lot of wrinkles about looking after himself and his elephant men and their families. His reading and writing of Burmese had caught up with his spoken language. I felt confident that I could leave him on his own, if I was given short leave or sent on the Andaman trip.

Fifty transfer elephants were due to arrive from Upper Siam before the break of the monsoon. They had been on the march nearly a year, having been much delayed by the rebellion. I knew they would be weary and in need of a considerable rest. The Siamese riders were only under contract and would have to hand over their charges to newly recruited Burmese elephant-riders from my own forest. U San Din, my Head Chaungoke, was to recruit the new elephant-riders.

I promised Archie that he should have charge of these elephants when they arrived, and the first assignment of his own was to reconnoitre suitable elephant rest-camps for hot-weather grazing.

It was as if I had promised a boy that if he gave up his rabbits he should have a pony. He had now put Anglo-Malayan girls and Ma Kywais behind him. Life was really taking shape. He had to 'cruise' a tract of country draining from the foothills of the Karenni Range. It covered at least fifty square miles, entirely uninhabited; and it was drained by a series of streams, running more or less parallel at ten-mile intervals, before joining the main Nancho River.

I already knew that for about five miles up-stream from where they joined the Nancho River there was good water and abundant fodder in the form of kaing or elephant grass. The country was flat, and our information was that above the area of elephant grass there was a five-mile stretch of dry Indaing Forest where the streams ran underground. Archie's main task was to discover whether water appeared again beyond the Indaing Forest, and if so whether there was suitable fodder. Reports from an Assistant who had shot over the area many, many years before even mentioned fair stands of teak forest.

The streams were named after a series of water-spirits. There was the Kyun Taw Yay Shin, or Teak Water Spirit; the Nat Taung Yay Shin, or Hill and Water Spirit and the Petyah Yay Shin, or Stinging-nettle Water Spirit, to name only three. It was reputed among my elephant men to be very bad for '*thut*' or goitre in elephants. This was more than Archie had bargained for. He had already seen and heard enough of goitre to last him his service.

We first scanned this vast area from the top of a high ridge in the Upper Mehaw Forest, looking east across the valley. It was spread out like a great green sea, stained with white patches of flowering bulrushes—a sign that the monsoons would break early.

I waved my hand towards it. "It's all yours, Archie," I said. "You've got three and a half months to learn all about it. And by

54

the time I come back, the new elephant-riders will be ready to take over. You will decide their camping sites."

I explored the first of the streams with him. We took the Petyah Yay Shin, which proved to be one of the eeriest streams I had ever camped by. The flow of the water was very sluggish. There were deep, canal-like backwaters with elephant grass eight to ten feet high growing right to the edge of the brackish waters. It was clear why the stream was named after the stinging-nettle plant. I have never seen it in such abundance, and it grew to the height of between four and five feet. Wherever it touched one's skin it raised a welt the size of half a crown. It had no effect on the elephants' skins. In fact they ate the Petyah plant, perhaps finding it rather stimulating as it stung its way down.

The problem of jungle food for the oozies was as important as that of elephant fodder. Were there fish in the creek? The oozies insisted there were none, and for that reason alone it was no place to camp in the hot season.

"All right," I said. "Let's see!"

We threw in a charge of dynamite with a couple of feet of fuse tied to floating bamboos. On the banks we all stood waiting, the oozies expectant and yet afraid they would be proved wrong. The banks shook with the first explosion and a column of water was shot into the air.

Once it settled, we saw a poor unfortunate stunned otter. It surfaced downstream and then disappeared into the bank. Where there's an otter, there are fish.

For quite a time there was no further evidence of life. Then a few small fry floated to the surface with silver bellies uppermost. The elephant men roared with laughter, as if to say, "Didn't we say so?"

Suddenly there was a tremendous splash. Two oozies had seen a huge fish surface belly uppermost. They had both jumped from the bank to grab it, but it dived again.

It came up some way off, and another two or three oozies plunged in. No luck. "There it is!" Another yell and a few more

were in. And soon the river was like a public bath on Bank Holiday, with oozies splashing, yelling and laughing.

Up to this point Archie and I had remained, if not aloof, at least
dry. But suddenly Archie dived, and when he came up he was
holding in his arms and gripping under his chin a fifteen-pound
mahseer.

With a last convulsive flick the mahseer was free again, but now
the oozies were all round, and between them they landed it.

By now everyone was fishing. The total catch was rather disappointing, but the mood of the camp was uplifted. As soon as the
river was clear once more, we tried deep-level tactics. We used a
short fuse and sank the charge with a weight.

Almost immediately there was an earth tremor, but only a blister
of water. All of us were now on the *qui vive*, and it seemed ages
before there was any result. Then suddenly there were cries.
"HOKE THEE!" "Hoke thee!" "Hoke Thee!" "Yes, there they
are!" "Yes, there they are!" And the stunned fish rose, not in

ones and twos, or even in dozens, but by the hundreds; one
pounders, five pounders and a few enormous mud-fish—filthy-
looking creatures with flat heads, but to the Burmese a great
delicacy.

What were we going to do with them all?

Ever resourceful and unexpected, my servant Aung Net produced, what to me was the wrong answer, my tin bath-tub.

"Blast you!" I yelled.

But it was down the bank and floating on the river, being loaded
with fish, some of which flipped themselves drunkenly out of it,
only to be hauled back if they were any size.

This was too much for Archie, who went off and returned with

57

his own tin bath. "My bath's as good as yours," he said, launching it on the deep.

None of that catch was wasted. What was not eaten fresh was cured in the sun. There would be contentment in his camp, I felt sure, provided that I left him enough explosives. Even Cæsar and Brutus had fresh fish for their supper that night as a change from Japanese tinned salmon at sixpence a tin. This was the jungle stand-by for dog-feeding when venison was scarce.

While waiting for final instructions from Rangoon I went with Archie up-stream to where the river became subterranean. He was more optimistic of finding good water higher up than I was. He had brought sticks of dynamite and lengths of fuse in the parcel with his lunch.

We trekked ten miles up-stream along a hot, pebbly stream-bed devoid of water. We were in a different world. No kaing grass grew. The river-banks disappeared into miles of leafless Indaing forest. We had had cool jungle breezes at our camp. Here the wind blew in hot blasts. Whirlwinds eddied the Indaing leaves up from the earth and carried them some way and then listlessly let them drop. The Great Danes kept running ahead for a few yards, and then, when they had found a lick of shade at the base of a tree, they lay down. When we came up, they went through the motions of keenness again. But their hearts were not in this excursion.

I was considering turning back when a barking deer bounded across the dried creek ahead of us. Archie immediately thought of the pot. The sight meant more to me because it promised water ahead. Soon the dry, sun-scorched pebbles were giving way to those covered with green lichen. I lifted some of them up, and underneath the sand was damp. Then we began to find pools. At first they were stagnant and foul. But higher up they grew larger and were interspersed with outcrops of rock. The river-banks appeared again. There were a few scattered clumps of bamboos, patches of kaing grass, even a few ill-formed teak-trees.

There was still no running water: just one stagnant pool after another. But in the pools there was the discoloration of a rich indigo, which meant only one thing: the tribes had been down from the Karen Hills to poison the fish. It was a poison they made from the bark of a tree, which worked in stagnant water but was too weak for a flowing stream.

Within two miles we were in mixed deciduous forest. We ate our lunch sitting on a rock in a small gorge overlooking a long, narrow run of deep, crystal-clear water. I told Archie elephants could camp here through the hot season.

"I wonder if there are any fish," Archie said. He had learnt that if he was to keep his elephant men contented, fish would be important.

I felt this might be my last day, and my thoughts were already leaving this forest, perhaps towards Ceylon or perhaps to the Andamans. "You find out," I said; "I want a swim."

So Archie went to the head of the gorge. I moved down to the pool at the bottom end, a couple of hundred yards away. I had grown fond of Archie, but all the same I was rather glad that I was leaving him soon. I had done the job of initiation which I had set out to do. But it was jolly exhausting and, to be frank, just a trifle boring. I could understand old Willie sending me off alone with that elephant that died of old age.

I stripped off my clothes and dived into the cool stream. I turned this way and that, weaving through the water like an otter and feeling the sheer joy of movement.

Suddenly something terrible happened. It was as if at the same moment somebody had punched me in the solar plexus, kicked me between the legs, wrenched back my shoulders, pushed down my head and tried to dislocate my spine. I doubled up and felt paralysed in all the places where a man ought not to be paralysed. I knew what Archie had done was to throw a charge in on a hell of a long fuse to kill a fish along the gorge, and he had damn nearly killed me.

I was paralysed in body and stunned in mind. As I sank below the surface, I was not thinking of myself, but of that great mahseer that Archie tried to catch in his arms and which we dragged

59

ashore between us; and of that concussed otter that dived to what I hoped was safety in the bank.

Water was not my element, and to be dynamited in it was a very horrible thing. It made everything go wrong, driving unseen feet between the legs and unseen fists into the belly, water into the lungs and the wish for life away.

As I flung up my arms, my wrist was caught and I was pulled ashore like that mahseer. Archie, who had for weeks been forced to listen to my lectures on first aid for man and elephant, then demonstrated on me a lesson which I had never taught him: how to bring life back to a man who has far too much water in his lungs.

CHAPTER VI

WHEN we returned to camp, I found waiting for me among my other mail a letter from P. N. C. The Andamans trip was on, he said. If I decided on a short leave, everybody would understand, especially after that unfortunate stabbing affair. I must be feeling like a good rest. But if I could regard the Andaman Survey as a sort of refreshing change, as I had hinted when I was down in Rangoon, so much the better for everyone concerned.

I had no intention of allowing any of my colleagues the chance of a paid holiday in the Andaman Islands. For Tun Gyaw and his fellow convicts the prospect of a long compulsory stay might be most deterrent—though it didn't seem to have deterred him from drawing his dagger in anger. But the period which P. N. C. proposed—a month in Rangoon preparing and three months in the islands—could not fail to be interesting, even if the climate was as unhealthy and the aborigines as unpleasant as everybody seemed to think they were.

I had already begun to make my preparations. When I reached

the Andamans, I would have to decide whether elephants could be entirely self-supporting on jungle fodders. Such problems did not arise in Burma, except during the dry and hot seasons, when elephants rested for three months; on our Andaman project, working all species of timber and not teak alone, we would have to continue throughout the season.

While Archie had been curing goitre, I had been collecting elephant fodders. I spent three days and nights continuously with a female elephant, moving as she browsed and collecting specimens of every plant she ate. I collected forty-eight species of common plants, as well as some others which I ignored because of their rarity.

When I went down to Rangoon, I took these with me and showed them to the Botanist of the Forest Department, who classified them for me and mounted them in a two-volume herbarium, which I took with me to the Andamans.

I have described in *Bandoola* how on my way out of the forest I met a girl called Susan, the niece of a Chief Conservator of Forests, with whom I had shot and fished. Molly Mia, whom I had always considered so devoted to me that she could be happy with no one else, immediately abandoned me for Susan. It solved the problem of what was to be done with Molly Mia while I was away. Susan offered to look after Molly Mia during my absence, and I completed my journey to Rangoon, relieved of anxiety about my dog.

Before I spoke to anyone else in Rangoon, I had a long talk with P. N. C. and Jeff, the engineer who was to sail with me from Rangoon. The two other Europeans we were to pick up at Port Blair in the South Andamans. There was Carl, a young Swede direct from the Swedish School of Forestry with special technical training in soft and matchwood timbers. And there was a young man called Bruno, who wanted to work for the Bombine. Bruno's father was a big noise in the small town of Port Blair and P. N. C. would have liked to do him a favour. Bruno's only qualification was that he had been sent down from Oxford for throwing a very distinguished visitor's dress-clothes out of a window before he could put them on and give a lecture.

"He hasn't done anything else, this Bruno?" I asked, hoping that there might be something more positive in his favour.

"If he has, we shan't employ him," P. N. C. said. "I've warned his father to that effect."

Jeff and I and the provisions and equipment were to go to Port Blair by the regular steamer service of the Indian Steam Navigation Company, which ran every fortnight.

Port Blair was the only port on the South Islands. From there to the northern Andamans was an open sea journey of nearly two hundred miles. For that, the Indian Forest Service placed at our service a steamer, misnamed a steam yacht, because she had a white hull and yellow stack. She was called *Surmai*, after the fish of that name. *Surmai* would dump us in the North Islands and would return after four months to collect what was left of us.

Up there we should need our own craft. We were operating from one island to another in the open Indian Ocean, where, even during the North-east Monsoon, strong breezes could blow up fierce ground-swells.

From Port Blair, P. N. C. said, we could hire a a copper-bottomed, deep-sea-going motor craft which the Forest Officer in that port guaranteed as suitable. Her name was the *Jarawa*, after a tribe in the South Andamans.

In Rangoon we had the luck to procure a newly-built ship's lifeboat. Teak from bow to stern, fitted with a 25-h.p. petrol engine, she was thirty feet overall length. She was a sturdy craft and very suitable for our purpose. Her draught was shallow, she was fitted with emergency water-tanks and all iron rations were stowed in specially built compartments in the bow. She was certificated by the Board of Trade for nineteen passengers. We bought her and named her *Madame X* because her beam appeared on first sight out of all proportion to her length.

It was not so easy to ship her to the Andamans. The captain of the *Shah Jehan*—the steamer of the Indian Steam Navigation

Company which was to take us to Port Blair—refused to load the craft, because of some Board of Trade regulation about deck space. It might, he pointed out, interfere with lifeboat drill or make it impossible to launch the ship's lifeboats in an emergency.

I have always found that when I am actually aboard a ship, I can find some way to overcome or circumvent difficulties of this sort. "Do it first and ask permission after." As it was, I had to take my problem to P. N. C., who handed me over to his personal assistant, known to all and sundry as 'He Man'.

How he earned this sobriquet was a matter of dispute. But once given, it was something he felt it necessary to live up to—and, I almost wrote, to love up to. He was as much at home in the Women's Snake-pit in the Gymkhana Club as he was in the jungle of a Men Only Bar.

He Man could think of nothing better than that he should sail *Madame X* from Rangoon to Port Blair; and of course, having reached there, he would have to take her up north as well. "Honestly, Bill," he said, "I can do it."

His instructions were to load the *Madame X* aboard the *Shah Jehan*, even if he had to get a special dispensation from the Governor. He did not need to go as far as that. In fact he solved the difficulty with despatch. But then he persuaded me to put up the alternative idea that he should take *Madame X* across to the North Andamans. This suggestion did not go down well with P. N. C. "If you can't do this job without He Man," he said, "I shall have to think again about whether you're the right man for it."

Next day *Madame X* was astride the teak decks of *Shah Jehan*.

"Too bad," said He Man. "You get the Andamans. And all I can do is look after Molly Mia for you."

"Susan's looking after her."

"In that case," he said, "I suppose I shall have to look after Susan."

It gave me a twinge of jealousy, because Susan and her uncle were coming back to Rangoon any day, and He Man's reputation was gayer than Lothario's.

We reckoned that we also needed a fast motor-boat to work in calm, sheltered waters. For this we bought a Chris flat-bottomed craft with powerful outboard engines and we called her *Hintha*, after the Burmese wild duck. The *Hintha* was also petrol-driven, but the *Jarawa* was a twin diesel. Th's meant that we had to plan our fuel supplies more accurately than if we had had to think only of petrol or only of diesel oil.

A far worse nightmare was that we had to visualise every possible contingency before we even left Rangoon. We could find out what requirements of ours could be met from Port Blair and what we should have to take from Rangoon. But once we had left Port Blair, anything which we had forgotten we should have to do without. As far as we were concerned, the North Islands were uninhabited territory. If we found aborigines, they would have nothing which we required.

At a pre-arranged date, more or less half way through the survey, two Southampton flying-boats were to be flown from Singapore by the R.A.F. to take oblique photographs of the forest areas which promised the best stands of timber. But it was no good hoping that the Southamptons would bring up anything which we might have forgotten. In those days the North Andamans were beyond the radius of contact with the mainland by radio, and we could not give any orders or make any reports on progress.

We gathered all the maps that we could find of the islands. But they had all been made by sailors, whose professional object was to avoid touching land. All the coastal soundings were marked and all the islands named, but apart from a few trigonometrical points there was no information whatever of the islands, no indication of rivers or contours, and no hint of the type of vegetation to be found.

Of course there were other sources of information than these naval maps. Everybody knew something about the Andamans, usually to their discredit, though no one whom I met had been

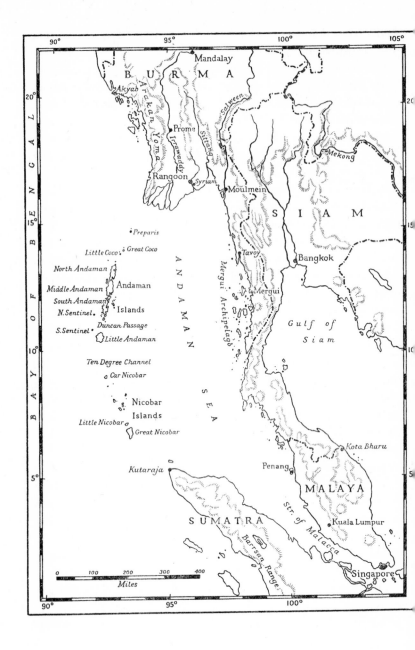

there. They implied, indeed, that they were places to which people
went, but did not return. Their reputation was as unsavoury as
that of Devil's Island in French Guiana.

We also gathered all the general maps we could find which
showed the Andaman Islands. On the big physical map of Asia
it was plain that the Andamans formed part of the mountain range
which ran from Arakan in Burma to the Barisan Mountains in
Sumatra. The central part of this had been submerged and the
island groups—the Cocos, the Andaman and the Nicobar groups—
were the still-projecting peaks.

There were two Andaman Island groups—the Great and the
Little. We were concerned only with the Great, which consisted,
very broadly speaking, of a mountain range 155 miles long and
nowhere more than eighteen miles broad. The North, Middle and
South Andaman were still almost one single land-mass with narrow
straits between them, formed by submerged passes. Rutland was
nearly as closely joined. The remaining islands were either individual peaks, like South and North Sentinel and Interview
Island, or collections, like the Archipelago and Labyrinth Groups.

The main map from which we had to work had been made for
the use of navigation, and not for foresters. The land was left
vague except for the odd triangulation point and imaginative
contours. The highest point in the North Andaman was 2,400
feet, in the Middle 1,678 feet and in the South 1,510 feet. The
east side of the islands was steep, and to the west they sloped gently
away.

There were two points of greater definition: Port Blair in South
Andaman and Port Cornwallis in North Andaman. Behind that
definition on the map we were to find that there was a great deal
more history than geography.

Jeff and I were not the first people to look at the map and dream
of the possibilities of the Andaman Islands. Those harbours were
some of the largest and most bountifully endowed by Nature.
Strategically it looked a most inviting base.

Yet something always went wrong with any scheme to bring the

Andaman Islands within the civilised order. Its aboriginal inhabitants still belonged to the Iron Age. They had an evil reputation from the earliest times as being cannibals. That of course was common enough in the days when travellers filled in the blanks with Anthropophagi. Marco Polo reported that the men of 'the long island' of 'Angamanain' had 'heads like dogs, and teeth and eyes likewise. They have a quantity of spices but they are a most cruel generation and eat everybody that they can catch if not of their own race.'

This reputation was perpetuated and heightened by the Malay pirates and slavers, who found in the Andamans the perfect hideouts from which to operate. So far from being eaten by the savage Andamanese, I suspected that they captured any they could lay hands on and sold them into slavery in Nicobar or Moulmein.

It is no wonder, perhaps, that the Andamanese developed a dislike of strangers who were so much more advanced than they were in civilisation and cruelty. They seem to have attacked the shipwrecked stranger as much as they attacked one another, quarrelsome people because full of fear and hunger. A more resourceful race might have come to better terms with the Andamans. But these squat Negritos were ignorant of agriculture and bad at fishing.

Towards the end of the eighteenth century, the Governor of Bengal saw the need for a harbour of refuge in the Andamans. He sent Lieutenant Colebrooke of the Bengal Engineers and Lieutenant Archibald Blair to explore the possibilities of founding a penal settlement there. The climate, at any rate in the pioneering days, would be too lethal and the rewards for private enterprise too meagre to draw free settlers there.

They chose for the settlement the area which in our time was called Port Blair. At the time of its foundation, in 1789, it was known as Port Cornwallis, and for two years it prospered round this southern bay.

But then it was decided to move the settlement to the place in the North Andaman now known as Port Cornwallis. Nothing was known in those days of the cause or carriage of malaria through the various anopheline vectors. It was thought to be borne on the miasma which hung on stagnant waters. The new Port Cornwallis was a secluded resort of the anopheline mosquito, rank with miasma. The prisoners fell sick too quickly to make it worth while shipping them. They were dead with remittent fever or enlargement of the spleen before they had earned their passage.

After four years in the North Andaman, the penal settlement was abandoned in May 1796, and it was not revived until 1855. In that year the Andamanese killed three and wounded four seamen of the *Fyze Buksh* of Moulmein. This determined the authorities to found a penal settlement which should itself act as a port of refuge in the Andamans and serve as a caution to the aborigines. Then the Indian Mutiny came to delay the establishment of the penal colony, though eventually it provided most of the early prisoners.

The intention was that, like the colonies of New South Wales and Singapore, it should start as a penal settlement, later to grow into a free colony, but for some reason this hope was not realised. It remained first and foremost a penal settlement, at least in the public imagination, as Devil's Island does. Despite its fifth-century name νῆσος ἀγαθοῦ δαίμονος—the Isle of Good Fortune— the Andamans had earned, and continued to hold, an evil reputation. The Burmese knew them by various opprobrious names: the Black Isles, the Isles of No Return, the Islands of Disease. A convict like Tun Gyaw banished to serve his sentence in Port Blair looked on it as a protracted death sentence.

My European friends seemed to consider that the assignment was one on which they should commiserate with me, 'four months hard labour'. There were jokes like, "Do you get remission for good conduct?" It was painful to see one after another of my friends in labour with this comic idea and to have to laugh, or at least to smile. I could not explain that to me the trip was an immense adventure, far better than any holiday in a hill station with not enough to do except drink too much.

There was certainly enough to do if we were to get off in time. It seemed to me that the time they had allowed me for assembling the stuff in Rangoon was not long enough for one even to think out what all one's requirements would be. Daily new difficulties arose to plague me. The worst was when P. N. C. called me in and said, "I'm sorry, Bill, but the Indian Government seems determined you should take armed guards. They're afraid there may be trouble with the convicts. And these Andamanese . . they don't really know how many there are left . . . but apparently they don't like strangers. . . ."

"And I suppose another Ferdinand Stipplewether to help me," I said. "You know as well as I do, P. N. C., that armed guards can be far more trouble than the rebels."

P. N. C. moved as much of heaven and earth as he could and the Government of India agreed that the final decision should rest with the man on the spot. "There's an Acting Commissioner in Port Blair," P. N. C. said. "Fellow called Alcock—Athelstan Alcock. Rather a queer customer, I gather."

"I knew an Alcock," I said. "A great shikari, isn't he?" I remembered a short leave I'd spent up in Simla and a tall, thin man in the Indian Political Service, rather weary-looking until he sat a horse or stalked a bison.

"I never heard he was a big-game shot. He certainly isn't now. There was a scandal of some sort. Somebody's wife. I was told all the sordid details, but I've forgotten them. But, anyway, I gather he's chosen the Andamans because Port Blair's so nice and quiet."

I thought no more about it. Alcock is not so very uncommon a name, but there was one thing that I was pretty sure of. There was a lot of flirtation in Simla, but my Alcock kept himself very much aloof from women. I had the impression that he was a man of the highest honour. He was incapable of having an affair with another man's wife, it seemed to me, because his regard for womanhood was so high that he couldn't love a woman he did not respect and he could not respect a married woman who did not cleave to her husband.

70

It was a pity that it could not be my Alcock; because I had got on well with him. We had shot together, and that can make for a certain warmth in friendship. I should have got my way with my Alcock about the prisoners.

Meanwhile, a frightening array of equipment and provisions piled up at the wharf in cases, crates and every conceivable type of container.

It was not difficult to cater for the Europeans. It was the multiple of the number of tins needed daily by four people and the number of days. Condiments for the Burmese convict rations were not so easy. My cook had to decide them; and this meant that the time had come when my servants had to be told that either we must part or they must accompany me to the Black Islands. I told them that during the expedition all rations would be free and, somewhat to my surprise, they professed to regard the expedition with as much enthusiasm as I did. My cook threw himself into the job of getting supplies for the convicts, but when he produced as his principal item two dozen sacks of chillies, I decided to seek advice elsewhere.

Everyone I met was bursting with advice; but I have often found that those who are most confident in advice have the least basis of experience. But, then, I have also found that people who really know about anything are often so inarticulate that they are less use than someone else with less knowledge but more imagination.

A few days before I was due to depart, I gave a 'What have you forgotten' dinner to a dozen friends, including He Man and Susan.

Susan arrived at the dinner-party like Diana the Huntress, with Molly Mia. I sat on her left, and on her right was He Man, who impressed the girls by biting the side out of his champagne glass and chewing it like wafer biscuit. He tried chewing Susan's glass, and I wasn't sorry when he cut his lip. "Look out, He Man," someone said, "or Molly Mia will start chewing you."

When the convivial stage of the evening was reached, I asked each of them to write on the back of their menus what they thought I might need on the Andamans, which I had perhaps forgotten. The conversation had been running on whether the death I was destined to die was from hunger or starvation on some deserted island or fattened up to make a Sunday luncheon for my convict coolies. The menu game, I realised, was merely going to extend the possibilities of innuendo.

As they were writing out their lists with guffaws and girlish laughter, Susan passed me a note under the table. I glanced down and read one word. SUSAN. "No, I haven't," I said, slipping the note in my pocket, "and shan't."

When the lists were all collected, each girl had written her own name at the top of the list with an exclamation mark. Except Susan, who had written: "Notepaper and envelopes."

The game ended with three serious suggestions. As a result next day I bought two hundred live chickens and a hundred and fifty live ducks, plus feed. From a keen gardener I collected two huge boxes of lettuce seedlings. "Pop 'em in the earth wherever your headquarters are," he said, "and don't forget they need a lot of water."

The third suggestion came from a young policeman called Roger. "If I was going to control a gang of convicts in the Andamans," he said, "there's only one thing I'd ask, and that's opium. Not as a bribe, but just to keep them going. They've got everything organised at Port Blair, but if you take them up to the North Andaman, they won't be able to get it for themselves, and they'll go crazy—the addicts, I mean."

"And do you think the Hon. Athelstan Alcock is going to let me bring in opium?" I asked. "Or will he provide it?"

Roger laughed. "Our Athelstan's a very strict geyser, so they say. You'd find yourself in the chain gang before you knew where you were. You'll have to smuggle the stuff in. I'll let you have it the day after to-morrow, if you like."

I appreciated Roger's point. The possible wrath of the Acting Commissioner if he discovered me dope-smuggling was nothing compared to the certain frenzy of a gang of addicts deprived of their opium. "But how do you do it?"

"I don't," he said, "but if I did, I might try walnuts. Of if you think that too slow, you could always stuff a football."

The opium arrived wrapped in banana leaves, and I had ready a sack of walnuts. One had only to split the walnuts in half, remove the nut and fill each half of the shell with the opium paste—which was like a black putty—and then glue the two halves together again. I fixed up a couple of dozen of these nuts and then retired to bed exhausted. At that rate, before I finished stuffing walnuts, the monsoons would have broken.

Finally, I stuffed a football-case drum-tight with the paste so that it looked fully inflated. In an open nailed crate, labelled ANDAMAN EXPEDITION in large stencils, it looked innocence itself. Only a very inquisitive person might wonder why it was necessary to take it out filled with air and then find, to his surprise, that it was a dead weight.

My last parting present was from my old friend the Senior Forest Officer, who was Susan's uncle. He gave me an excellent dinner, and after it produced a box the size of a small coffin. He opened it as if it were a treasure-chest. "There you are," he said. "Haven't used it since I was it Mergui fifteen years ago. But it's all there."

It was a rusty tangled mass, shark hooks the size of shepherds' crooks, tangled wires, a harpoon gun as well as the general gear.

"Maybe Susan'll give you a hand at unravelling it," the old man said, and went off to smoke a cigar.

I had better things to do with Susan than sort fishing tackle. We neither of us declared our feelings outright. It was not necessary. "It's no good taking notepaper," I said, "there are no mails where we are going."

"There's a Southampton flying-boat, isn't there?" she said. "And remember I'm staying with my uncle for another year."

"And I'll be going on leave before then," I said. "I was hoping to see you in England."

When I said goodbye, I just kissed Susan on the forehead, making all the fuss of Molly Mia. There was no need to say more. and I did not realise at the time how much that said. I was too busy, for one thing.

All next day I supervised the loading of stores, equipment and gear. That night I slept aboard, and next morning Jeff joined me and we sailed on the high tide, before noon.

CHAPTER VII

I HAD been assured that I should be able to get the fuel oils, petrol and diesel that we needed when we arrived at Port Blair. This had relieved me, because no insurance company would give us cover if we shipped it in drums with the other stores and equipment aboard the *Shah Jehan*.

Shortly before we were due to sail, word came from Port Blair. We were quite wrong. We could draw fuel oils in drums from Port Blair only if we brought the equivalent in bulk to replenish their stocks.

In the Rangoon River off Syriam we had to pick up an oil-barge, which was to be towed by the *Shah Jehan* across to Port Blair. The sight of it being towed alongside by a cheeky little tug roused all my scepticism. It looked to me less like an ocean-going craft than a whale that had succumbed to the harpoon.

"What do you think?" I asked Jeff, who was leaning over the rail beside me.

"I was thinking how like the 'double' in *The Specialist* that thing at the back is." He pointed to a sort of deck-closet in the stern which sported a red flag of danger.

It was plain soon after we got the barge in tow that the 'double' was in fact the living quarters of a couple of unfortunate lascars who formed the crew.

We dropped slowly down the Rangoon River, and when night fell we were still in the muddy waters of the delta.

By next morning we were in the Indian Ocean and the pilot had left us. One did not have to look out of the porthole to know one was at sea.

I felt sorry for those two lascars, but not so sorry that I wanted to see how they were faring before I took my own breakfast.

Jeff and I were both placed at the Captain's table. He was a little wizened man, who clearly did not owe his appointment to his social graces. He stonewalled any effort at conversation and perhaps felt it would be indiscreet to betray any interest in his passengers. If they wanted to tell him their business, no doubt they would do so. But sufficient unto the meal was the evil thereof. 'With any luck,' his silence seemed to say, 'we'll know as little about one another by the end of the journey as we do now.'

The Captain tantalised me, not because I thought that there was any particularly interesting secret locked behind his taciturnity, but because I wanted to discover what would dissolve that rather grumpy expression into pleasure. I could not believe that it was impossible to rearrange even his features to show good humour. But certainly we failed during breakfast. "I think you'd find it easier to make the eggs and bacon laugh," Jeff said.

There was a heavy north-east swell, and when we went on deck we found that the reason why we wallowed and proceeded so

slowly was because there was a following sea. Jeff and I went to
the stern to see how the barge was faring.

It was most alarming. One moment we would appear to slacken
speed and the barge would make way on our stern, the towing-
ropes would fall slack, the barge would ride dangerously forward;
and then the next moment the *Shah Jehan* would appear to shoot
ahead, taking up the slack so that the cables snapped out of the
water. It looked as if they would part or else the stern would be
torn out of us.

"Anything wrong?"

I looked up. It was the Chief Officer, a man with a Presence.
The Chief looked and behaved as if the *Shah Jehan* was his.

"It's obvious something is going to give," I said. "I was just
wondering what will happen to those two unfortunate lascars if it
gives in the middle of the night."

"Don't you worry," said the Chief. "We'll play a searchlight
on them as soon as it gets dark. They're not scared."

Jeff laughed. "We could do with toughs like them during the
next three months," he said.

The Chief inquired what we were going to do, and soon we
were swopping yarns of sea and jungle. One of his stories was

about a transport which caught fire off the coast of Aden during the 1914–18 war. He was Chief Officer then, and the ship was loaded with British prisoners of war.

"And the O.C. Troops was a friend of mine, a Gurkha officer named Tommy Tucker," I said.

The Chief Officer remembered Tommy Tucker very well, as he had come off in his lifeboat, and by the time they were rescued from the remote shore on which they beached, Tommy had allayed the terrors of the Turks and started to teach them Rugby football.

This mutual friendship led us to the bar, and the subject of the miserable little skipper cropped up. It took all sorts to make a world, the Chief said, and though the Captain might appear rather short, once you got him on his subject there was no stopping him.

"And what is his subject?" Jeff asked.

"Birds," said the Chief. "He'll be asking you up for a drink. You'll be surprised when you see the bridge. Like a blooming apiary!"

"Don't you mean aviary?" I said.

"No, an aviary's what you keep bees in," said the Chief.

When I left the Chief at the end of the session, he caught sight of my precious seedlings in my cabin. "Blimey, what's this?" he said. "Garden of Eden?"

I explained the plan. One was a box of cos, the other of cabbage lettuce. We should have salad wherever we went.

The cabin was like an oven, and though I had watered the seedlings before breakfast, from the water carafe in my cabin, they were already beginning to wilt. "They won't reach Port Blair at this rate," the Chief said. "You'd better let me put them in a nice cool place. Want to be very careful with them lettuce. People think lettuce is easy. But you've no idea. No idea."

I agreed with the Chief, partly because it was plain that my cabin was one of the many menaces to lettuce; and also because once I get aboard a ship, I come to rely on the officers and crew not only to convey me to my destination, but also as experts on any subject they set up to know. I would have pitted my knowledge of lettuce against the whole complement of the *Shah Jehan* ashore. But we were at sea. "I'll see they're looked after," the Chief said.

During the afternoon the lettuce seedlings disappeared from my cabin and the weather deteriorated. The two lascars were occasionally visible apparently swopping seats in the double. It looked as if there was quite a lot of sea being shipped by the barge. But I had given up worrying about salt water in the petrol, or even the total loss of the barge.

"I'll never forgive myself," I said to Jeff, several times, "if those two lascars lose their lives."

Towards sundown we received an invitation to take a drink with the Captain in his cabin on the bridge. As we went into the cabin my eye was met by that of an African grey-blue parrot, perched on an upright stand near the door. "DoyouknowtheCapeofGoodHope?" I heard the parrot say.

Pride and joy rearranged the creases on the little Captain's face. "Ha! ha! ha! You know, that bird's more intelligent than I am," he said.

We looked at the bird, whose unwinking gaze was baleful, and then we looked at his gleeful master. He seemed unable to realise that there was nothing funny in the phrase which it proceeded to repeat. "DoyouknowtheCapeofGoodHope?" But even if the Captain was right, as Jeff said later, it wasn't a very intelligent bird.

"I expect you'd like to see the bridge," said the Captain, and he led us into what I had always believed to be a sort of nautical holy of holies.

But this was, as the Chief Officer had said, a 'blooming apiary', with a dozen large cages full of canaries, yellows and reds, rollers, hooped, feather-footed, top-knotted.

The teak floor was spotlessly clean, but it was littered with minute chippings of newspaper. The Captain caught my eye. "Breeding," he said. "They make their nests out of newspaper. Tear it up in little bits."

79

"How interesting!" Jeff said.

"My birds prefer the London *Times*," he said, "but I can't always get it." He was glowing with the thought of his canaries' intelligence, or good taste, or political reliability. I was not quite sure which. But all the same I was impressed by his love of these birds.

Those two lascars tossed aboard the oil-barge left him unmoved. He would get them to Port Blair in safety—as he did. But all he cared about was these birds, the colours he could crossbreed, the sounds he could get them to copy. The only person I have ever met like him was a very dull man who married a very beautiful but stupid Burmese girl and who derived great pleasure out of hearing her repeat his opinions.

I noticed that in the corner of the bridge were the two boxes of lettuce seedlings. The Chief Officer had obviously asked permission for them to be kept there in the cool; at the same time I think he had told the Captain how keen Jeff and I were on cage-birds.

"I can't say how good of you this is," I said, pointing to the seed-boxes.

"It's nothing," he answered.

He was right. During the night he let loose his parrot, who ate up every seedling, no doubt asking after each precious plant went down "DoyouknowtheCapeofGoodHope?"

"That proves it," Jeff said.

"Proves what?"

"That the parrot's more intelligent than the Captain. I bet, if the parrot was looking after the seedlings for us, he wouldn't have let the Captain loose."

But that was our only disaster. The cables had not parted overnight, the wind had dropped and the sea was glassy, with little or no swell.

Our first sight of land was two small islands, the Britton Islands, then Long Island.

Approaching the coast of the main South Andaman Group, we

saw they were covered with dense natural forest. But close to
Port Blair there was a fringe of coconut plantation. A dredge was
working among the mangrove swamps. Above some corrugated-
iron roofs stood the tall stack of a saw-mill. Scattered up the
steep slopes of the settlement were several pleasant bungalows,
the residences of officials. At the end of the promontory was a
huge wooden building, which was obviously part of the jail.

We anchored in the calm water of the sound off Chatham
Island. Lying at anchor near the sawmill was the S.S. *Maharajah*,
a 3000-ton steamer built for carrying convicts. Alongside another
jetty was a steam yacht, the S.Y. *Surmai*, which the Indian Forest
Service had promised us. She stood so high out of the water
that it looked almost as if she might turn turtle. That, I thought,
would be remedied as soon as we had loaded our equipment
aboard. She was a trim-looking craft, with rows of white life-
belts, and awnings fore and aft. Her recently painted yellow mast
and stack gave her the air of a yacht.

The Chief Forest Officer came aboard the *Shah Jehan* with a
few Indian officials in uniform. To my delight, they wanted to
avoid all unnecessary fuss and suggested that if we transferred our
stores and equipment direct on to the *Surmai*, there would be no
need for any Customs inspection.

Jeff took over the work of transhipment, while I went ashore to
see the Chief Jailer about the convict labour, to meet my two
assistants and to pay a call on Athelstan Alcock at the Residency.

The invitation from the Acting Commissioner was presented
by a Sikh in red uniform heavily decorated with gold braid. The
envelope was impressively sealed, and I expected something far
more formal than the simple note asking me to come up and see
him and reminding me that we had perhaps met in Simla. There
was nothing in the letter to endorse P. N. C.'s gossip about Alcock's eccentricity. It was charming, friendly and very normal.

The *Jarawa* took me ashore. This was the deep-sea launch we
were hiring for the trip. She was after my own heart, a 30-foot
launch with twin diesel engines and a copper bottom. She took a

crew of four, two bunks in the built-in cabin and two others forward. There was a minute galley and aft a spacious railed platform. She romped ashore from the *Shah Jehan*. There was no doubt she could travel. But it was clear that we could not load her on the *Surmai*.

There was a young Anglo-Burman police officer waiting for me on the quayside. He told me that he had been detailed to conduct me to the jail. I took to him immediately, as I have done to all Anglo-Burmans I have ever worked with. They are given the dirtiest jobs, which they never hesitate to do, loyally, courageously and good-temperedly.

As we walked towards the jail, the Anglo-Burman begged me, if I got the chance, to take him as the officer in charge of the convicts.

"If there is to be anyone," I said, "I'd like it to be you. But I don't want any armed guards. If you'll back me on the question of no guards, I'll back you personally as officer in charge of the convicts."

I asked him the principle on which they had selected the prisoners for me. He answered that they had tried as far as possible to pick their men from the good-conduct convicts. But they had had to take other factors into consideration as well—age, physical fitness and jungle experience. "We've got two men who have worked for you," he said. "One of them said he was a Sinôke, a man called Nga Moh."

I couldn't remember his name, and this surprised me, as I prided myself on knowing all the Sinôkes, or elephant headmen, who had worked for me.

"I think you'll remember the other one's name," the Anglo-Burman said, grinning. "Tun Gyaw."

"Am I having him?" I asked.

"Not on your life. I mean, even if he hadn't done . . . well, what he did do to you, he's only just arrived. He's earned no remission for good conduct."

"He could be very useful," I said. I remembered his knowledge

82

of trees and jungle lore; and I felt that if I trusted him this time he would not let me down and I should have made some amends for what was my guilt in the fight which we had had together.

"You wouldn't want to take him with you, anyway!"

"Why not?" I asked. "I am quite sure that Tun Gyaw never intended to murder me. But these other convicts may include quite a number of deliberate murderers."

The Anglo-Burman laughed. "There's a lot to be said for that. But I could never get Tun Gyaw on a working-party. It would cause too much hard feeling. If you took me, I might be able to bring him along as one of my personal servants."

"If he could be one of your personal servants, why couldn't he be one of my convict labourers?"

By that time we had reached the jail and were informed that the Chief Jailer was waiting for me.

As soon as I met the Chief Jailer, I realised that we talked different languages. It was understandable. His job was to see that the prisoners came to no harm and caused no trouble. The authorities had worked out a form of discipline which answered very well in Port Blair. He disapproved of the whole project. It would be disturbing. There had been great eagerness on the part of the prisoners, all of whom were prepared to give their parole, provided only that they could have a holiday away from the boredom of Port Blair. Those who were left behind might prove restive, and those who went might find it difficult to settle down again on their return. I suspected that all these things were at the back of his mind, as they were at the back of mine.

But we did not talk in those terms. The Chief Jailer told me what a dangerous gang of dacoits and murderers I should have working for me, and that he would take no responsibility for the safety of our party unless the convicts were accompanied by adequate guards. I replied that I was perfectly happy to take the risk of our party being murdered and that the Jail Authorities would be exonerated of all blame. "I understand that they have given their parole," I said; "they know that they will be paid for their work when they return to Port Blair, and even the most desperate of them is not foolish enough to think that it would be possible for him to escape and survive. The jungle will prevent their escaping far more effectually than any armed guards."

We kept at it for about an hour, and he finally said, "Before you make up your mind, you had better come and look at them." It was said as if this would convince me, if nothing else did.

The selected prisoners were being paraded somewhere in the prison. To reach them, we went through long corridors and across several courtyards. We passed various groups of prisoners and I kept my eyes open for Tun Gyaw, but there was no sign of him. It was the first time I had ever been in a penal settlement, and I never want to enter one again. As we passed them, the prisoners looked at us sullenly, as if they would willingly have murdered us. I thought that if I had been in that prison I might well have looked the same, at the sight of someone with the exquisite privilege of liberty.

At last we came to a small open courtyard where my Anglo-Burman friend was standing beside a group of squatting Burmans. He came forward to salute, and I was taken up to the gang. I hadn't thought how I was going to deal with them. Without thinking, I addressed them as I would a group of my own men, with the normal Burmese greeting: "Ahlone mah t'lah?" Are you all well?

I could feel their shock. With some it was twenty years since they had been spoken to in that way, as if they were free men. They looked at one another and at their jailers, and their faces were wreathed in smiles. Without realising it, I had stumbled on the way to treat these men, and any fears that might have been aroused by the menacing looks of the other prisoners were immediately dissipated. I knew that I could do anything with these men because I was giving them three to four months of freedom on parole. No guards. Quite certainly no guards.

I was attracted by an old man with steel-grey hair and a mandarin moustache. He had a striking face, old and lean. To relieve

84

the embarrassment caused by my first greeting, I pointed to him. "What's your name?"

"Nga Moh," he said. He immediately added that he had been a Sinôke in charge of the Bombine elephant camps in the Shan States. It wasn't one of mine. The Anglo-Burman police officer had made a slight mistake, or Nga Moh over-stated his claim.

"Very good," I said. "From now on you are chaungoke of this camp." A chaungoke in elephant camp language meant Head of Everything.

Then Nga Moh did a surprising thing for a Burmese convict. He stood up and came and stood by me, facing the gang. He wasn't a prisoner any more, and I expected him to speak to the others. But this was too great a liberty. I told him to ask them if they were willing and agreeable to follow me under him as leader. As one man they answered, "Thabaw too bah thee," which means only 'Very willing', but it was said so fervently that it sounded like a deep-felt response in a Buddhist monastery.

Then I gave them a short talk, explaining that we would be leaving next day and that I would look after them, if they served me well.

When we left them, I asked the Chief Jailer whether my Anglo-Burman friend could come with us. About that the Chief Jailer was quite firm. "He will be in charge of the prisoners on board the S.Y. *Surmai*," he said. "But from the moment they are disembarked they will be your sole responsibility. I cannot allow one of my officers to be placed in the anomalous position of having to control convicts without guards."

"It was the best I could do," I apologised to the Anglo-Burman.

He hadn't been expecting anything else. "Do you really want to take Tun Gyaw?"

"Better the devil you know," I answered. "That is, if Tun Gyaw would like to come. Tell him I think he could help us."

It was now nearly sundown. I picked up Jeff, and together we went to the Club House to meet Carl and Bruno. After that I had to go to the Residency. I tried to persuade Jeff that he should meet the Acting Commissioner. But he was adamant. "If you think I'm going to put on a tropical suit to meet the Hon. Athelstan Alcock," he said, "you've got another think coming. I'll stay at the Club House and get to know the boys."

The Port Blair Club House was like any up-country club in India. The big night was the night the English weekly illustrated papers arrived.

They clearly had not come on the *Shah Jehan.* We could not see anyone at all for some time. Then we noticed an old Indian butler with a long beard. He tottered over to greet us. He looked as if he had served his twenty-five years in the prison and then, as happened frequently, lacked the courage to go back home.

"Are there any sahibs here?" we asked.

There were two in the billiard-room, and the butler would show us the way.

As we passed through the library, we stopped to admire a table. It stretched the whole length of the reading-room, twenty-eight feet in length and four and a half feet broad, and the top was made from a single plank.

"Padauk!" Jeff said. "If we can find a stand of timber to yield wood like this, our work ahead is going to be easy."

"That table, sirs," said the butler, in English that was almost too perfect—"that table, sirs, was presented to Lord Kitchener when he visited the penal settlement many years ago. Some say that it was too expensive to ship to India, but others think Lord Kitchener overlooked it."

While we were still admiring it, two young men appeared at the door and came to introduce themselves. The first, short, stocky with bright blue eyes full of mischief and self-assurance, introduced himself as Bruno. Carl was almost twice his size. He had obviously only just arrived in the East from Sweden. His bare arms were still pale. But his shoulders were broad and square, and I took to him at once.

Bruno had spent the past three months with his father in Port Blair. He had amused himself chiefly deep-sea fishing from his father's launch, the *Jarawa*. The *Jarawa*, I resolved, should be one of the first of Bruno's cares. Bruno already understood her better than any of us would before the end of the trip; and if anything did go wrong with the hired launch, it would be far better if Bruno was at the helm.

Bruno could speak good Hindustani, but he had no Burmese. That was a pity, but I thought he would pick things up quickly. He was a practical all-round young man.

Carl was more of a specialist. He had recently qualified as a wood technologist in the Stockholm School of Forestry. He had spent the last month studying all the main species of Andaman trees and woods. He spoke English with a pronounced accent, rather slowly, but also precisely. How serious he was it was difficult to judge, because his gravity might be caused by his fumbling for English. As a timber-man I felt that I would trust him. He would under-estimate rather than over-estimate. He would not hazard a guess. Bruno, on the other hand, would hazard anything. He made a useful contrast to Carl. There would be plenty of scope for both their temperaments before we were through.

"Tell me," I said to Bruno. "When I knew Alcock, he was a bachelor . . . that was some years ago." I did not openly want to ask what had happened, but Bruno immediately rose. It was not, I think, that he was interested in the scandal, but that the tragedy had stirred him.

Apparently Alcock had fallen in love with the wife of a tea-planter whom he had met in Simla. He was not the type of person to have affairs; nor was she, though her marriage was violently unhappy. If they had indulged the sort of affair that was only too common in India, it would probably have ended soon without any scandal.

Alcock and she tried to repress the feelings which they felt for one another. Their attraction mounted to a passion which neither of them could control. Yet both of them believed that they were morally wrong in loving one another so much.

In going to the husband and announcing their love, they made a far greater scandal than if they had been discreetly adulterous. Alcock said openly that he was prepared to sacrifice his professional career, and seemed positively upset to find that this was not necessary.

People in fact were sympathetic to a couple who had tried so hard to live according to the dictates of conscience, only to have them countermanded by ungovernable passion. They were in no mood to ostracise the romantic couple. But Alcock himself had felt that he had done something which was reprehensible. He imagined that in India he and his wife-to-be would never be free from gossip, and he had asked to be posted to the Andamans. He hoped that in crossing the Sea of Bengal they would leave scandal behind.

Tragically, within a week of their marriage, before ever they had sailed for the Andamans, his wife fell ill and died. Alcock took up his residence at Port Blair, a shattered man, convinced that his wife's death was God's punishment for adultery. "You may find him," Bruno added, "just a wee bit odd."

CHAPTER VIII

As I walked up to the Residency, I thought over what Bruno had told me. Even if it were true, I should have preferred to hear it after I had seen the Acting Commissioner. I could not feel at ease as I walked up to the huge glass conservatory which ran along the front of the Residency.

I felt relieved to be received by a uniformed Sikh and taken along in the usual, over-formal manner to sign the visitor's book, a red-leather-bound volume like the register in an expensive hotel. A pen was placed in my hand by the orderly and I signed. A silver salver was presented, and on it I laid a visiting-card from my pocket case. The orderly disappeared.

As I waited for him to return, I resolved that I would play my interview the formal way. The Chief Jailer had as good as granted us permission to take the prisoners without guards. The Acting Commissioner would reiterate all the warnings we had already received and make sure that if anything went wrong the blame would rest with us. I would give him my assurance, and take my departure as soon as possible.

The orderly returned and bowed, indicating that I should follow him. We crossed two imposing reception-rooms and came to a door on which the orderly tapped. I noticed that the door had heavy teak panelling of great beauty.

I heard no sound from the room within, but the orderly turned the handle, opened the door and stood aside for me to pass. Then he closed it behind me.

I found myself in a library which was very small compared to the rooms through which I had come. The Acting Commissioner was standing on a small mahogany step-ladder. I did not recognise him at first. He was going slightly bald, but his ginger eyebrows more than made up. And he had a long, sandy, walrus moustache, and sandy hairs on the back of his freckly hands.

If I had not been announced beforehand, discovering him in this position of vantage—which he did not abandon—could have been explained as chance. But he had had my card. It was on the desk by the window. So, on hearing that I had arrived, the Hon. Athelstan Alcock had climbed his little library ladder and re-moved a book from the shelves. It showed a theatrical sense with which I would not have credited him. "Good evening," he said, in a voice which was devoid of welcome or of the recognition which he had accorded me in his note to the *Shah Jehan*. "Come in."

"I'm afraid I'm disturbing you, sir," I said.

He gestured me to a chair, as he descended his ladder. "I have plenty of time to hear of your plans in the North Islands."

I explained my instructions: to ignore all previous forest work-ings in the South Andaman and concentrate on the other islands; to look out for at least ten different species of Indian trees; to estimate the yield per acre and to report on the possibility of using elephants to extract the timber. But I refused to sit down.

The Acting Commissioner behaved as if he had heard all this.

"And is that where your investigation ends?" he asked.

"We have only three months," I said.

"I have to warn you that if you take the prisoners without guards," he said, "we accept no responsibility for them. You will have to immobilise all your craft, or they'll steal them and leave you stranded."

"We shall take all precautions," I said.

With a slight change in his voice, he said, "You're quite right, of course, to go without guards. But it's my duty to warn you. Things may go wrong."

"They're less likely to go wrong if I take them on parole without any of the associations of Port Blair."

"You mean, things would be less likely to go wrong if they were ordinary people. But they're not. They're dacoits and murderers. They aren't normal."

"Which of us is?"

"Well, you're not a dope addict," he said—"at least, I hope not."

"Meaning?"

"It is not for the authorities to provide opium for convicts. But it would be folly to prevent those obtaining it who would go crazy if deprived of their supplies."

"I don't think any of your men need go crazy," I said.

The Acting Commissioner smiled. "Have a drink?"

I nodded, and he poured us both a liberal glass of whisky. As he raised his glass, he said, "Here's to your expedition! I wonder if you realise how greatly privileged you are."

"In what way?"

"You are being commissioned to explore the interior of the Andamans; and that is something which none of these authors here did." He waved to the library shelves. "The Malay pirates knew the islands well enough from the point of view of anchorages, but they wrote nothing and spread a pack of lies about the Andamanese. There have been a number of ships wrecked on the coast . . . but of course, the shipwrecked mariners were just spoiling to get off. And the expeditions—Colebrook and Blair's in 1789 and Mouat's in 1857—they were just to explore the possibility of a settlement. They were not scientific."

"Nor is mine," I said. "It is purely to find out about timber extraction."

"As if they couldn't have attached a botanist, a zoologist, an anthropologist, a geologist, and really made something worth while. It is such a waste of a splendid opportunity. It may never recur. You realise that?"

"I don't think anybody in Rangoon really thought about that, sir," I said. "After all, the Bombay Burma is a profit-making organisation; it is not interested in scientific exploration as such."

"But don't you see," said the Acting Commissioner, "the Andamanese are the most wonderful study of an Iron Age civilisation. I should think they are unique. And they're dying out; they're dying out fast. You may not see any of them at all." The Acting Commissioner spoke with the passion of a fanatic, who cannot understand that his interests are not shared by everyone. He seemed to have read everything that had been written about the Andamans. "There was some splendid work done in the nineteenth century," he said, "but anthropology was in its infancy. They were still in the stage of measuring skulls and taking temperatures and average respiration rates."

I suggested to him that he was the best person to organise an expedition of the type which he thought might be needed. Why didn't he go himself?

The moment that I asked the question, I realised that I had touched him on a tender spot. "Of course," he said, "you would not know. It was all planned; to be our honeymoon. . . . Do you believe in Divine Providence?"

I made a non-committal answer.

"It's quite plain you've never read about the shipwreck of the *Briton* and the *Runnymede*." He climbed up the library steps and fetched down a large green volume. He passed it to me with the air of a headmaster giving a schoolboy his first prize. "I'll give you this. I've got two copies. It's very rare. You take it on the voyage with you. Portman, who compiled it, was the officer in charge of the Andamanese at the end of the last century. It's the only place I've found the contemporary account of the *Briton* and *Runnymede*. And it has such a lot of useful information about the Andamanese; and advice. Such as don't rape their women—I mean don't let the convicts. Andamanese girls may not be very beautiful. But remember these men are sex-starved. If you're without guards, you will be responsible. There must be no breach of the peace."

I assured him that there would be no breach of the peace if I could avoid it, and that I would bring back all the information I could about the people, the flora and fauna; though it was understood that this was not my primary concern. I thought that the best thing might be to let him have a copy of the diary which I intended to keep, but I did not commit myself to this. There might be things which it would be better for him not to know.

As I finished my drink and made ready to leave, he walked over to the desk and took up a large envelope. "I wonder if you would mind posting this for me," he said.

"Of course not," I answered, though I wondered why he could not have one of his servants do it for him.

It was not until I was on my way that I looked at the address on the envelope. Then I read:

> Mrs. Athelstan Alcock,
> Port Cornwallis,
> North Andaman.
> *By Hand.*

The Indian butler at the Club House told me that the others had gone on board the *Surmai*; so I went down the hill towards the port.

In the evening light I could see Chatham Island set in the lovely sea. The evening was still, and there was a gentle breeze which made my tropical suit tolerable for the moment. Even the ugly buildings of the prison were softened in the yellow light.

I thought how deceptive it all was; what misery lay hidden behind those prison walls, what torment there was in the soul of the Acting Commissioner, into what fury this calm harbour was recurrently lashed by hurricanes.

The others were in high spirits when I went aboard.

"How did it go?" Jeff asked. "Bruno's been telling me the Indian Postmaster's got a sackful of letters addressed to Mrs. Alcock in Heaven."

"Anyway, they're unstamped," laughed Bruno, "and they don't pay postage dues where she's gone."

They pressed me to have a drink, but I said that I wanted to change first. I went to my cabin and took off the uncomfortable suit and tie. The envelope I hid in one of my cases, beneath a pile of shirts; the large green volume on the Andamans I placed on the rack above my bunk.

Into what separate compartments our personalities are divided, I thought. The Acting Commissioner had been very shrewd in his remarks, for example, about opium addiction. When he spoke of the scientific value of our expedition, he was sensible enough, except in his refusal to recognise that our Company had quite enough to do discovering what was necessary for our own purposes without wasting time on general fact-finding. Yet as regards his wife there was an enclosed area of his mind in which sanity did not rule.

I wondered how true this was of the convicts we were taking with us. I was assuming that if trusted and treated decently, they would respond in the same way. But what justification had I for considering that Tun Gyaw was a saner person than the Acting Commissioner? Perhaps I was altogether too optimistic and trustful.

I said nothing to the others of my misgivings. There were too many practical things to discuss.

All gear, provisions, equipment and kit were stowed aboard the *Surmai*. As the *Jarawa* was too large to be loaded on the *Surmai*, there was nothing to do but take her under her own power. Bruno

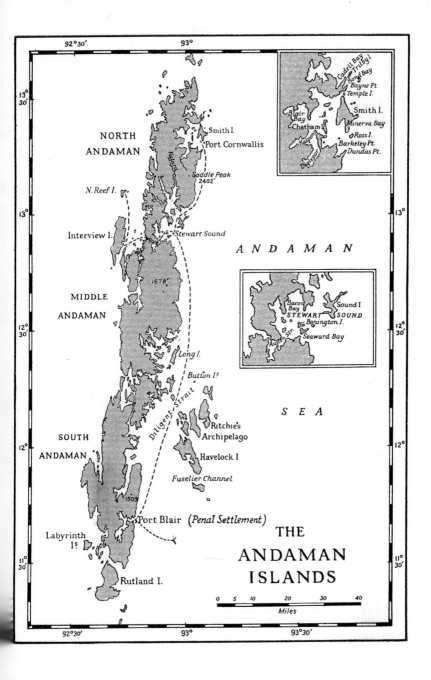

13°
30′

NORTH
ANDAMAN

Smith I.
Port Cornwallis

Saddle Peak
2402′

N. Reef I.

13°

Interview I.

Stewart Sound

A N D A M A N

MIDDLE
ANDAMAN

1678′

12°
30′

Long I.

Button I⁵

SOUTH
ANDAMAN

Diligent Strait

Ritchie's
Archipelago

Havelock I

12°

Fuselier Channel

S E A

1509′

Port Blair (*Penal Settlement*)

Labyrinth
I⁵

11°
30′

Rutland I.

THE
ANDAMAN
ISLANDS

0 5 10   20   30   40

Miles

Cadell Bay
Trilby I
Bond Bay
Bayne Pt.
Temple I.
Smith I.
Blair
Bay
Minerva Bay
Chatham I.
Ross I.
Barkeley Pt.
Dundas Pt.

Bacon
Bay
Sound I
STEWART   SOUND
Bonington I.
Austin Str.
Seaward Bay

13°

12°
30′

12°

11°
30′

considered that this was quite practicable, and it was decided that I should go with him, while Carl and Jeff sailed on the *Surmai*.

No date was fixed for our relief, except that we should keep a look-out for a relief ship from March 15 onwards; we sailed on November 15—my birthday.

At mid-day I watched the Anglo-Burman policeman march the convict gang down to the *Surmai*. They were a sad sight, moving like sheep being driven to the butcher's, jerkily. They did not know what was expected of them; then, as soon as they realised what they had to do next, they shambled off with a pathetic eagerness. When ordered to cross the gangway from the pier to the well-deck, they broke into a run, and I expected any moment one of them would fall into the harbour.

Once aboard, the convict gang was put to work rearranging the deck cargo of oil and petrol drums, so that they could be roped securely. The S.Y. *Surmai* looked as though she would roll in the slightest sea. For her size, she was of shallow draft; indeed, she had to be, to coast off these shores with shallow channels, sudden reefs and shoals.

The convicts were not my responsibility until they were handed over at Port Cornwallis. I saw them off on the *Surmai* with an easy conscience, expecting that the *Jarawa* would go in company with her.

I found that Bruno and the Serang of the *Jarawa* had other plans. They had no intention of following the *Surmai* on her deep-sea route to the east of Ritchie's Archipelago. They proposed instead to hug the east coast of the main group, passing through Diligent Strait to the west of the Archipelago. It was a course with which both of them were familiar, and, seeing the comparative frailty of the *Jarawa*, I had to agree that it was sensible to keep her as far as possible in sheltered water.

I had also to agree that it would be sensible to lay in some odd stores for the voyage—just in case we did not succeed in meeting the *Surmai* at Port Cornwallis. While Bruno was having them brought from the Prison Officers' Canteen to the *Jarawa*, I took his suggestion and went to see his father.

"You can understand the old man's pretty worried about me," Bruno said, winking. "I'm almost as wild as he was at my age."

The old man had applied to have Bruno accepted as a Forest Officer in Burma, but P. N. C. had told him that everything would depend on what sort of report I gave him. "You've got to be strict with that boy, Mr. Williams," he said. "What he needs is discipline. We all do in our family. And don't you be afraid of giving it to him."

If the discipline had been applied to old Bruno, as he recommended it should be applied to his son, neither of them would have been in Port Blair.

Many, many years before, when serving as a master carpenter on a German ship, he had touched at Port Blair. Now it so happened that the Port Officer, who was also a sawmill engineer and Forest Officer of the South Andaman, needed a barge in which he could transport timber from the coast to the mill. He knew that it had to be capable of sea towage, but how to set about building it he had not the least idea. And it so happened that the master carpenter of the German ship confided to the Port Officer that before the wanderlust took him he had served his apprenticeship in a sailing-ship-building yard in Stettin, and he had also worked in a barge-builder's at Kiel.

When the German ship sailed the next day, the master carpenter was nowhere to be found; otherwise he might have been disciplined for trying to jump ship.

The master carpenter changed his name and settled down in Port Blair, where he proceeded first to construct some barges as fine as any plying on a German canal. Then, perceiving that there was a need for a Jack-of-as-many-other-trades as the Port-Officer-Mill-Engineer-Forestry-Officers, he set about fulfilling as many of them as possible. He had made far more money in Port Blair than he would ever have done in Kiel or Stettin. He had become a solid citizen, the sort of man who highly disapproved of master carpenters jumping ship.

When he retired from being Chief Forest Officer, he took over the contract for extracting timber, and a part of the Port Blair development had been named after him. He really was, in his own view, a solid citizen, and it was his pride that he had sent Bruno to an excellent English public school and then to Oxford. He was bitterly disappointed when Bruno turned out to be a chip off the old block.

To me it was tragic. He had sent Bruno away as soon as he was ready to go to a prep school. Though there was this deep psychological kinship, they had never known one another. I knew Bruno better after twenty-one hours than the old man did after twenty-one years. All Bruno was suffering from was too little love, not too many opportunities.

"That boy has got to be taught to play the game," said the old man. "He's got to be taught to keep a straight upper bat." (His command of the clichés of British fortitude was still not perfect.) "I want you to beat the very best into him."

"I'm not going to do anything of the sort," I said. "That son of yours is going to take me to Port Cornwallis in the *Jarawa*. And I'm quite sure that he will do so. If he doesn't . . . then neither of us will have to worry about his problem any more."

The whole attitude of the old man changed. He had imagined that I wanted to think the worst of his boy. Now I had to listen to what a wonderful son he was, how marvellous in his handling of a boat.

By the time Bruno joined us, the old man was telling me about Port Cornwallis. He had been there once. How many years ago? That was difficult to say. Time passed so quickly. But what a harbour! Who had said it was large enough to hold the whole British Navy? It was like an inland sea. It teemed with fish and sharks. I've always thought it was the breeding-ground for the sharks of the Indian Ocean.

The sun had practically set before we departed, with only old

Bruno to wave us *au revoir*. I did not feel quite the confidence in young Bruno that I had expressed to the old man. But the Serang, the old man assured me, was a fine navigator and knew the coast well up to the Middle Andamans.

The Serang certainly looked impressive. He wore a smart black alpaca coat reaching down to his knees and fastened down the front with polished brass buttons. His legs were clothed in tight-fitting white trousers. His feet were bare and on his head he wore a red Mohammedan fez. He and the three members of his crew were the only four Indians we had on the trip. They had worked for years for the Government at Port Blair; but had followed the old man when he retired from Government service and set up on his own.

As we went full ahead through the sound and towards the open sea, Bruno, the self-appointed cook, lighted up an antiquated and rusty oil-stove, announcing that he was going to prepare eggs and bacon.

I left him to it and joined the Serang in the cramped wheelhouse. As soon as we entered the open sea, I felt the force of the Serang's argument that we should keep to the leeward of the Archipelago. We struck a strong north-east breeze which livened the *Jarawa* in no small way . . . we were to go head on into that until we found the shelter of Havelock Island, in the south of the Archipelago. If we followed the west coast of that island, we should find ourselves in Diligent Strait by daylight, said the Serang. But seeing through what a maze of small islands we had to thread our course, I hoped that we should do it before daylight ended.

We were soon in a heavy sea. Having eaten his bacon and eggs, young Bruno relieved the Serang at the wheel. He cut down speed, at which I was pleased. But he put the *Jarawa* to each oncoming wave as if he were nursing a hunter over a stone wall. He chatted the whole time, talking about the islands of the Archipelago. It was on one of them that the *Briton* and the *Runnymede* had so providentially been wrecked. He said that the Fusilier Channel, which we were now passing, acted as a funnel for the north-east breezes, and in about an hour we should be out of the weather. It sounded as if he knew what he was talking about, though I felt that if he had a fault, it was to make plans, and not be prepared to change them if the weather changed.

I decided to go back to our own cabin. Mention of the *Briton* and the *Runnymede* reminded me that I had the story of their wreck in the green book which the Acting Commissioner had given me.

It was no easy task passing along the deck to the cabin in that sea, but there were good hand-grips along the hatch. I could feel the motion of the *Jarawa* as I lay down on my bunk to read the green book, and it was not very long before I became oblivious to everything around me, in re-living one of the strangest shipwrecks in the history of navigation.

It was a story which I shall re-tell, since very few of my readers can have heard of it, and it became inextricably bound up with my own experiences at this time; for just as I came to regard this period of my life as an experiment in trust—the trust between man and man—so the story of the *Briton* and the *Runnymede* stood for the highest trust of all—the trust of man in God.

What gave the story an immediate significance was that though the ships had been wrecked so many years ago, the violent storms which caused the wrecks had taken place in November. And we were now in November. We ourselves might at any moment run into similar weather.

CHAPTER IX

ON the morning of 12 August 1844, Her Majesty's 80th Regiment, about a thousand strong, marched out of Sydney Barracks to embark for Calcutta. They were in four ships—*Royal Saxon*, *Lloyds*, *Enmore* and *Briton*—and they left Sydney together on the 15th, having said adieu to the colony on the completion of seven years' service.

They had from the start baffling winds and dirty weather. The passage through the Torres Straits, at all times tedious, took eighteen days.

On September 11 the four ships lay to off Booby Island, each ship sending a boat ashore to communicate with the Post Office. Seventeen days later they were together again in Kupang Roads, Timor Island. But after this they gradually parted company, and the *Briton* reached Singapore alone.

The *Briton* was a North-American-built barque of 776 tons measurement and registered A1 at Lloyds. This was her second voyage. Captain Bell was her master, and he had a crew of thirty-four, men and boys. Of the troops, there were eight officers besides Major Bunbury: Captains Bert, Sysers and Montgomery; Lieutenants Leslie and Freeman; Ensigns Hunter and Coleman; and Assistant Surgeon Gammie. There were twelve sergeants, four drummers, two hundred and ninety-three rank and file, thirty-five women and forty-three children—a complement of four hundred and thirty-one souls in all.

After leaving Singapore they were wind-bound for several days before they got into the Straits of Malacca. As they got clear of the Straits, they naturally expected to fall in with the North-East Monsoon, but the wind kept variable and unsteady, not blowing from the same quarter for two days together.

Saturday, November 9 dawned cloudy and threatening. Captain Bell could not take observation to determine his position. The wind remained west-south-west, as it had been the day previous, and the weather continued to threaten. Captain Bell took in the royals, flying jib and gaff-topsail. At 5 p.m. the barometer began to fall. There was small rain with heavy gusts of wind.

At 1 a.m. on Sunday the 10th, as the gale was increasing, they furled the main and foresails and close reefed the topsails. At 4 a.m. there were heavy squalls. The spanker and gaff-topsail blew out their gaskets and had to be cut away to save the masts. As day broke the squalls increased in violence. The foresail blew out its gaskets and was cut away; the parrels of the main topgallant yard broke and left the yard swinging by the halyards.

By 11.30 a.m. the gale had increased to a hurricane. The fore-topmast was blown over the side and followed soon after by the main and mizzen-topmasts, which were snapped off close by the cap, the former taking with it the main yard, broken in half in the slings. In less than ten minutes the *Briton* was a wreck fore and aft.

Shortly after noon the squalls abated almost to a calm.

Congratulating themselves that the force of the gale was broken, all
hands went to work to clear away the wreck. A new spanker was
bent and another foresail got up ready to bend. Loose spars were
lashed to the ringbolts and the Major's horsebox was secured with
extra lashings.

As they were doing this, the ship was invaded by an immense
number of birds, so completely exhausted by the storm that the
need to rest overcame the fear of man. Several were caught by the
soldiers and the children, including hawks and golden kingfishers
and goatsuckers.

It was impossible to light a fire in either of the galleys, so the
men were served with biscuits and a glass of rum each. All their
clothes were wringing wet, but no one complained, and each was
prompt to give his help either in clearing the wreck or helping at
the pumps.

At 3 p.m. the weather lowered, the barometer dropped and it
was clear that the hope that the gale had blown itself out was forlorn. Squalls came back, with small rain and thunder and
lightning.

Within an hour the gale had increased to a hurricane which proceeded to strip the *Briton*. First to go were the two quarter-boats,
then the meat-safe and the hen-coops. Then the cuddy-skylight
was whirled off, and as the sea was by now boiling up as high as
the poop, a tarpaulin had to be battened over the cuddy-hatch to
keep the water out.

At 5 p.m. the ship rolled so heavily that the Major's horsebox
came adrift. It burst open and the horse fell on the deck. As it
struggled, it was thrown by the next lurch down the hatchway
amongst the soldiers and its forelegs were broken. It was impossible to rig a purchase to hoist it upon deck, so its throat was
cut and the carcase lashed to leeward as securely as possible.

Night came without any abatement. The barometer was still
falling and the squalls were terrifying beyond description. Yet
Captain Bell and his crew buoyed up their spirits with the hope
that such violence would have vented itself by the dawn and that

with the whole day before them they might get sufficient sail on the *Briton* to keep her under command.

Monday broke black and put paid to their hope. The gale, if possible, increased. The ship continued to labour and rolled heavily. The tarpaulin was ripped from the cuddy-hatch. The spars broke adrift and carried with them the cooking coppers (which were smashed to pieces), the galleys, the long-boat and the other horsebox. As the ship rolled, they, together with some thirty fathoms of chain cable belonging to the working anchor, which was on deck, were thrown from side to side with such violence that they feared momently that the bulwarks would be carried away. Nor was it possible, with so many heavy objects loose upon the deck, to venture to secure them, while the high seas were running. Fortunately about 11 a.m. the gale lulled partially. The long-boat, which was stove in, was thrown overboard; and then the other horse, which—poor creature—had been crushed in its box by the long-boat. The decks were cleared of lumber as far as possible, the soldiers assisting the crew and working the pumps. Many of them were severely hurt, being jammed by the spars and so on. One poor fellow had his leg broken.

At noon the sun came out for a few minutes and the Master tried to get an observation, but he could not see the horizon. About half a mile to the eastward a barque was sighted with only her bowsprit and main and mizzen lower masts standing; and a short time after this a brig was descried, totally dismasted. Both vessels were labouring severely, and the sea was breaking over them. There was no sign of activity.

Another tarpaulin was battened over the cuddy-hatch, and to keep it from being blown away again a door with some strong staves was nailed over it.

At 2 p.m. the barometer started to fall once more. The gale had been blowing for thirty-eight hours with only two short lulls. The men were issued with biscuits and a glass of rum. Fires could not be lit in the galleys, and men were offered cold raw pork. They declined it.

The rain started again about three, with thunder and lightning as before. By 4 p.m. the gale had once more become a hurricane and the ship was rolling heavily.

At 10 p.m. there was a lull for a few minutes. Then the wind veered round to east-north-east and blew with greater fury than ever.

The ship was now on the opposite tack, and the remaining spars and gear which had been secured to leeward broke adrift. Between decks, Major Bunbury's dead horse was forced from his lashings and began to lurch this way and that, carrying the arms-racks away and the lockers fore and aft, wherever he went enlisting a confusion which followed him about in his mischief—knapsacks, arms and accoutrements. Several men were hurt and one had a leg broken, before they succeeded in lashing the horse to the mainmast. The task was made more difficult because the ship was taking a good deal of water on board at the time and this kept pouring down the hatchways.

Towards midnight the squalls grew awful, with thunder and lightning. Part of the bulwarks were blown away, the poop began to crack and the fore-part to give way. The cuddy-tables and seats were wrenched from their fastenings in the decks and thrown to leeward. The more anyone knew of ships, the less he expected to see the morning. As the *Briton* trembled from stem to stern, her bell tolled mournfully with every gust, as if, thought Captain Bell, 'to warn us of our approaching destruction'.

The married soldiers had gathered in and around the hospital with their wives and children. One of the women read portions from the Bible aloud, after which they joined in prayer to be delivered from this hazard and sang a hymn for those in peril on the sea.

It did not seem possible that they could be saved. The ship threatened to break up every moment. The starboard topsides and covering boards were started and the water poured in in great quantities. The men snatched blankets, loose coats or whatever else they could find to stuff in and stop the leaks.

With each squall the poop gave more and more. The Master took his chronometer, sextant and charts down the after-hatch into the lower cabin, telling the officers in the cuddy to be ready to go below, as he was afraid the poop was no longer safe.

At midnight the hurricane was still raging furiously. The ship was making much water and labouring heavily as squall after squall struck her almost without intermission. The thunder and lightning were incessant, and the barometer fell to below 27 inches, the oil leaving the tube of the sympiesometer altogether on occasions. The thermometer stood at 84 degrees, and it was stiflingly close.

About 12.30 the ship struck. The sea, breaking over her at the same moment, threw her on her beam ends. The larboard after-cabin was swamped and raised from the deck. The Master's cabin also floated. The door of the cuddy jammed and could not be opened. One of the windows and the steward's pantry were stove in. Both mates were washed out of their cabins. One scrambled into the cuddy through the broken window, while the other got down the steerage hatch. The spanker boom broke into three pieces, one of which struck the man at the lee helm, carried away several of the spokes and jammed the wheel.

These were moments of awful suspense. With the ship on her beam ends, the crew and passengers alike clung each to whatever he could for support, expecting that every next moment would dash the ship to smithereens and send them to eternity.

The boatswain shouted for all hands to scramble up to wind-ward, hoping that perhaps she might right. This did not succeed, but the violence of the hurricane forced the ship somehow off the reef she had struck and into smoother water, where she righted herself.

Now the leak between decks was so enlarged that one of the soldiers went running to the Master to say that they feared the ship was breaking up. The sea was pouring in so fast it defeated all efforts to stop it.

The Master went below straightway with some of his officers, and under their instruction the men collected their blankets, loose coats and any suitable material on which they could lay hands and forced them between the covering boards, whence the sea was rushing in.

The lower deck was flooded, the water washing from side to side. The Master returned to the cuddy and informed the Commanding Officer that the pumps must be manned. One of the officers scrambled out on deck through the window. But he was forced to return almost at once. The night was very dark and the decks so lumbered up it was impossible to find the pumps.

A second attempt was made from between decks, and this succeeded, the party ascending the hatchway and contriving to reach them.

The night was so dark it was impossible to see more than a yard except during flashes of lightning. These revealed trees close on the larboard side, and it became clear that the ship was ashore. The wind continued to rage and spray to break over the ship, but by 1 a.m. the ship was steady, though the storm continued to rage with rain, thunder, lightning and violent squalls of wind.

The barometer started to rise, and by 2 a.m. it was up to 27·60. The hurricane had blown itself out after raging for over two days with a violence almost unremitting. By the time it left, the havoc which it had wrought had reduced the *Briton* to an utter wreck and smashed every boat on board. Had she remained upon the reef, she would have gone to pieces before the night was out.

It was too dark to see exactly on what land the ship had run aground; but there appeared no longer danger that any moment she might sink. So the ship's officers, who from the commencement of the gale had taken nothing but part of a cold fowl and some biscuits, after congratulating one another on their miraculous escape and inwardly giving thanks to Heaven for it, took some ale and wine and water. Then they lay down, and so completely was nature exhausted that in less than half an hour every soul on board was fast asleep.

Awaking at daybreak, they saw to their astonishment the reason for the trees which had appeared so close in the darkness. The gale had driven the *Briton* high on shore into the centre of a mangrove swamp, and there she was, a ship of 770 tons, plumb in the middle of a wood.

On the shore, about a quarter of a mile away, lay the barque they had seen the day before. At low tide a party of soldiers were lowered from her poop and waded over to the *Briton*. The officer who accompanied them said that the barque was the *Runnymede*, out of Gravesend for Calcutta with detachments of the 10th and 50th Regiments, under command of a Captain Stapleton of the 50th.

All that day, November 12, it rained without stopping. Over the quarter-deck of the *Briton* a topsail was spread for an awning and the broken pieces of the coppers were collected to make a stove. After some contriving, they succeeded in getting a kettle of water boiled and part of a broken boiler propped up to cook the meat for the men. About noon dinner was served, of which they stood in great need, having tasted nothing but a little biscuit for seventy-two hours.

A muster of livestock revealed only a solitary pig. Everything else had died or been washed overboard.

The debris from below was brought up and thrown over the side. The between-decks were swabbed dry and clean and the stores in the hold were checked. The Second Officer reported to Captain Bell that everything had been turned out of place, a great portion of the bread, flour, sugar and other stocks was found to be damaged, if not ruined. Also many of the casks of beef and pork had been stove in, which was a sorry prospect for a company of over four hundred souls stranded on a reef.

That evening the gale rose again and Captains Stapleton and Doughty with the troops and crew left the *Runnymede* and came aboard the *Briton* for safety. The *Runnymede* was on the edge of the reef, and they feared she would go to pieces during the night.

During that evening they exchanged their news. Those aboard the *Briton* learned the *Runnymede*'s story: how they had set sail from Gravesend on 20 June 1844, with troops of the 10th Regiment: thirty-seven privates, two women and a child, and of the 50th Regiment, Ensigns Venables, Du Vimal and Purcell, 105 privates, eleven women and thirteen children, with Dr. Bell, the ship's surgeon, in medical charge.

Their voyage had been more than usually unfortunate from the outset. They met nothing but light or contrary winds. The passage had been delayed so much beyond the average that many of the stores were exhausted. It was decided to bear up for Penang, at which port she came to anchor on October 29.

Having filled her water-casks and taken in the supplies necessary, she stood to sea again on November 3.

As with the *Briton*, the weather began to turn from moderate to unsettled on Friday, November 8, and the day following trouble started. The fore-topmast-staysail split in a heavy squall. The whole of Sunday was one loss after another, of sails and masts and gear, with the wind and rain so severe by ten o'clock of the Sunday night that men could not hold on to the poop and had to be employed in bailing water from the 'tween decks, which had been forced down the hatches. But the ship was still tight and proved herself an excellent seaboat.

Monday morning the gusts were so terrific that no one could stand on board to man the pumps or clear the wreck. The starboard bower anchor was hanging only by the shank painter, and as the ironwork was knocking into the ship's side, the chain was unshackled and the anchor cast adrift.

At noon the hurricane was still raging in gusts. The crippled state of the ship made her completely unmanageable, but she rode like a bird over a confused sea which ran from every point of the compass. At this point those aboard the *Runnymede* saw a large barque, which was the *Briton* drifting past with topmasts and main yard gone; and over to leeward was the unidentified brig, totally dismasted.

By 4 p.m. the barometer had fallen to 27·70, and the mineral sympiesometer left the index tube. The hurricane blew with such force that the front of the poop to leeward, the cabin door and the skylights were blown away. They expected momently that the poop would be torn off. Captain Doughty said that the force of the wind was so violent that he knew nothing with which to compare it, unless it were that the gusts were like the crushing blows of some metallic body.

Everyone, soldier and sailor, did all in his power to keep the ship free of water. But it was impossible to stand at the pumps; and the water being principally in the 'tween-decks, it was bailed out by the soldiers, as far as possible. About midnight the rudder was carried away.

At 1.30 a.m. on Tuesday the 12th they felt the ship strike, and the men joined themselves to the women and children in prayer, though it seemed impossible that the ship should not sink and all lives be lost. "But it pleased Almighty God to decree otherwise," said Captain Doughty, "for although the ship filled up to her lower beams with water, she was thrown so high on a reef that all the force of the water was broken and smoothened, and the bilge pieces keeping her upright, she lay comparatively quiet."

And so, like the souls aboard the *Briton*, which had struck almost the same place in this enormous ocean but an hour before, those aboard the *Runnymede*, having let go the larboard bower anchor to prevent the ship beating over into deep water, fell asleep from sheer exhaustion, ignorant of their true plight and too tired to care.

At daybreak the hurricane had abated, but there was still much rain, through which to leeward they saw the line of shore, and with the increasing light, to their dismay, a large barque held aloft the trees, with troops aboard her.

The *Runnymede* was so grounded on the reef that she was nearly dry aft. An officer and twelve men were sent over the stern to communicate with the barque wrecked in the trees, and they returned later with the news that it was the *Briton*, with soldiers of the 80th Regiment under the command of Major Bunbury and short of everything.

As has been related, that night the two groups joined forces aboard the *Briton*, whose position was the less precarious as regards the sea. Those aboard the *Briton* were pleased to hear that there was a fair stock of provisions, especially flour and biscuits, which could be landed for their benefit.

Major Bunbury was placed in supreme command of all troops and seamen, whom it was agreed should be made subject to military law during the emergency. The crews of both ships were given as their first task the salvage of as many stores as possible from the *Runnymede*. To extend the shelter on the *Briton*, another sail was spread across the forepart. Two warps from the foremast and mainmast heads were made fast on shore, and the fore-yard was got over the starboard side to shore the vessel up and prevent her falling over.

Wet clothing and blankets were brought up to dry and lines were rigged fore and aft to hang them on. A fatigue party started to make a causeway running through the mangrove swamp to the shore. An observation made on Wednesday, November 13, established their position Latitude 12°1′ N., Longitude 93°1′4″ E., which proved that they were on one of the islands of the Andaman Archipelago.

On the afternoon of the next day the causeway was completed through the swamp to the shore. On the beach were found the bodies of two Andamanese, and above them in the bush lay parts of the wreck of their country boat. The two corpses were buried by a fatigue party.

The only boat remaining sound between the two ships was the *Runnymede*'s long-boat, which three carpenters were detailed to put into a proper state to proceed as soon as possible to the nearest port to get help. The carpenter's mate was put on to cutting a large hole through the larboard side of the main deck to admit air and facilitate the unloading of supplies, etc.

The number of the shipwrecked was six hundred and eighteen, men, women and children, and as important as making ready a craft to summon help was the search for fresh water and food.

On Thursday some excellent prawns were brought in, and on Friday some pigeons were shot, much like the English brood birds in appearance.

An exploration revealed that the havoc wrought by the hurricane had spread across the whole island. Not a leaf was left on the trees, nor was a tree unbroken. They lay about in all directions, some torn up by the roots, others crushed down. Many were of the largest size, perhaps a century old. Canes and bamboos crushed and twisted made it impossible to touch the earth. To get through, they had to clamber along the fallen timber.

As a result of the exposure, several of the officers and men were suffering from swollen feet. Dr. Bell feared an epidemic with so many crowded on board the *Briton*, so the detachments of the 10th and 50th were sent ashore to make an encampment for themselves on a slope facing the beach, and the same afternoon—November 16—the cooks went ashore to fix the coppers saved from the *Runnymede*, it being feared that they might set fire to the deck of the *Briton*, since there was no means of fixing them there.

The next day all married soldiers were sent ashore to rig tents for themselves and their families; and to improve the ventilation air-ports were cut in the 'tween-decks. Fatigue parties were employed in bringing more stores from the *Runnymede*, clearing the bush around the shore and searching for fresh water in the vicinity. Some officers, exploring along the beach to the northward, found fresh water there and an oyster-bed and shot some more pigeons. Two sailors started to make a canoe out of a log.

On Sunday the whole company celebrated Divine Service on board the *Briton*, giving thanks to Almighty God and reading the forms of prayer for the preservation of their lives.

Some natives appeared on the shore to the south and tried to surround two sailors collecting shell-fish. But they dodged away, and when the savages saw an officer coming after them with a small party, they put off in their canoe.

That night either the same or another canoe of natives attempted to approach the *Runnymede*, but they fled when a few shots were fired in their direction.

The Commanding Officer, who had just previously issued an order commending both troops and crew on the cool and courageous way they had behaved during the gale and the resourcefulness and initiative they were displaying ashore, expressed his regret that the natives should have been fired on. Every attempt should be made to conciliate them, in order to induce them to bring in provisions and indicate sources of fresh water. At the same time no one should venture too far from camp.

That same day the first detachment court-martial assembled on board the *Briton* to try some men charged with insubordination and pilfering beer from the cargo of the *Runnymede*.

The doctors reported that "the position of the *Briton* in a mangrove swamp would prove injurious to the troops if they continued to occupy it as a barrack and hospital". So two companies were ordered ashore to clear a space for an encampment to accommodate the healthy, while the sick were transferred to the *Runnymede*, which was now firmly embedded in sand.

On Tuesday the 19th, one week after the wreck, the first parade was held. The appearance was not military. The greater part of the men's uniform and equipment had been lost or destroyed during the gale. But the Commanding Officer felt it necessary to remind the men that they were under military discipline. Four court-martials were held and many men punished for insubordination.

Nothing more was seen of the Andamanese until the afternoon of Thursday the 21st, when a party of men searching for shell-fish were attacked by several natives, four of them being wounded by arrows, one rather seriously. The alarm was sounded. The men stood to their arms. But though a party was dispatched in pursuit, "the black rascals had escaped into the jungle, luckily for them, or they would certainly have got a Roland for their Oliver".

That night a guard was mounted on the beach below the camp to keep the savages at a respectful distance. Feeling had changed towards them. They were "naked, regular savages in both appearance and habits, and no doubt cannibals". There seemed little chance of receiving any assistance from them.

A Board of Survey had been set up to examine into the state of the stores saved from the wrecks and report on the best scale of issue, reckoning for forty days. Having taken an inventory, the Board recommended and the Commanding Officer approved an alternate scale.

1st day—½ lb. bread, ½ lb. beef, ½ gill spirits, ½ oz. tea and ½ oz. sugar.

2nd day—½ lb. flour, ½ lb. pork, ¼ pint peas, ¼ oz. coffee, ½ oz. sugar, ½ gill of spirits.

Even this reduced scale would last only thirty-six days—until December 27. Nor could it be hoped to supplement it greatly from the island. On first arrival there were occasional dishes of prawns, crabs and other shell-fish; but the supply soon ceased from the number searching for them. For two miles either side of the camp the beach was stripped of shell-fish and to go farther, or even as far, without arms was dangerous. A few wild pigs had been seen on land, but there seemed to be no fruit or vegetables that could be eaten.

By Saturday the *Runnymede*'s long-boat was nearly ready for sea and men were employed in collecting stores for her and making preparations for sending her away.

For the first time two canoes of natives were seen together. Next day, after Divine Service, which was held on board the *Briton*, natives came close, collecting pieces of wreck, especially iron hoops and nails. Two men were sent towards them with an old jacket as a present, "To see if it would be possible to conciliate 'Blackey'." They placed it on a broken stump and retired to a short distance and made signs to the natives to take it. 'Blackey' was clearly far more interested in something useful like iron. They took the jacket down, trampled on it and proceeded to attack the two men. Then, seeing the cover party raise their firearms, the natives made off and hid in the bush, leaving behind them part of a bow and a bundle of arrows. From this it was plain that they understood the lethal uses of firearms, though they were quick to attack those they found unarmed.

The next day—Monday, November 25—the long-boat was launched from the deck of the *Runnymede* at noon on the flood tide. A gang provisioned and watered her, and at 5 p.m. there embarked Captain Hall and Lieutenant Leslie of the 80th Regiment (the bearer of the dispatches), the boatswain and five sailors. Within an hour she was off, *The Hope*, happily named and cheered by hundreds.

The night covered her before she was below the horizon. Of the company that stayed behind many prayed as they went to bed, and the next morning the first thing that each did on waking was to look to sea for sign of *The Hope*, which had disappeared.

After dinner that day three officers strolling on the shore sighted a wild hog. Silently they moved so that they were between him and the bush. Then he winded them and away he went, a charge of shot and ball flying after him as he passed each in succession. One of the bullets lodged in his head and sent him staggering among the logs.

A small King Charles spaniel, the favourite of the Regiment, rushed among the logs and got the hog's ear between his teeth. At this moment a man ran up with a large stick to dispatch the hog, and not seeing little Billy the spaniel in the dusk, he struck him on the head and killed him instantly. The regret at poor Billy's fate was felt by all in camp. Small as rations were, they would sooner have lost a day's supply than their favourite dog.

The hog was brought into camp. He had large tusks and weighed about 80 lb. The meat proved nearly as hard and tough as his hide, which was half an inch thick. But tough as he was, he was extra to the meagre ration.

Now that *The Hope* had left, the carpenters turned to laying down the keel of a new boat. The canoe on which the two sailors had been working was nearing completion, when she took fire and both her gunwales were burnt.

The water had always been of poor quality. There was much dysentery, of which one man died early on. Now the wells and water-holes began to fail, despite the efforts to deepen them. On Tuesday, December 3, two officers in search of water found a running stream under the hills. But it was a mile from camp, and very difficult to reach, because the jungle was so dense.

Heavy rain fell during the night, and the wells and water-holes filled. It was most welcome, though the tents, made from old canvas, all let the water through.

Short rations and heavy fatigues began to tell on the men. The shore was covered with them at each low tide searching for shell-fish. It was perhaps as well that they did not find many, as in their weak state the shell-fish disagreed with a lot of them. To give them an incentive the Commanding Officer ordered that a bottle of beer a day should be issued to each of the carpenters and other artificers building the boat.

On December 6, several men were admitted to hospital with fever and affections of the head. A Detachment Order was issued "prohibiting men from bathing in the heat of the day, or otherwise exposing themselves in the sun".

The sailors' canoe was finished, and proved far better than was expected after she had been damaged by fire. Her first trip was to the northward oyster-bed, from which she returned with a fine cargo. Everybody's spirits rose as the horizons expanded. The search for food could be carried out over a much wider area now. The canoe was vastly improved by the fitting of wash-boards, a false keel and stern-post and the addition of a large sail. In her a party of officers crossed to the island that lay northwards. What they found there was of little use. In the bush they saw some wild cat, like a panther. They also saw bundles of pigs' heads tied together with cane and laid in heaps and also stones hung by rattan from the branches of a tree—the uninviting signs of some primitive religion. But it was good to be able to cross to another island, and there were also some excellent oysters on the rocks, so they made a fire and dined off them.

On Sunday, December 15, Divine Service was held as usual. It was twenty days since *The Hope* had left and it was decided that from the next day rations must be reduced by one half, which filled everyone with dread, it being so near to starvation diet and the shell-fish as good as exhausted.

At about 11 a.m. there were two heavy shocks of earthquakes. The *Briton* shook so violently that all hands ran up from below, fearing she would fall over.

The last shock had scarcely subsided when from the look-out trees on the right of the camp where the men had established of their own accord a sentry, relieved every hour, came the cry, "A sail! A sail!" The cry was taken up and ran across the encampment from one end to the other. The *Runnymede* hoisted her ensign and fired a gun, which was the signal already agreed on for 'a sail in the offing'. The camp was in a commotion, with everyone stopping the business that had been in hand and straining to see where this sail was sighted.

The anxiety was not prolonged. Within a quarter of an hour she had rounded the point and was visible to all.

At 1 p.m. she came to anchor abreast of the *Runnymede* in fifteen fathoms, with men on shore cheering like mad while the ship saluted her with twelve guns. The whole camp was like a fair in its excitement, the people hurrying and firing in every direction, and shouting with delight when they saw that at her stern she was towing the long-boat, *The Hope*.

The ship was a small schooner of seventy to eighty tons, belonging to the Honourable East India Company, named *George Swinton*, after the Secretary to the Government of India in the Secret and Political Department, 1824.

The canoes went off, like a fleet of ancient British coracles, and returned bringing Lieutenant Michael of the 17th Madras Native Infantry with dispatches from Mergui for the Commanding Officer.

The Hope had arrived at Mergui on the 6th, twelve days after leaving the Andamans. Her crew had suffered from sun and fatigue, since, the wind being either light or foul, they were obliged to pull the greater part of the distance.

Having reported the plight of the *Briton* and *Runnymede*, they were given a lighter boat and proceeded on to Moulmein, where they could find a relief ship. The *George Swinton* then sailed for the Andamans laden with provisions, which were the cause of great rejoicing.

All talk of cutting the rations was abandoned. Half a pound of biscuits and a glass of spirits were issued as an extra to all hands, and joy would have been unbounded had not a soldier of the 80th been drowned in the surf while bathing.

From that time forward until the departure of the last transport from the island three weeks later, the sojourn of the shipwrecked was free from the fears that no help would come or that supplies would give out beforehand.

The daily ration was increased out of the supplies landed from the *George Swinton*, and thoughts were even turned to the welfare of future shipwrecked sailors. The seeds of melons, limes, pumplenose and other fruits had been sown by officers in different parts of the island. Perhaps, speculated Captain Bell, they may "prove a benefit hereafter to some unfortunates like ourselves".

It seemed to me unlikely that we should find any traces ninety years later, unless the Andamanese had developed an agriculture in which they were deficient in 1845. Captain Bell described how in the brief space between the hurricanes and their departure the jungle had altogether changed its appearance. Melons, limes and pumplenose would, I was sure, have been swallowed up. Indeed, as I read further I discovered that the author of the book had explored the site fifty years later and found no sign of the fruit and vegetables they had planted. Though wide clearings had been made, the jungle had swallowed them up. No trace could be found either of a plaque on which was recorded the small number of those who died on the island.

The remains of the *Briton* were still visible, lying on the reef at the mouth of a creek and mangrove swamp. Small mangrove trees had sprung up on and round the remains. Of the *Runnymede* there was nothing surviving.

But though the Acting Commissioner at Port Blair had been so interested to see whether we could find any remains of the ship-wreck, it was the story itself which stayed in my mind.

That trust which I believed in as the basis of the relation of man and man, and man and animal, seemed here to be extended to the relation of man to God—the astonishing answer to prayer. And this was what impressed the captain of the *Briton* when he wrote his account on arrival in Calcutta on January 18 1845.

How apparent throughout were the kind and merciful acts of providence. Two transports from opposite quarters of the globe were lost on shore within a quarter of a mile of each another, each possessed of stores etc., which the other was deficient in, thus mutually affording that assistance which was most required. Had the vessels been separated, or wrecked on different islands, in all probability how different would have been the result; how fearful the loss of life, had not the hand of God been mercifully extended towards us.

None would have been left to tell the tale of their comrade's fate and sufferings. Six hundred and twenty souls are cast on a most inhospitable and proverbially unhealthy island, short of every description of provision and comforts, exposed to heavy fatigues under a tropical sun, constantly wet for the first fortnight while landing stores through the surf from the *Runnymede*, scantily clothed, badly fed, and pestered and annoyed by savages; yet wonderful to relate, during the 54 days they remained on the island only seven adults and a few children died, scarcely a common average! What may not indeed be accomplished by British soldiers and British discipline in times of trial and difficulty such as these. In that short space of time a considerable portion of the dense jungle was cleared from around the encampment, wells were sunk, a workshed, sawpit and forge were erected, and a boat capable of carrying 25 persons completed.

As I finished reading the graphic narrative of these old ship-wrecks, I was forcibly reminded by the resounding thud of a heavy sea that the *Jarawa*, which, compared to the *Briton* or *Runnymede*, was a mere shell, was off the same treacherous shores on which they were wrecked. And it was the same season of the year.

Alcock had specifically mentioned the *Briton* and *Runnymede* when he gave me the book. He had obviously wanted me to read it, but for what reason? To scare me, because he was jealous that I was making a voyage which he felt he could have taken more profitably? To give me heart, from the example of the salvation of two vessels more hardly pressed than ours was likely to be? (After all, we had no sails to be blown to shreds, could not be crippled by dismasting, could run with more ease to shelter.) Was he a lover of literature, who liked the story for its sheer excitement? Or was this part of his lunacy, a piece with his letter to be posted to his wife?

I was shaken by the story, but I consoled myself by remembering how frequently it happens that reading heightens present discomfort. I once spent thirteen weeks in hospital in Mesopotamia with enteric, allowed only fluids and dreaming of roast beef and Christmas pudding. I couldn't pick up a book without coming on gargantuan feasts or delicate dinners, descriptions of food and drink that set my salivary glands working overtime. If I was camped in some lonely jungle, depressed and longing for good companionship, I would receive from home a parcel of ghost stories or a copy of *Dracula*.

It was childish, I told myself, to be afraid. No harm had come to me yet, and it was pure superstition to believe that because a cyclone had struck two ships in the middle of the previous century, a cyclone would strike the *Jarawa* also.

But all the same I had had enough of my own company. So I opened the cabin door to the whirr of the wind and the hiss of the beam sea and scrambled along to join Bruno and the Serang at the wheel.

CHAPTER X

I HEARD the signal bell ring from the wheelhouse. I looked through the porthole, but I could not distinguish Havelock Island in the darkness. I went up again to Bruno, who explained that the Serang wanted to change our bearings and for a time we would be in a beam sea. "I can imagine the old *Surmai* rolling in this," he said.

From the way we ourselves rolled, it was not difficult.

Bruno handed her over to the Serang, and we both stood on deck. There was a sound as if a terrific gale was about to break on us. It reminded me of a tropical thunderstorm crossing dense forest with a torrential downpour—an incessant drumming roar. I asked what it was.

"That's the sea," Bruno said, "breaking on the coral reefs."

"It sounds dangerously close," I said.

Bruno laughed. "It's miles away. Anyway, it'll be calmer soon."

He was quite right, and as we reached smoother water, Bruno and I turned in, leaving the Serang to follow the coastline of Havelock Island, 'feeling' his course by the sound of the breakers.

I was up at daybreak, and what a dawn it was! Sitting on deck sipping a strong cup of tea from the galley, I watched the daylight develop the picture of the emerald-green islands, the long white line of breakers roaring on the reefs at least a mile from shore. It was a wonderful sight, and I felt that even if from that moment everything went wrong, the trip would have been worth while. I felt so much at peace with the world that when at last Bruno appeared, still rather sleepy-eyed, I congratulated him on the wonderful job of navigation he and the Serang had done.

He had not been accustomed to receive congratulations. His father had always pointed out how far short of perfection he fell. He flushed with pleasure.

"In return for those kind words, I'll cook you a first-class breakfast," he said.

"Why shouldn't I catch you a first-class breakfast to cook?" I asked. We were approaching the narrower part of the Diligent Straits, where there was a decent chance of a fish.

The *Jarawa* tackle was in almost as big a mess as Susan's uncle's (which I had left aboard the *Surmai*). But eventually I was rigged out with sea-rod and line, a wire trace and a hook baited with a piece of red flannel.

I cast it over the stern, and it was not many minutes before the bait was taken with a suddenness that jerked me hard against the safety rails.

I could not see what I had hooked, but whatever it was, the fish was a fighter. I gave it the reel as it dashed off, and then as it slackened I brought it in again, until it made another dash.

It was wonderful sport to play. I felt it gradually weakening, and after each outburst I brought it a little closer to the boat, till at last I had a glimpse of a blue shape, that suddenly leapt silver from the sea about five feet in the air and then dived like a gannet.

"A surmai!" shouted Bruno. "That's the last kick."

It was, but not in the sense in which Bruno meant it. I felt the rod was going to be torn from my hands; and then where the surmai had dived was a swirl like the vortex of a whirlpool and I saw the ugly white belly of a shark rolling over.

I reeled in. On my hook was hanging the surmai's head, but our breakfast, that fine silver-blue body, had been severed behind the gills, as if with a hatchet.

I was so angry that I fished for an hour with a wire line to a shark hook, using the head as bait. But never a bite did I get. "They don't like heads any more than you do," Bruno said.

By afternoon we were again in the open sea with a fair swell off the east coast of the Middle Andaman, keeping half a mile outside the breakers. The reef looked almost continuous and the jungle came dense and tangled right to the very shore, in those cases where it did not march out into the sea in the form of a mangrove swamp.

"What do we do if the diesels fail?" I asked.

"Well," said Bruno, "they say no sharks go inside the breakers."

We made such good time that we decided to put in at Stewart's Sound, just to the north of the Middle Andaman. Old Bruno had established a small logging camp and mill there at one time. It was the farthest north that any timber had been extracted and it had been abandoned some years before because it was not profitable. But the timber bungalow, though decrepit, was still standing.

Bruno was anxious to show it to me, because it was the farthest north he had ever been; and I was not sorry to look it over. As our main interest was in the Port Cornwallis area in particular, and the

North Andaman in general, I intended to look over this previous operation and see whether there was anything I could learn from it after we finished in the extreme north.

In the Burmese jungles I had seen many places where the jungle tide had come in with such speed and persistence that it broke the hearts of men trying to keep it out. But I have never seen such a dreary and desolate place as this was. What made it more shocking was that the approach was so beautiful. We passed over shoal patches where the water was the palest of green in colour and of a crystal clarity, through which we could see the undersea gardens so rare and brilliant with their weeds and molluscs, shells and flaunting fish that one wished to change elements to enjoy the submarine beauty to the full. And ashore the brilliant greens of the victorious jungle proclaimed the supremacy of this vegetable empire.

Among this only what was man-made was vile. We steered for a jetty, to which ships had made fast. It was still standing, but as we drew close the stench of rotting wood became almost unbearable. Then we saw that the wooden piers had been riddled by teredo borers. It was unsafe to attempt to scramble up them. They would crumble and snap.

The old bungalow on the hillside was still standing. What insects and vegetable parasites were working on the destruction of its individual timbers we did not go ashore to discover. But from the *Jarawa* we could see that the jungle had reached out its suckers and tendrils to encircle the building and threatened to crush it into collapse.

There was still sufficient evidence of human habitation to make the silence and absence of animal life eerie and frightening. It was a warning of the futility of our thinking that we might conquer this vegetable kingdom, where so many before us had been defeated. My impulse was to move on as quickly as possible.

But Bruno urged that we should stay at anchor for the night. The course from here to Port Cornwallis was new to him and the Serang. They would feel more at ease navigating by daylight. He added—what to me was an argument as potent—that if we sailed up the North Andaman in daylight, we could get a far better estimate of the mountains and forests which it was our main purpose to survey.

So we lay up in the dead-calm water, fishing while there was still light and having wonderful sport. After it was dark we discussed what must be our first task on arrival at Port Cornwallis: to find a source of fresh water large and constant enough to supply our complete party without running dry. I think I had alarmed myself by reading of the water shortage which nearly proved fatal to the shipwrecked passengers of the *Briton* and *Runnymede*.

"And we must see to it," said Bruno, "that the *Surmai* doesn't go off and leave us before we have found a camping site close to fresh water."

I was afraid that in order to be quite sure of fresh water, we might have to camp far up one of the tidal creeks which drained into the harbour. Apart from the inconvenience of being away from the sea, such a site would probably be infested with malaria.

At dawn next day we were at sea. Soon the northern range of mountains came into sight, with the Saddle Peak rising to the height of 2,400 feet.

From this east side it was richly timbered, but very difficult country. There were few covers. The cliffs everywhere were steep and in most places precipitous. Along the top of the cliff-line we could see the huge boles of the silver-barked gurjan standing like sentinels guarding the enormous thronging forest which ran all the way up the mountain slopes, so thick that even through binoculars we could not see the bole of a single tree. This was virgin forest. The timber was there. The problems would be how to extract it and how to live while doing so.

We kept an eye to the east, as we hugged our way along the reefs, but there was no sign of the *Surmai*. Nor was there any sign of her as we rounded Dundas Point into Port Cornwallis.

As we came in bearing west, south of Ross Island, the magnificent natural harbour of Port Cornwallis reminded me of Falmouth. I was rather surprised not to see a lighthouse, or a castle, or a fort; only a scatter of forest-clad islands and to the west the high ranges of the main North Andaman.

This inland sea was as calm as a mill-pond. We skirted Minerva Bay and anchored off Smith Island so that we could take our bearings and absorb the details of this astonishing anchorage.

There were vast areas of mangrove swamp that looked forbidding, but the western shore of Smith Island was a sandy spit which made us think that a stream might flow beneath it. We decided to try to land. As we neared the shore we sounded from the bow every yard or so. Then, finding we were over a coral reef, we dropped anchor and went slow astern, moving inshore the while. It was one of the advantages of the *Jarawa's* protected propeller.

It was like sailing on a huge aquarium. There were fish of every shape and hue: little bright fish darting in myriads and lustrous blue fish with long fins and tails like flowing drapery. The water was quite clear and appeared to magnify everything.

We backed slowly towards the steeply sloping sandbank. Ten yards away and we still had a couple of fathoms. The water was so lovely and the day so hot that I was tempted to dive in and swim the last ten yards. I must in fact have made a motion as if I was going to do so, though the sight of the shark that had taken my surmai was a counsel for caution.

"Look out!" Bruno shouted from the wheelhouse.

I looked, and saw that the place was teeming with sharks. They seemed to be attracted by our copper bottom, as if the *Jarawa* was a giant goldfish. They would come flashing up, scrape themselves against the keel and then be gone as quick as lightning.

I waited until I was within jumping distance of the spit. I leapt and sank through the wet sand to the knees. It was like powder, but easy enough for me to move up the slope. I made straight for a gap visible in the edge of the jungle. There were sat-thwa plants growing there like gigantic pineapples. They frequently grow beside streams in Burma.

127

Almost immediately I came upon a small rocky stream-bed, which I followed for some time until I came to a fair trickle of water. I leant down and drank from it like a wild animal, and like a wild animal, glanced round to see that nothing was hunting me. It was sweet water, and I went back immediately to tell the good news.

Within half an hour of arrival we had picked a suitable temporary camp-site. As the *Surmai* was still not in sight, we agreed to do a run around the harbour, keeping in view of the entrance so that we should not miss her arrival.

This first survey showed us that the curse of our work would be the vast fringes of the mangrove separating the sea from the shore. Because the tide was midway and still dropping, we kept well offshore.

We turned beyond Chatham Island and were passing what was marked on our maps as the mouth of the Kalpong River. According to the map, the Kalpong River was joined by a large tributary called the Diglipor, which drained the northern slopes of the Saddle Peak.

We shut off engines so that we could have a better look at this river-mouth. The mangrove trees here grew to a height of between twenty and thirty feet above the sea-water level, standing on their myriad roots like a crowd of women on stilts with their skirts held up. There were a few sandbanks showing, and odd tree-trunks stranded on them, which had been washed down-river during the last monsoon. I scanned the whole coastline slowly with binoculars and then I suddenly stopped. Something on a mud bank at the water's edge had moved. Without taking my binoculars off it, I said to Bruno, "I saw something move, I think. Yes, I did. It's a full-size crocodile."

"No," said Bruno. "No crocs in the Andamans."

"See for yourself." I passed him the binoculars.

The moment he saw it was true he wanted to shoot it. The crocodile was 400 yards off and my rifle was sighted only to to 300. It was quite unsuitable for long range. But he pressed me so earnestly that I fetched the rifle from the cabin, loaded it and handed it to him. He lay flat on the hatch, with the intention of showing off his marksmanship. I was prepared for almost any fluke of luck, but not for what actually happened.

The crack of that rifle-bullet echoed round that huge, still harbour, magnified by the mountains. What happened to the crocodile at which he aimed neither Bruno nor I ever noticed, because there must have been hundreds of others lying with their snouts out of the water waiting for the tide to recede so that they could bask in the sun. Frightened by the noise, they backed suddenly into deeper water, and it appeared as if the edges of all the mud-banks were suddenly boiling. Then, quite as abruptly, there was nothing—all movement stopped. There was not even the sign of a bird—just a deathly stillness.

Young Bruno was even more amazed than I was, because I had seen similar sights when I was in India, shooting the crocodile in the Hoogly Delta.

As we moved on, I noticed that Bruno was nursing his jaw in the cup of his hand. "That rifle can't half kick," he said.

The siren of S.Y. *Surmai* interrupted him. She was hove-to at the entrance to the harbour. When we reached her we saw that the whole party had come to the prow to wave to us.

Bruno brought her in, acting as pilot with the *Jarawa* as the pilot brig. It was a tedious job, as she moved at a snail's pace. But eventually she anchored in what we called The Roads, off Smith Island, where there was a small anchor marked on our map, showing that at one time Lieutenant Blair had anchored there during his coastal survey.

As soon as we boarded the *Surmai*, I noticed how differently the convicts were moving. They were men now, not sheep. They moved as individuals, and the old convict, Nga Moh, came up of his own accord to tell me that they were all well. I heard them chattering among themselves in Burmese, like schoolboys on an outing. The only one of the Port Blair party who looked miserable was the policeman, who had to return on the *Surmai*.

Jeff came fussing up. "Are we to off-ship tonight or wait till the morning?" he asked. "Have you had a chance to look round?"

We talked it over with the policeman and decided that it would be best to get as far forward as we could that day, but not to disembark the convicts until the next day. "And then, immediately the *Surmai* sails, make it plain to them that they are stuck here for three months."

The school of sharks which I had seen when I leapt ashore came to visit the *Surmai*. The convicts noticed them and, I think, regarded them with more respect than they had for all their armed guards. There was no escape by swimming; that was plain to them.

Jeff said that the *Surmai* had rolled so much that he had been afraid that she would capsize or that *Madame X* would break loose and charge about the deck.

The lascar crew of the *Surmai* first launched two of their own lifeboats. Then they got *Madame X* into the water. It was a busy little fleet, of which the only boat which looked out of place was the Chris Craft speed-boat *Hintha*.

We turned the engines of our craft, attached the ropes for towing the ship's lifeboats, and Jeff and Bruno did a practice run, so that we could move without a hitch next day.

Meanwhile Carl and I made another survey of the proposed camping-site. It seemed as if God had created the spot for our purpose. There was a large patch of open sand, very firm, near to the jungle edge and within 300 yards, up the rocky stream, a good-sized pool with ample water. If not perennial, it would last well into the hot season, by which time we hoped and expected to be relieved.

We all had a meal aboard the *Surmai*, and after it Jeff suggested that he took me on a brief reconnaissance round the harbour in the *Hintha*. Jeff was a master at handling speed-boats and he had used this particular craft in her trials on the fast tides of the Rangoon River. My job consisted merely in exploring in more detail the coastline of the harbour which we had scouted in the *Jarawa*. I had a vague feeling that Jeff resented this *Jarawa* excursion, but it seemed so silly that I did not pursue the thought. Perhaps the sight of a bay so calm was all the temptation he needed.

He opened her out and with her twin propellers churning deep furrows we were off like the *Bluebird*. The echo was appalling— compared to Bruno's rifle-shot, an uninterrupted stream of heavy machine-gun fire.

We made direct for Blair Bay, a clear, open stretch of water unmolested by a single ripple. As Jeff opened the throttle full out, she got her nose right up. I could share Jeff's delight at shattering the silence of that great anchorage with the power of the speed-boat. It was the twentieth century proclaiming its confidence where the eighteenth and nineteenth centuries had been defeated. The swifter, noisier, more thrusting we were, the happier I was. After all, my belief in this whole expedition was that we were going to succeed where our forefathers had failed.

The tide had turned. It was well up again and the sea was hiding the bare legs of the mangroves. Their lower branches now were almost at water level.

Occasionally I signalled Jeff, who was at the helm and engines in the stern, to steer to port or starboard. But there were no floating objects to avoid. We ran close in to the mangrove in Blair Bay and throttling down turned for Smith Island again. We were gathering speed again with full throttle, when I suddenly saw a few green leaves just above the water. We were heading for a mud-bank. I stood up, trying to yell above the roar of the engines and signalling 'cut out'.

It was too late. Jeff threw her helm over. We did a water skid of twenty to thirty feet and all but capsized. As she flattened out, she did another skid along her bottom in about a foot of water, churning up an evil-smelling, muddy sediment. Then we came to rest.

Bubbles of gassy water gurgled up all round us. We were hard fast, stuck in the mud while the shallow water closed round us again. The engines stalled, and there was a moment of silence before we both gave vent to what might in other circumstances have sounded like an oath, but in this case was more a prayer for help.

My fear was that the tide would not lift her, however much more it had to rise. I was afraid the suction of her bottom on the mud would hold her down and the water, instead of lifting her, would pour over the sides.

We sounded the mud with the boat-hook. It went sheer down as easily as into water. There went the hope of hopping overboard and pushing her off. We were marooned. The light was fading fast and we could only pray that someone on the *Surmai* would notice we were missing.

For more than an hour we stirred the muddy water with the boat-hook, hoping that if we kept some circulation round the bottom of the craft we might lift with the tide. We were more successful with the prow than with the stern. The weight of the outboard motor was too great. We tried starting the motor, but though the mud was too liquid to take our weight, it was too solid to be circulated by the pump. By shifting our weights we could alter the tensions in the other parts of the craft, but the dead weight of the engine was like an anchor. We debated whether we should take off the motor and sling it overboard, but decided that this should be a last resort.

"This is a damn fine start," Jeff kept muttering, "a damn fine start."

I remembered what old Bruno had kept saying about his son. "The trouble about him is he's such a lazy young devil." It was already dark and probably young Bruno had retired to his bunk, and was sleeping as deeply as he had the night before.

When I repeated this to Jeff, he said, "It isn't his fault. I immobilised the *Madame X* before we left, and he'd be crazy to try the *Jarawa* in the dark."

"What about that searchlight?" I asked.

"I haven't fitted it yet," Jeff said, "and unless you told him, Bruno doesn't even know we've got one."

"Then the only chance is the lifeboats, rowed by the lascars," I said.

We had no torch, no visual means of indicating our position, not even a match to light a petrol-soaked rag. Every half-hour we shouted as hard as we could and then listened intently. Hours passed without success, and it was not until about an hour before dawn that we heard the yelling of voices. We stood up and started to yell in answer, at first without waiting for them to stop; and then, returning to our senses, we waited for their listening periods before replying.

It was impossible to tell whether they had heard us. The eerie echo of our own calls across the water was maddening. We could see a light—probably a torch, as it seemed miles away. There appeared no sense in its waving and there was no means of our replying in kind. There was no sound of an engine, so the rescue party was clearly in one of *Surmai*'s lifeboats. "Damned if I know what they're doing," Jeff and I kept saying.

It was not until later that we realised that they were lost also. They were at that moment less concerned in finding where we were than in learning where they were. They did hear us, however, and came in our direction. In the distance I made out a voice calling "Thakin! Thakin!" I recognised who it was, and called back "Aung Net! Aung Net!"

I had shared a great deal with Aung Net. On one occasion l had saved *him* from drowning. I don't know what he expected had happened to us—perhaps that we had been attacked by crocodiles or sharks. "Bah pyet the lai?" he yelled. ("What has happened?")

"We're stuck in the mud," I said in Burmese, and then I added in English to whoever was in command, "Go easy or you'll be grounded yourselves. "

They got to within fifty yards. We could see them dimly in the starlight. We could talk without having to rise our voices too loud. But between us we could not think of how they were to rescue us or the Chris Craft. They had no rope and we were separated by a sea of mud fathoms deep. And once again the tide was dropping.

Jeff explained to young Bruno how to mobilise the *Madame X* and told him to muster as many ropes and anchors as he could, including the spare anchor from the *Jarawa*. Then, as soon as day broke and they could see their way, they rowed the lifeboat back to the *Surmai*.

Our anxiety relieved, Jeff and I were able to think of more trivial matters, such as how hungry we were. We had plenty of time to think of that, because it was not until midday that, after several abortive attempts, Bruno got us a line from the *Jarawa* and towed us off on the flood tide.

CHAPTER XI

THE Anglo-Burman policeman was sarcastic about our ability to look after his convicts, when we couldn't even take a turn round the harbour without running aground. "You know you ought to have me stay with you," he said.

We had lost half a day on the sandbank, but the convicts worked magnificently, and by the evening we had everything off-loaded and ashore. When it came to waving the *Surmai* goodbye, the convicts all lined up and waved with such heartiness that it was quite clear that they wouldn't care if they never saw the ship or the Anglo-Burman again. It confirmed me in my conviction that I had been right in cutting every association with the penal settlement and starting them off afresh.

That night we pitched a large tent for the four of us. The convicts had cover under tarpaulin sheets. Everybody was dead tired, and we decided to postpone all sorting, stacking and organising until the next day.

The convicts still had a day's ration of their prison fare. While they were eating it, Nga Moh came and asked what they should do after the meal. I answered that there was no more work to be done that day. But I wanted to talk to them all. "Before I talk to them," I said, "I want them to arrange themselves into 'waings' of six men each." I had noticed that some of the men had surly, brutal faces; what I regarded as 'criminal type'. But most of them were simple-looking Burmans very similar to those I had employed in the elephant camps in Burma. I felt that I could rely on them implicitly.

I used the word 'waings' deliberately. It was the Burmese term for a gambling ring. Maybe they had not gambled in Port Blair, but every Burman is a gambler casually. I handed Nga Moh a pack of cards for each 'waing' and two Burmese cheroots for each man. He left me as happy, as he would have said, as a 'tiger with two tails'.

If they had been given any cheroots during their imprisonment, they had had none of the quality of these. Nor had they seen a pack of cards.

By the time that I went over to speak to them they were sitting in their selected groups under their chosen leaders. It was a little democratic revolution, under my designate Nga Moh. Nga Moh did not squat. He came and stood by my side as I made my announcements.

It was not a speech. It was just a collection of pronouncements, made on behalf of myself and the chief jailer; the Charter of Parole, so to speak. It could almost be reduced to numbers, though I did not do so.

1. Any one of you who earns a good report from me will be remitted one year of his sentence.

2. Each one of you will be paid two rupees a day, which you will receive when you return to Port Blair. There will be no money in camp, because there is nothing for money to buy.

3. You will receive to-morrow morning a new pair of shorts, a new vest and a new blanket.

4. For your work you will be issued with a Burmese jungle knife (dah) which must be returned each evening, after work.

5. None of you may enter our camp unless ordered to do so for some specific job.

6. You may not under any circumstances speak to the camp servants.

7. You must report any complaint to Nga Moh. He will report it to me and I will deal with it.

8. You will get good food and plenty of it.

9. You must not leave camp except with one of the Thakins.

10. Your main work will be to cut paths through jungle.

11. If any of you is sick, I will be the doctor.

12. You cannot escape. To try would be suicide. I am your friend and will get you home as soon as I can.

I finished by asking whether there were any questions.

I was pleased that there was not a long pause before a man—who looked as if he had murdered his grandmother for her wedding ring—asked, "Can we fish?"

"You can not only fish," I said, "but I will give you hooks and lines."

"If you decide that the forest can be worked," said a second, "can we come back here and work in the timber camps?"

"Yes," I said. "I promise you that."

"Are you going to bring elephants?" a third asked.

"If there is enough fodder to feed them."

"I was an oozie once."

"Then you can help find where the fodder is."

"I was a store clerk once in the Mogok Ruby Mines," said another, "I would like to do work like that."

"If you can write Burmese," I said, "give me a list of all the men here, what they did in Burma and where they came from."

He was at once given an exercise book and writing materials.

After that there was silence. I thought that there were no more questions. But then something happened that was typically Burmese, but at the same time was terribly like what one might expect from a Cockney crowd. A voice was raised. "Bo Gyi!" That was the term which was reserved more or less as a term of address for the head of a dacoit gang. Immediately all the rest turned round to the man and grins came over their faces. "Bo Gyi, have you any watches to mend? Before I came to this place I was a watchmaker in Mandalay."

In this strip of shore on Smith Island, the idea of a convict soliciting work as a watchmaker was so absurd that we all burst out laughing, even those convicts whose faces seemed set in a permanent mould of surliness.

Some puritans I have met hate laughter because it is not a moral thing. It is beyond good and evil, in a dimension of its own, a dimension I feel which is not so very far from God, when it is free from malice. At least I thanked God for the great wave of laughter that rose in the gathering twilight. The watchmaker from Mandalay had made us all free in the brotherhood of laughter. And I left them then to their cards, knowing that unless something went very wrong, we were going to get on with one another on quite a fresh basis. It was as if we had been translated to another planet, where the errors and crimes committed on earth no longer mattered.

But there was another group that I had to reassure before I went to bed, and that was my own servants. With one exception they had all been with me in Burma, and they had come with me of their own accord. My cook Joseph was a Kalabai, an Indian born of a Burmese mother. He was a Christian and spoke English, Burmese and Hindustani equally well. I never spoke to him in any other language than English, of which his mastery was perfect; nor did I tell him what to cook. Left to himself, he took pains and produced a variety of dishes.

His assistant was San Pyoo, a one-handed Shan. There were no fingers or thumb on his left hand. He had been born with a stump, which he used with devastating effectiveness. He could punch flour and water with the stump into the most submissive of puff pastry. His right arm was of great power, as it had to do so much of the work of the left. With one slash of a dah he could sever any creeper. Whatever the leaf or shrub, he was as ready as Tun Gyaw with an answer to the question, "What's this and what's it good for?" Imagination was always ready to make good the deficiencies of knowledge. I always treasured his reply when I asked him about a very rare and loathsome fungoid growth. "If you boiled it for two hours, it would make a good eye-lotion."

My personal boy was Aung Net, whom I had employed since he was a kid of fourteen. He was a gossip, a simpleton and the butt of other servants. But what he lacked in intelligence he made up in loyalty.

Finally, there was Po Sine, my gun-boy, my shadow, a jack-of-all-trades who was useful in a hundred different ways. He climbed trees like a monkey. He was a great hunter. His knowledge of jungle lore appeared infinite. He was never idle. If there was no job he had been told to do, he was whittling a piece of stick to make it into a whistle or making a trap to catch some animal or bird.

He was already at work on a fish-trap when I joined them. I explained that they were to have nothing to do with the convicts, except that San Pyoo was to issue their rations every day.

"Who'd want to have anything to do with a gang of murderers?" Aung Net asked, as usual saying the first thing that came into his head.

I was glad he had done so. He was used to my telling him off and it gave me a chance of warning the others that there was to be no loose talk about convicts and murderers.

"You remember Tun Gyaw?" I said.

From the expressions on their faces it was plain they had not forgotten.

"Tun Gyaw is one of the convicts I have chosen," I answered.

The three Burmese said nothing. Joseph, in English, asked me what Tun Gyaw was going to do. "Tun Gyaw knows more about

139

elephant fodders than any of the convicts except Nga Moh," I said.

"Chauk-thee, I am afraid," Aung Net said.

"Why should you be afraid," I asked, "when it was me he tried to stab?" The others laughed, and I knew that I had won them over to accept Tun Gyaw. "We say in English 'Better the devil you know than the devil you don't know'." I explained that Tun Gyaw would be able to mix with the other prisoners and he could tell us what they were saying, so that if there was any conspiracy, he could report it to me. They thought this was a very wise and cunning scheme, though in fact it was an idea which had only just come into my head and I never used Tun Gyaw as a stool-pigeon.

The person who really distrusted Tun Gyaw was Joseph. Perhaps he remembered Tun Gyaw's defence, that he never intended to stab me and had only brought his knife to murder Archie's cook. Joseph may have feared that Tun Gyaw would do to my cook what he had failed to do to Archie's.

By the evening of the following day the camp was properly organised. Petrol and oil drums were neatly arranged in a dump at a reasonably safe distance from camp and fenced off against interference. Perishable supplies were also fenced off and where necessary shaded against the heat. Equipment was stored in another enclosure.

The convicts looked smart in their new shorts and vests. To the gang leaders we presented shirts, which made them feel proud and enabled us to identify them more easily. The convict stores clerk also asked to be given a shirt in recognition of the importance of his position. I gave him one in exchange for a list of names, ages, villages and pre-conviction occupations. I glanced down it. "Where is the watchmaker?" I asked. "I can't see a watchmaker anywhere here."

The clerk, whom we christened Saigyi, smiled. "He is listed as a travelling actor, Thakin."

Saigyi proved a clerk of the highest competence. Within another day he had a general list in Burmese of everything in camp. He had a natural sense of where and how goods could be stored and he carried in his mind a detailed picture of where everything was kept, so that he could go to it without reference to his lists.

The Serang and crew of the *Jarawa* never came ashore. As Indians they had no cultural contact with the Burmese, and they seemed to live in dread that their craft would be stolen by an escape gang of convicts, who would murder them or throw them to the sharks.

Madame X was kept permanently immobilised, except when in actual use. She was moved alongside the *Jarawa*, both well off-shore. With the *Surmai* and her lifeboats gone, our little fleet of three looked pathetically small, and our four dug-out canoes were no craft for an escape by open sea. These we merely drew up above the level of high tide. The idea that they or our stores might be plundered by the Andamanese never entered our heads, though earlier voyagers had related such awful tales of their attacks.

The only living creatures we had seen on land so far were sand-crabs and shell cowries. Everybody else was too busy to pay much attention to them, but Aung Net was delighted. Acting like a schoolboy, his ambition was to catch a sand-crab. From well up the beach he would spot one between him and the sea. Immediately whatever he was doing was forgotten. Quietly, walking on tiptoe, Aung Net would move slowly towards the crab, whose only indication that it had observed Aung Net was its utter stillness. As it stayed motionless, a gruesome creature with piercing black eyes and long, spindly legs, it looked for a moment as if it had decided to stand and repel attack.

Then, always at exactly the right moment, like a playful puppy, it would bolt for the edge of the sea, with Aung Net suddenly going flat out to catch it. He might as well have chased a grouse on the wing. High off the ground on its stilt-like legs, it would scutter sideways, and at the very moment when it looked as if Aung Net would gather it like a rugger ball, the crab would reach the soft sand by the water's edge and with one convulsion of its

legs be buried from view. Over and over again Aung Net tried;
over and over again he failed; over and over again anyone in view
would stop and laugh at him. It made no difference. Nothing
would discourage him.

Though he caught no crabs, he brought an astonishing collection of different cowry-shells to me, to admire their wonderful
shapes and colours. Some were as large as my fist, and if I had
had the time at my command which Athelstan Alcock seemed to
think, I should have made a collection of shells. As it was, the
rumble of Time's winged chariot rather frightened me. There
seemed so much work to do and so very little time in which to do
it before the Southampton flying-boats were due.

There were five different types of jungle area. On the muddy
flats along most of the sea-coast and on the tidal creeks was the
mangrove forest. Just above high-water mark, and adjoining the
mangrove forests, was a narrow belt of mohwa (*Mimusops lit-
toralis*), which composed the littoral or beach forest. Neither of
these was of any interest to us as timber. The two main species

of which we were in search were gurjan and padauk. In some
areas were dry, deciduous padauk forests; and in others evergreen,
broad-leaved gurjan forests. But more interesting than either of
these from our point of view were the mixed deciduous and evergreen forests to be found on the deep alluvial soil in the valleys.
Here both the gurjan and padauk reached the best height-growth.

We were to estimate a census of the tree population, dividing
them into hard and soft woods. Eight hardwoods—gurjan,
padauk, koko and chuglum predominating—and two soft woods—
thit pok and papita. All other trees were listed as 'miscellaneous'.

There are few Burmans who do not know every main tropical
tree, as instinctively as they know the points of the compass. This
sense of direction is fantastic; almost as if they have some sense
like the magnetic needle which responds to the north. In any

ordinary conversation on direction, even in the densest jungle, a Burman will tell you to take the north, east or south fork, not the left, middle or right one.

We called the convicts together and explained to them the method of taking a strip enumeration. This is done by keeping a compass-bearing straight into the forest for a given distance—say a mile. On either side of that mile-long distance—say for the breadth of a chain either side—every listed tree is recorded, with its breast-high girth measured by a wooden calliper.

These callipers were simple contrivances, consisting of a wooden pole with one fixed arm at right angles at one end, and another sliding arm which could be moved freely to and fro. The stick was marked in inches. The fixed arm was placed against the bark at one side, while the other arm was moved to touch the bark on the opposite side. The diameter was read in inches. Taking the diameters, we could at the end of a day's work, calculate the volume of the tree in cubic feet, provided that the height was estimated to the first branch.

More than half of the convicts volunteered as spotters of the species and proved to be able to identify correctly. Every Burman can read and write Burmese, whatever his status in life; so there was no trouble in getting capable calliper readers. Others were told off as 'line-cutters', to clear the jungle on a dead-straight line, as if clearing an ordinary jungle path.

Carl, representing a large Swedish match concern, was interested only in soft woods, though in each sample hard and soft woods were enumerated. He had an auger with which he bored into every soft-wood tree he saw, in order to extract from it a sample core of the wood. One of his first tasks was to learn the Burmese names for the soft-wood trees. He had already learnt their names in English, but he was not very good at pronunciation. This was not due to bad teaching. After the three and a half months we spent together, he still pronounced English with as bold a Scandinavian accent. "Ze vood must be vight, you know, for ze good match."

He loved to take different matches and deliver us lecturettes on the oriental psychology of the match-stick. "Here in ze east, you know, ve vant ze molti-porpoise match. Ve vant ze match vich light ze fire or ze cheroot. But ze Indian must have ze steek vich he can split, to make ze toozpick. No split, no buy. In Sveden ve understand; in Japan, no. Zey make ze pretty, ze cheap, ze coloured. But no good for ze toozpick. No good to clean ze vax out of ze ear. No."

Our rehearsal was completely successful, except in one respect. The first canopy, or first floor of jungle foliage, was so intense that we could not estimate accurately how high the clear boles rose in many species.

There was a long discussion as to the average height to be used for gurjan, which at breast height had often girths between five and six feet in diameter.

We eventually decided to reckon on sixty feet as the average to the first branch. This gave us a volume of 900 cubic feet of timber and the colossal weight of eighteen tons.

This immediately raised the question, supposing that we found there was the fodder to support elephants, could any elephants that we might import shift such heavy timber? But I did not try to find the answer yet. We had first to see whether there were enough trees to make the project pay.

By the end of a few days the convicts had had enough practice at enumeration to know that we could split up and do far-reaching areas around the harbour. We organised ourselves in four parties of twelve, each under one European.

Working around the harbour was going to be far more difficult than on Smith Island, because we had this accursed fringe of mangrove to penetrate before we could do anything.

This wasn't our only worry. There was Carl's appetite, for example. He took eating very seriously. He was no gourmet. Bulk was what he needed. The first three mornings at breakfast, while everyone else was discussing the work ahead, Carl concentrated on Grape-Nuts. The sight of an unfinished tin of his concentrated breakfast food seemed to outrage his sense of frugality. The idea that we might have some more of it next morning never occurred to him. He must have thought an opened tin was thrown away, if it wasn't finished.

I looked with horror at the inroads he was making, knowing that at this rate the Grape-Nuts would not last three weeks, let alone three months.

Worse still, Carl was not a dry feeder. For every deep helping on his tin plate he needed half a tin of milk to float it and then enough sugar to sink it again.

I realised that Carl would have to be told, but some way had to be found to do so without causing offence or humiliation. If Carl went into a sulk, the spirit of the expedition might be ruined.

I drew Bruno on one side and we cooked up a plot. The same age as Carl, Bruno could take liberties which an older man could not.

Next morning when Carl asked Bruno to pass the Grape-Nuts, Bruno took the full tin and poured the contents into the tin plate until it was piled high like a cereal Vesuvius, and running down the sides.

Carl laughed and clapped his hands. It was a wonderful joke. Taking the tin of milk, he made a crater in the centre of the volcano and filled it up with milky lava. As Carl was nearing the end, Bruno said, "What's our ration of this stuff, by the way, Bill?"

Very deliberately I said, "It's one tin a week for each of us. I think we'd better each have our tin now and write our names on them." I turned to Aung Net and told him to bring me four new tins from the store.

The trick worked wonderfully. Carl thought I was angry with Bruno for his stupid prank, but he took note of the ration. Then he transferred his ravenous appetite to bread. Our supplies of flour, I reckoned, could stand up to it.

A far worse threat to our flour supplies developed very soon. Saigyi came to me with a long face to announce that we had been invaded over-night by rats—not ordinary rats, but bamboo rats.

146

All our cereals had been placed in one large dump on corrugated-iron sheets and covered with tarpaulin. Rat poison was not a thing I had thought of in Rangoon, and when I saw the chaos beneath the tarpaulin, I was filled with an emotion not far from panic. Every flour-bag had been punctured, or rather torn savagely apart, and an alarming proportion of the flour eaten or ruined. I could not have believed that it was rats, if it had not been the myriads of half-webbed footprints.

I remembered a story which had been told me by an old planter called Thom in the Karenni Hills. The bamboo forest had flowered and died, and armies of rats, driven by hunger, invaded the paddy-fields in such numbers that they were impossible to control, the rice crops were utterly destroyed and the Hill tribe had to evacuate the area.

We were in an area which we could not evacuate. We luckily had a reserve stock of fifty tin chests of Swedish biscuits, presented by some of Carl's friends in India. Each of these was as large as a tea-chest, so that even if all our flour was eaten, we should not starve. But the thought of being stripped by these bamboo rats challenged us. They had started on the soldered corners with their incisor teeth.

It was Tun Gyaw who solved the problem. With their half-webbed feet, bamboo rats cannot walk a tight-rope. The thing to do was to re-bag the flour and hang it from wires suspended between trees, like washing on a drying-line. When this had been done for flour and biscuits—our main ration for the four Europeans—we examined the rice-bags. They had not been attacked yet, but clearly they would be the next objective. I knew I had made a good impression on our forty-nine convicts, but it would not stand up to the loss of our rice.

To sling the hundreds of bagged rice between trees was out of the question. "What about oil-drums?" someone suggested. Not nearly enough of them were empty yet to act as rice-bins. But from the mention of oil-drums came an idea which Jeff immediately put into action. Four huge rafts were made by lashing softwood timber from the jungle to oil-drums, and these were anchored just below low-tide mark. This took three days, a sizeable chunk of three months; especially since we had fixed for the Southampton flying-boats to come and take their photographs of any rich stands we had found by December 20.

The very next night we were again invaded by rats. With one barrel of my shot-gun, Po Sine bagged sixteen of them. The convicts were pleased, because bamboo rat is considered a Burmese delicacy. Carl was forbidden to try them! But Aung Net was given two, provided he promised he would not let Joseph pop one into our soup.

After that we had no more trouble from rats. But the ducks and chickens began to disappear. The ducks had been well penned inside a bamboo fence; the chickens were at large scratching about as they might in a farmyard. Po Sine was told to keep a look-out. We suspected that the convicts were at the bottom of this.

Late one evening, when the four of us were relaxing after a hard day's work, Po Sine came up and quietly asked me to come with him. It was rather as he had come each month to show me the new moon. The Burmese had a superstition to match the British one that you mustn't look at the new moon through glass without turning your silver. The Burmese superstition was that you must see the line of the sickle moon without anything breaking it, no easy task in the dense Burmese jungle. Po Sine never failed to find some open sky over a creek-bed. It amused him to tell me to close my eyes and lead me out as if I was blind and then tell me when to look up and open my eyes.

He led me to the chicken-house with eyes wide open. It was made of bamboos and leaves, with long perches inside. There were no eggs to bother about. All our birds were cockerels. We had brought our eggs in enormous earthenware jars, filled up with isinglass.

Po Sine stopped in front of me and pointed. All I could see was half a dozen cockerels—the late grubbers who would any moment follow the rest to roost. But these late grubbers were not scratching and pecking away. They were sharply alert. For a moment I thought they were observing Po Sine and me. But I knew this was not the real reason. We did not inspire fear, and these birds were terrified.

I looked into the branches of the trees above. Perhaps there was some bird of prey—an owl or hawk—perched there. But there was nothing.

Then, looking at where Po Sine pointed, I saw something. It was at the base of a tree: the largest monitor lizard I have ever seen: dark grey, with a dry, wrinkled skin. The ordinary water monitor in Burma is a beautiful creature with yellow markings, edible, and with eggs that are considered a delicacy. This creature was an overblown version of the species I had seen in Ceylon, where the Sinhalese protect them as destroyers of vermin. Since the innovation of television, adventurers describe them in Children's Hour as dragons.

He was motionless, his head and shoulders were raised by his forelegs, as if standing on tip-toes. In slow motion he did an arms-bend and then raised himself again. I watched fascinated. The monitor crouched and singled out a cockerel. Po Sine stood with his dah ready to go in to the attack and save the precious bird, but I held his elbow. This was worth watching.

Slowly—painfully slowly—the monitor crawled forward on its belly towards the cockerel, so intent on the kill that it did not notice us. The cockerel did not move. It was stupefied with fear and, I thought, mesmerised. But I was wrong. The cockerel suddenly made a move for safety and the monitor, prepared for this, leapt forward and, pivoting on his forelegs, slashed his powerful tail right round and knocked the cockerel senseless. In a flash, the lizard had seized the cockerel in its jaws and was off, while the other cockerels screamed and fled.

Within half an hour Po Sine had shot the thief and brought him back to camp. Or perhaps it was not the thief, as there were plenty of other lizards. They were such a plague, that Joseph's only solution was to feed us chicken or duck at every meal, hoping to get them into our bellies before the lizards got them into theirs.

Repulsive as they looked, these monitors were eagerly sought after by the servants and the convicts. Aung Net disposed of this first monitor and he became Casualty No. One. He became so bilious that a quarter of a pound of Epsom salts was needed to save his greedy life.

CHAPTER XII

CAMP had now settled. Our teething troubles were over. As a general hut we had built a large 'basha' of bamboos, thatched with grass. The camp began to look more like a small village. It was time for us to start our enumeration work.

We decided that Jeff with young Bruno and a cutting party should 'cruise' Chatham Island, doing a strip enumeration from south to north. From the sea Chatham Island looked fairly flat. What we had to find out was whether there was enough timber there to make it worth while felling the whole island as a mill site.

Carl and I were to penetrate as far up the Diglipor River as we could at high tide and cut an entrance into a right-bank tributary towards the trigonometrical point Jire Miku (2,247 feet) on Saddle Peak.

I could never have believed such mangrove swamps existed. From a distance they looked like bushes, but once we entered the tidal river of the Kalpong, we were in a forest of mangrove trees which, as the tide rose, appeared impenetrable.

We saw dozens of crocodiles. I was as keen as Carl was to get one specimen for identification, but I had to insist that it was futile to try with anything but a rifle.

For our work, the *Madame X* was perfect. But the voyage was very monotonous, with thick mangrove on either side. Our fear was that we might be completely stranded when the tide dropped.

We entered a side-stream which was so overgrown it was like passing up a vegetable tunnel. After a time we ran out of the mangrove and found a complete change of forest. We were obviously reaching the salt-water tidal limit. We anchored *Madame X* and disembarked.

Mud-banks had given place to shingle and clean sand. I tasted the water. It was brackish but fresh.

Immobilising the launch, we followed the river-bank until after a mile or so we had gradually come into a new world of clean, beautiful forest. Familiar grasses, creepers, bamboos and canes grew to the river's edge. We followed the creek-bed until it forked. Here I decided we could make a temporary camp, from which we could both operate, one party going up either fork and returning to camp at an agreed time.

As I went up the left fork, I kept my eye open for any signs of animal life. There were no tracks of animals in the creek-bed and very few birds. The only bird I recognised was an imperial pigeon, perhaps the same breed as those that the crews of *Briton* and *Runnymede* had eaten with such relish.

While we were still going up the creek, and before I had even looked at my watch to see if it were time to turn back, we almost panicked on hearing voices. It was Carl's party! We had passed on either side of a large island and met at the head of it.

We decided to cruise this large island by returning together along its centre. It was high ground and would provide a fair indication of the mixed trees.

The cutting party set to work and made good headway despite the heavy undergrowth. The convicts moved ahead, slashing a line so that we could readily recognise and calliper-measure each species of tree.

The jungle gave place to an area of tall grass in the centre of which there was a large pool. By this I realised that at the height of the monsoon the whole island must be under water.

One bank of the pool was steep, where the flood-current had exposed the roots of a large letpan tree. Carl took a test bore from this tree, while I went round to the shingle side.

To my surprise, I saw a mark on the shingle rather as if a heavy tree-trunk had been recently dragged into or out of the pool. I called to Carl to come and look. "It's a crocodile," I said. "Either entered or left the pool this morning."

A closer examination showed that this was the entry track and there was no exit trailer. The crocodile was somewhere in the pool. That was the only explanation, and yet we were miles above the tidal limit. "What a pity we've only got a shot-gun with us," I said.

But Carl was still hankering after his crocodile. He looked round for one of the convicts to cut him a bamboo with his dah, but the convict parties had moved well ahead.

I cut a long bamboo with my knife and sharpened the point like a spearhead. With this Carl scrambled back to the letpan tree and starting probing downwards into what was obviously the deep part of the pool. There was no reaction, so I cut another bamboo spear and waded in on the shingle side and started to probe as well. "I bet you anything you like there's a crocodile here," I said, prodding away.

Carl was sceptical. "Vot for he want to be alone?" he asked.

"Perhaps it's come up here to make a nest, lay eggs or . . ." At that moment the pool heaved in a churning mass, the bamboo stick was snatched from my hands and I beat a rapid, and rather

153

indecorous, retreat out of the water well back on the shingle. It was not merely a crocodile, but a monster.

Carl nearly fell backwards, laughing—but we were both terrified.

By the time we had both recovered, the crocodile had returned to its lair, the water was calm again and I might almost have imagined that the whole thing was an illusion; if it had not been for the bamboo which had been chewed to pieces.

Carl came round to my side of the pool with the shotgun and gave me his bamboo. His plan was that I should lure the crocodile out and he would shoot it. He had no knowledge of firearms, and I told him that it was quite useless with a shot-gun. I could not see what we could do to get this crocodile. I cut and sharpened another bamboo as reserve and poked futilely around.

This time the crocodile did not seize the bamboo. He came straight across the pool towards us, lashing his enormous tail, his head well above water, and barking in a peculiar sort of snarling rage. Carl gave him two barrels of No. 6 shot in the muzzle, but it bounced off like rain off armour-plate. He came on, all twelve to fourteen feet of him, and we took to our heels.

I fully expected the animal to attempt escape by the same route that it had entered the pool. But instead of going up on the shingle, it stopped at the water's edge and did what the lizard had done to the cockerel. With astonishing agility and power, it made a complete pivot on its forelegs, lashing round a complete circle with that eight-foot tail. It missed us by yards, but it needed no imagination to realise what would have happened if that enormously strong and heavy tail had touched us. It immediately retreated into the pool again, backing towards the deep water beneath the tree.

The sound of the two shots brought back the whole excited convict party to see what had happened. When they learnt that in the pool there was a 'mee gyaung yay' or enormous crocodile, they needed no orders. They took up position as spectators on the edge of the jungle, in easy dodging distance of cover. I was annoyed that they had come back; they would be worse than useless in helping to kill the wretched crocodile, yet now they were here, we were committed to trying.

I thought of the Sinhalese method of inserting a stick sharpened at both ends inside a dead dog. The crocodile snapping at the bait impales its jaws. Unfortunately there were no dead dogs handy at the moment.

The only convict who offered assistance was Tun Gyaw, who came forward waving his jungle-knife and offering to kill the monster, if it appeared again.

"Have you ever seen a crocodile?" I asked.

"No, Thakin."

"Well, I have," I said, "but not like this one. You might as easily kill it with a dagger as with that dah."

I went back to my prodding and once again the crocodile emerged, once again Carl gave him both barrels, once again the crocodile pivoted on his forelegs, scattering the shingle with his tail, like shrapnel.

But this time he scattered the convicts as well. Shrieking, they rushed in the direction of the open creek. I was glad I had immobilised the *Madame X* and had the parts in my pocket. Otherwise they would probably not have stopped until they got back to Smith Island. There was one exception to this. Tun Gyaw had taken prudent evasive action, but he was still with us. He was not in the least bit frightened, which surprised me, as I had always thought of him as a man of bravado rather than courage.

By now even Carl realised that there was no hope of getting the crocodile with the shot-gun. In fact I saw, to my amazement and terror, that he had passed the shot-gun to Tun Gyaw. Carl probably had not even realised that Tun Gyaw was a convict. He probably thought he was on the same level as Po Sine. I had of course mentioned no word to any of my companions about Tun Gyaw's stabbing attack on me, and since none of them spoke Burmese, there was no means of their learning except from Joseph, who was discretion itself.

At that moment, I could have cursed myself for keeping silent. I suddenly saw an explanation of Tun Gyaw's staying behind, which was far more sinister. He wanted to get hold of a weapon, and he had succeeded. He had Carl and myself in his power, if he chose to exercise it. The only thing which might restrain him was the presence of the crocodile. If I tried to get the shot-gun away from him too obviously, I might put into his head ideas which were not there at the moment. The only thing that held him was his belief that I trusted him. The most dangerous thing of all would be to destroy that belief.

I tried to get him to drop the shot-gun, suggesting that he should run back to the launch and get a rope with which he could lassoo the beast. But he took no notice, as if he thought that suggestion as silly as I did myself. Then what about the boathook from the launch, to jab in the reptile's gills?

Before I could translate that into an order, Carl, who had been prodding excitedly in the pool, suddenly gave a yell. The water churned and those great open jaws reared out. Carl turned and on the loose shingle stumbled, righted himself, and then tripped and sprawled.

The crocodile, infuriated, saw what had happened, and instead of spinning on his forefeet, which would have battered Carl unconscious, it dashed forward, with that queer snarling noise, ready to take Carl in its jaws.

Tun Gyaw ran forward; from the way he held the shot-gun, I feared that he would shoot Carl dead or pepper me. He was as dangerous as the crocodile. "Don't shoot!" I shouted, "don't shoot!"

But at that very moment he let off the first barrel, followed immediately by the second. The muzzle of the shot-gun was almost touching the back of the crocodile's head.

The crocodile gave a strange cry, which was a sort of compound of anguish and surprise. It stopped in its tracks, concerned now only in getting back to the pool. Its tail swung as it pivoted, Tun Gyaw flung himself to one side to avoid being struck, and the shot-gun crashed on the shingle.

Carl was on his feet again. He rushed to Tun Gyaw. I did likewise, picking up the shot-gun and reloading it. Tun Gyaw helped himself up and readjusted his lungyi, which had fallen loose. He walked with a limp, thinking that if he had been hurt, it would pain him less. But in fact he had not been struck by the crocodile.

We turned to the pool wondering if there would be another attack. Now that I had the gun, I felt I must be prepared for a shot as courageous as Tun Gyaw's. "If it charges, you must run away as decoy," I said to Tun Gyaw in Burmese and repeated it to Carl in English.

But instead of that ominous churning, there came only the sound of gurgles and from under the bank rose large bubbles. "Tun Gyaw," I said, "you've really wounded him."

We probed again, but for a long time there was no reaction. Then there was a movement, and we were ready to bolt, but no attack took place. Instead the surface of the pool parted and floating like a water-logged tree-trunk appeared the white underbelly of the crocodile.

"Belly upwards," Tun Gyaw said, with raw Burmese humour. "Must be a female."

"What does he say?" Carl asked.

The thought of having to explain this Burmese joke in basic English was depressing. "Tun Gyaw saved your life," I said and, turning to the convict, I told him the same thing from both of us.

Tun Gyaw smiled. He was pleased to be praised, but he was far more interested in seeing the wound at the back of the crocodile's head, so close that every shot had entered in a space not much larger than the diameter of a tennis ball.

I was relieved by the return of the other convicts and their expressions of admiration of Tun Gyaw and disgust at the crocodile. During the remainder of our stay in the Andamans, we saw thousands of crocodiles. But we never bagged another. We did not try very hard, as we thought that another could only be an anticlimax after this fourteen-footer.

That evening we returned to camp with heartening information. The supplies of elephant fodder were sufficient to support quite a large strength of elephants and there seemed to be ample fresh water from perennial springs. We had done more than merely bag a large crocodile.

Before returning, we had to wait for the tide to come well up again. On the way back to Smith Island, I watched the convicts. It was almost impossible to believe that they were the men who had shambled aboard the *Surmai* at Port Blair. They had regained their sense of freedom and independence. For their sake I hoped that the verdict of the survey would go in favour of the Andamans, because it could mean a form of hard labour which was paid and which was not degrading.

Back in camp, we found Jeff and Bruno ill-disposed to listen to our crocodile story. They had caught an assortment of fish and actually bagged a wild pig. I remembered the toughness of the pig which the officers of the *Briton* would so willingly have exchanged for their pet dog. I imagined that Jeff and Bruno's wild pig was just as tough. The convicts, who would have rioted if they hadn't been allowed to eat it for supper, did not complain, however. It was the thinnest wild pig I have ever seen. It had really reduced itself to the bare essentials. If it had grown any skinnier, it would certainly have stopped being a pig, and perhaps have stopped being anything else, except a corpse.

We shot hundreds of wild pig in the weeks to come. None of them looked in condition. But we all succumbed to roast pork in the end, in spite of the risk of tape-worm if one eats it undercooked.

That evening we worked out the yield of Chatham Island according to Jeff's enumerations of timber. If the rest of North Andaman was to prove no better than Chatham Island, we should have been wise to stop work at once.

But that night our concern shifted from timber-yield to more irritating matters. During the night young Bruno started to scratch. He made such a noise about it that he woke us all up.

"For goodness sake," Jeff said.

"I'm sorry," said Bruno, "but this itch is driving me mad."

"And your scratching is driving *us* mad," said Jeff.

By torchlight I had a look at Bruno's body. His skin reminded me of Archie's the first night we explored the Petyah Yay Shin. "The Petyah's the worst of all stinging nettles," I said; "it leaves minute prickles from the serrated leaves in your skin."

"I'm not interested about that," Bruno said, tearing at his skin with his nails. "How do you cure it?"

"What we do in Burma," I said—"in fact the only thing that gives any relief—is to rub the affected parts with the long, oily hair of a jungle Burman."

"What a pity none of the convicts have long oily hair; otherwise Bruno could go and have a good rub and we could get a decent night's rest," said Jeff.

Bruno was in such a state of irritation that at last I woke up Joseph and asked him for some olive oil, which I rubbed on Bruno's back and chest. It gave him some relief, and we all fell asleep until shortly before dawn, when Jeff began to scratch and swear, making, as Bruno said, a far worse fuss than he had.

I thought it rather strange that if they had both been stung by nettles, it should have taken so long for the prickles to have made their effect on Jeff. Indeed, I was rather surprised that he had been stung at all—once again it was the torso which was affected, and whereas Bruno was almost hairless to the hips, Jeff was covered with a thick mat of hair over chest, arms and even back.

I examined Bruno again more carefully, and I found that my first diagnosis had been wrong. It was not the petyah sting. Both of them were covered in myriads of bamboo ticks, so tiny that they were almost invisible to the naked eye. The day before, they had both stripped to the waist, and in walking through the forest they had brushed against nests of these ticks, hanging from the branches of the trees. Probably this was the first time in the history of the North Andaman that bamboo ticks had been offered such delicate fare. Whatever follies of personal hygiene the original settlers of Port Cornwallis had committed, walking through tick-ridden forests stripped to the waist was not one of them.

The two victims did not seem interested in these reflections of mine. What was the cure for bamboo ticks?

The application of pure spirits of turpentine was the only thing I knew to make the bamboo tick give up the ghost, and the sting of that was nearly as painful as petyah leaves.

We sprayed them both from an atomising spray-gun and soon cleared the bald torso of Bruno. But the unfortunate Jeff went through agony as we drenched his fur mats. "Which only goes to show," said Bruno, "how unwise it is to be unsympathetic to the ills of other people."

These were not the only casualties. Next day our convicts were ill, and among them Nga Moh. This greatly alarmed me, because I had come to rely on Nga Moh for the complete administration of the convict gang. I did not know what crime he had committed, but I could not believe that it had been a very serious one, because as well as high intelligence he displayed a great strength of character. I trusted him completely.

There was no doubt that Nga Moh and the others were very sick men; I could see that by their colour, which changes very quickly when a Burman is ill. And yet there was nothing obviously wrong with them.

I drew Nga Moh on one side and asked him what was wrong.

I was not surprised when he told me that he had run out of opium. What surprised me was that he knew I had some. How he knew this I never discovered. "There will be much illness in the camp, Thakin," he said, "unless you can issue opium to those who use it."

I had worked out the morality of this. I was not prepared to hand over opium to him unless he would promise on oath before Buddha that he would give it only to those who were already addicts. If I did not give it to the addicts, I felt that I should be as guilty as if I did give it to those who were not addicted.

Nga Moh gave the promise, and there was indeed no temptation that he should break it, as I pointed out that my supplies of opium were limited and they had got to last until they returned to Port Blair.

That day Nga Moh and the three other sick men recovered and several others who had begun to wilt suddenly appeared refreshed and healthy. There was no more sickness among the convicts during the rest of the expedition, and I won for myself a reputation as a good doctor which I could never have sustained without my football.

CHAPTER XIII

As we worked further from our base camp on Smith Island, we devised a bivouac system of camps where we could stay two or three days. By this method we caught up our initial delays and found ourselves ahead of the schedule which we had worked out, based on the total mileage of strip enumeration needed for making a reliable calculation of timber supplies.

One of our main tasks was to locate the varying types of forest. At first, we felt that if we could have had one of those flying-boats to do an aerial survey beforehand, it would have made our task much easier. But the most important function for the aircraft was to fly over the stands of timber after we had located them, and from oblique aerial photographs we should estimate the extent of the areas.

My collection of sample elephant fodders established beyond doubt that we could graze at least a hundred elephants in the jungles surrounding Port Cornwallis. There would be ample fresh water in the dry season, though in the hot season it might be necessary to work on the 'well system' of watering. In streams where water became subterranean during the dry season, water could be found at a depth of four feet or so. I had found in dry-zone forests of Burma that excellent results could be obtained by allotting each elephant its own well. Prospecting for fodder and water was an operation distinct from timber-cruising; but in the course of following streams up their full length, I came across many areas worth listing.

At an encouraging speed we were building up reports under different headings, on the basis of which the powers that were would have to decide whether it would be economic to exploit these forests.

Each time we crossed Port Cornwallis harbour, we fished our way over. It was some of the finest sea fishing I have ever had. Our choice of fish was always abundant, and though between us and the lizards we had finished the chickens and ducks, Po Sine kept us well supplied with imperial pigeons. Wild pig were abundant. It was their farrowing season and weaners were two a penny.

We were so well ahead of schedule that I decided that we could afford to take a day off. Jeff elected to stay in camp to work on his report of the saw-mill capacity which would be required.

Carl had repeatedly expressed the desire to try spearing fish and, borrowing one of the crew from the *Jarawa*, he went to Minerva Bay, along the coast of Smith Island, on the *Madame X*. I had long wanted to visit a place called Bond Bay, which lay south of Cadell Bay, in the shelter of Trilby Island. Bruno elected to come with me, and on the *Jarawa* we passed between Smith Island and the mainland, a treacherous waterway, into the more open sea by Temple Island. It was not long before we reached Bond Bay, where we anchored and fished for a time. There was no fringe of mangrove swamp here and the stretch of sand was so inviting we decided to land.

As we neared the shore, moving slowly and cautiously, easy

ahead–half astern–easy ahead, sounding our way across the most gorgeous coral reef, I looked up from the bow and saw quite distinctly a naked human figure run from one part of the jungle fringe to another.

"Full astern!" I yelled to Bruno. "Andamanese! Pass the binoculars!" At the same time I flung the anchor overboard.

Bruno was in the bow beside me in a matter of seconds, adjusting the binoculars and muttering his disbelief. "But you're right," he said. "There's a hut, a sort of wigwam."

He passed the binoculars to me, and through them I saw another figure running, as if to warn others. Sure enough soon a little party of four naked natives collected outside the wigwam.

We were about 600 yards away, and I passed the binoculars back, saying as a joke, "See what an extraordinary navel that chap on the left has."

"It isn't a man," Bruno answered seriously. "That one's a woman, and so is the one next to her."

They came half-way to the water's edge across the sand and then halted. We waved, but they did not wave back.

"My old father said they were all dead," Bruno said. "He won't believe this. Unless we take a head back, to match that old crocodile head you've got buried in the sand."

I suggested that we should go ashore and fraternise, but Bruno was adamant. "Haven't you heard?" he said. "If there's one thing an Andamanese hates more than another Andamanese, it's a European."

To show that we had friendly intentions, we decided to send some things ashore. There was an empty wooden Johnny Walker crate in the bows. I held it up to show them, and into it I placed a few stores, a roll of fishing line and two or three hooks, and then launched it overboard.

Through the binoculars we could see little detail because they were so bunched together. They were obviously curious, but very suspicious of us; after all, they knew even less about us than we did about them.

Bruno said that he thought their intentions were hostile. I was not so sure. There were plenty of well-authenticated accounts of vicious attacks by Andamanese on Europeans. But as with the *Briton* and *Runnymede* parties, it had always begun with a European attacking the Andamanese in the first place. It was probable that our particular group had never seen a European before. There might be a tradition of fear of strangers handed down from previous generations, but there was a chance that we might be able to establish trust between us and perhaps find out a little more about this dying race.

They watched the box drift ashore, but they left it for some minutes before any of them moved. Perhaps they feared it contained something dangerous.

As we put our stern to the shore, as if we were going to leave, two figures left the group and walked towards the box. There was no doubt they were women. They were naked except for a leaf as a *cache-sexe* and their breasts were plain to see. They appeared to have negroid or negrito features.

The women snatched the box and ran with it up the beach as if they were stealing. They all crowded round it, obviously examining the things inside. But there was no wave of gratitude; nor did they use the catamaran canoe, which we could see drawn up beside the wigwam, to come out and thank us.

"They look damn suspicious," Bruno said.

"The reason for that might be that they don't know what's in the box," I said. "We're assuming that they know what a fish-hook is. But they are probably living in a pre-fish-hook age. And how are they to know that the stuff we've sent them is food? They probably don't even know how to open a tin."

Bruno and I had an argument whether we should stay the night there. Bruno pointed out that we could sleep aboard and that they would not dare to leave while we were in the bay. We should be pinning them down. On the other hand, if we went back to Smith Island, we'd find them gone by to-morrow morning.

I over-ruled Bruno. I had already spent one night away from

the main party on a mud-bank with Jeff, and I knew what chaos it might cause. I could envisage the anxiety of Carl and Jeff and perhaps some misguided attempt to find us by searchlight during the night. But I also thought that our chances of establishing good relations finally with these Andamanese depended upon our going away now. I was sure that Bruno was right and the Andamanese would escape as soon as they could. That could be taken for granted. But if we allowed them to escape this time, instead of pinning them down, they would be more inclined to trust us the next time we saw them.

"But supposing we don't see them again," Bruno protested.

"In that case," I answered, "we shall have to content ourselves with not having made enemies out of them. Supposing we stirred up their enmity now, we might endanger the whole timber operation if the company decides to move in."

Bruno laughed. "You needn't worry about that. This is all the Andamanese there are left up here. I'm jolly surprised we found them."

"If I remember," I said cruelly, "there were no crocodiles in the Andamans, according to your sources, but we've seen thousands of them."

When we got back to the Smith Island Camp, our news did not cause the stir we expected. Jeff was still immersed in his calculations, and Carl had a graphic story of his day's sport. Hanging from the branch of a tree was a 200-pound shark which he had caught with a leg of wild pig as bait. He had also collected a most beautiful assortment of corals and shells. But what he wanted to talk about more than anything else was the octopus which got away. He had speared it in Minerva Bay, and each time that he told us about it, it grew larger, until, as Jeff said, "It sounded as if it was a jolly good thing that it *did* get away."

Carl wanted to go back to his spearing ground next day, but he was over-ruled, because we wanted both launches if we were to persuade our Andamanese to make friends.

We set out at dawn, and we scrutinised every yard of shore that we passed. Now that we knew that some Andamanese existed, we imagined that they might be anywhere, and in almost any numbers.

If these innumerable islands had not been so begirt with mangrove swamps, we should have regarded the search as hopeless. But most of the shore was made impossible for us, and so even more impossible for the Andamanese.

On the mainland to the west of Temple Island there was a long stretch of sand. At the suggestion of Bruno, Carl and he landed at one end and walked the length of it to see whether they could detect any footprints. Jeff and I followed them off-shore, speculating on the possibility of our discovering a really large settlement—or unsettlement—of Andamanese. "I don't see how it is possible," Jeff said. "There can't have been enough people from outside for them to hate and kill; they might have spared one another." There were no signs of footprints on that beach.

We sailed round Bayne Point into Bond Bay. The wigwam was still there, but the catamaran had gone. There was no sign of life. We concentrated our binoculars on the shore and made going away movements with the craft, but it provoked no reaction, so we went ashore.

Bruno was a great believer in the treacherous Andaman theory, so we told him to go ashore, telling him that we would shoot any Andamanese before they roasted him alive. Bruno was to walk across to the wigwam, while a small picked party, including Carl and myself, Po Sine, Nga Moh and Gyaw, waited at the water's edge to cope with any unpleasant incident. Jeff stayed in the bows of the *Jarawa* with the binoculars in one hand and a megaphone in the other.

Bruno was conspicuously without arms. He did not even carry a stick, and he stripped to the waist. Bruno reached the wigwam and very soon signalled us up. There was no sign of anyone. As we approached, I formed a theory that it was not we but the stench which had driven them away. They were great mussel and oyster eaters. Near the wigwam was a mound of oyster and mussel shells at least five feet in height. They had heaped sand over them at intervals, intending to keep bluebottles away. But they had clearly not associated the gentle with the adult fly. The heap was a fly factory, engaged in full-time mass reproduction.

There were myriads of fish-bones of all shapes and sizes, bones of wild pig and smaller bones which we took to be those of bamboo rats.

Anything that could be of use to them they had taken away. There was no sign of our Johnny Walker box or its contents. They had launched the canoe at the height of the previous tide, so that there was no sign of foot-prints or of the canoe having been dragged below high-water mark; just the marks where it had rested by high-water level.

We went back to our craft and decided to scout north towards the western shore of Trilby Island. But we soon turned back. The mangrove swamps seemed everywhere, and there were no beaches where the natives might land.

It was not very difficult to detect possible landing-places. The mangrove swamp eliminated so many. Anything the least out of the ordinary was marked out by absence of mangrove.

A spot at the southerly tip of Trilby Island attracted our attention, and we manœuvred inshore, to the delight of Carl, who had brought his spear with him and was eager for another octopus.

"Look over there," Bruno shouted, pointing to a very small beach.

He snatched up the binoculars, but even with the naked eye one could see a group of Andamanese carrying a canoe over the sand towards the jungle's edge. They must have seen us at that moment, because they dropped the canoe and bolted for the jungle.

"It must be the same lot," Bruno said. "There's our Johnny Walker box on the beach."

"How do you know it's Johnny Walker, at this distance?" asked Jeff facetiously. "They may drink some other whisky."

We decided that the best thing that we could do was to take

another box ashore in the *Madame X* and then withdraw, without even examining the canoe, and wait and see what happened. The natives had hidden themselves in the jungle.

We anchored both launches alongside each other well off-shore and waited for at least an hour, taking turn and turn about with the binoculars and the fishing-rods.

At last two figures appeared out of the jungle. Once again it was the women. They seemed to do the fetching and carrying in the family, at least if there was any danger attached to it.

First they carried the new box into the jungle, and not long after they reappeared, two very black figures against the white coral sand, and went to the canoe. This they launched and with expert strokes brought it rapidly towards us.

When they came close, they both made signs of drinking. We had obviously cornered them on the shore of a small island where there was no drinking-water. Equally obviously they regarded us not as enemies, but as people who might supply their wants. They must have opened the tins and found they contained food.

I half filled two bottles with water, corked them and threw them over to the two women. In a quiet voice I said to Bruno, who was on *Madame X* with Carl, "You two push ashore and cut them off."

The two women seemed quite unalarmed by the departure of the *Madame X*. They did not return our smiles, however. "Perhaps the Andamanese don't express friendly pleasure by smiling," Jeff said.

In fact they made no gestures at all either with their features or their hands. They were the most phlegmatic people I have ever seen.

Their faces were negroid—or rather, taken in conjunction with their diminutive physique, negrito. Both the women had faces which to our taste were very ugly, but the younger one, whom I judged to be unmarried, had a beautifully proportioned body.

Bruno and Carl went ashore, and were met by the rest of the Andamanese family: two males, of whom the more remarkable

was an aged man with a rusty old spear, who was clearly the leader or paterfamilias. On his shoulder he carried a newly-killed wild pig. Both of the men tried most earnestly to communicate with Bruno and Carl, but without success. Neither side could understand the other.

When we were all ashore, however, we managed to convey to the Andamanese that we wanted them to come with us, and we had apparently built up enough trust for them to agree. We had no clear idea what we intended to do with them. Perhaps they could be useful with their knowledge of the islands, but I doubted it. Perhaps it was the promise which I had given to Athelstan Alcock that we would find out as much as we could about the natives and would not do them any harm. Or else it was the challenge levelled by the centuries of fighting between the Andamanese and the strangers who landed on their shores. Was it possible to build up some relationship between ourselves and these Iron-Age survivors without some disaster intervening?

As we took their canoe in tow and started for Smith Island, the old man began violently to gesticulate, pointing to the canoe and then towards the mainland. It was not clear what he wanted, but we humoured him, and were rewarded by finding a canoe which they had just completed, lying at the edge of the jungle on a strip of sand. We took that in tow as well, though we found that an Andamanese canoe with outrigger is not an easy tow with a fresh breeze.

We piled all their household effects aboard the *Jarawa*. It was a pathetic collection of tropical junk, but it was all that they and their ancestors had accumulated over the millennia between them and extinction. It was little wonder the race was dying out.

I eyed them curiously, because they were the survivors of a disaster centuries old. Some remote ancestors had either been marooned upon these islands by a subsidence of the mountain range or had possessed the wit to reach here without the wit to leave again. Perhaps they lacked the will, because they were able to sustain easily the very simple sort of life to which they were used. On a diet of mussels, oysters, wild pigs and bamboo rats, life was easy to sustain, provided numbers were kept down. But to sustain any higher form of civilisation, based upon agriculture, was extremely difficult. If there were two families trying to live in a bay which could support only one, how much easier it must have been for one family to kill the other than for both of them to devise ways of increasing their food supplies.

It was a common thing to regard these people as primitives untouched by civilisation. But as I looked at them, the women squatting on their worldly possessions in postures which outraged the modesty of Nga Moh, I thought that really they might be some of the earliest human decadents. In the Pleistocene Age they might have been in the forefront of humanity, at least judged by standards of living. Their downfall was due to the opulence of the foreshore. They were not so much Iron Age men as Musselmen living at the end of the Oyster Age.

As we drew near Smith Island, we became aware of an acute problem. The two women might belong to the Oyster Age and be as ugly as sin, but one thing was self-evident, and that was their sex. To place them close to a camp of enforcedly celibate convicts was asking for the sort of trouble which makes newspaper-owners millionaires.

At Nga Moh's suggestion we dropped them off at a beach on Smith Island well short of our camp. We took their canoes with us, but we left them many luxuries the uses of which we had demonstrated while they were on the launch.

What they treasured more than anything else was an earthenware bowl, the shape of a large fruit dish, in which burned, or rather smouldered, a few pieces of touchwood similar to charcoal, which they fed continually as if it were a God of Fire. The Andamanese had a sort of Promethean legend that fire had been stolen from heaven and since then had never been allowed to become extinct. They seemed to regard themselves as keepers of the flame. When we showed them how to make fire by striking a match, they were not in the least interested, which I thought evidence of their good sense; for what was the use of their learning to strike matches, if after we left there were no more matches to strike?

I had read that supposing their fire went out, they could get fire from another family. That was in 1899. But in the meantime it looked as if the other families had died off. Certainly there were none with whom they were in constant contact; nor in the rest of our time did we see any other Andamanese.

Bruno, who had a strong line in dumb crambo, undertook to explain in sign language that we should bring the canoes back at noon next day. The time being 5 p.m., Bruno pointed to the westering sun. With the downward movement of his hand and arm, he made it set. He closed both eyes, and leaned his cheek against both folded hands. Then he turned to the east, opened his eyes and rubbed the sleep out of them. He warmed his hands at the rising sun and then pointed it up the sky till noon.

They watched him with great interest and Bruno said to them in English, "That's to-morrow noon."

They nodded and grinned.

"You see? They understand!" Bruno said triumphantly.

"Perhaps they just think you're funny," Jeff said.

But Bruno was not to be distracted. Keeping the sun at high noon with one finger, with his other hand he pointed first to the canoes and then to the shore.

Once again they nodded; a certain proof that they understood, Bruno said. Jeff suggested that perhaps they wanted to get rid of him before he went completely insane.

We handed back their canoes next day. Their fear of us had gone, and they were even more curious about us than we were about them. The men knew every beach in the Port Cornwallis area, and they might have been of great assistance to us if we had been able to master their language. Unfortunately we never got beyond sign language. It could not be said that we made friends with the Andamanese; they were more like mascots, whom we liked to have with us. The two most popular were the young girl and the old man. They would both spend whole days with us at

174

camp or at work, watching what we were doing with an interest that was intelligent a lot of the time. The old man we named Friday.

It was not till the day before the Southamptons were due that Jeff suddenly said, "Good Lord! what'll Friday do when the Southamptons come? Do you think we'd better send them away?"

"Don't be silly," Bruno said. "I'll explain it all to him." And the next time the old man came in to camp, Bruno gave a wonderful imitation of being two Southampton flying-boats in the air and coming down on the sea. It was very funny, but Friday looked blankly from Bruno to us and back, as if Bruno had gone demented!

"He hasn't understood a thing," said Jeff. "The only way for it is for me to explain to him so that he can follow it stage by stage." Jeff had been a pilot in the First World War, and he took charge of buoying the harbour to show the Southamptons the way in. He insisted on taking Friday with him and 'explaining it stage by stage'.

Bruno said it was much funnier than his dumb crambo, because it lasted longer. "He can't understand why you haven't any hooks and bait on the buoys and markers, Jeff."

I asked Tun Gyaw if he had ever seen a Southampton flying-boat. He hadn't; and he made it plain he did not expect to see one at Port Cornwallis. That it was possible to fly he accepted, but that it was possible to fly across the sea and find a particular place in the ocean was more than any sane man could believe.

But they appeared all right; two hours before we expected them, at that. The two Andamanese men, who had arrived in camp that morning to cadge salt, looked up at these strange roaring birds 3,000 feet up in the sky, and before Bruno could explain that this was the meaning of his dumb crambo and Jeff that this was what he hoped to catch with his buoys and markers, the two Andamanese were tearing down the beach, yelling "Hoo! Hoo! Hoo! Hoo!" like a war cry. They launched their canoe, leapt into it and started paddling as if they were in a canoe race, the prize for which was life itself.

We all of us, convicts included, roared with laughter, and after they had disappeared from view we gave them no more thought, because the first of the flying-boats was already losing altitude and manœuvring for position.

As the hull of the Southampton touched the water, there were exclamations of "Ma lai!" (Oh mother!) from the convicts. It taxied down the waterway to make the way clear for the second Southampton. The roar of the engines was deafening, reverberating back across the water from the mountains. Some of the convicts who had been laughing loudest at the two Andamanese, shrieked and rushed for refuge in the jungle. As soon as the second had landed, Jeff and Bruno went out in *Madame X* to pilot them to shallow anchorage near our camp.

The Southamptons had only a few hours' flying to do for us, but they stayed for two days. We regarded the way they had hopped up from Singapore in a few hours and worked day after day way above the earth to which we were bound as a most romantic and wonderful thing. To them it was a boring routine, except when it was broken by assignments among men like ourselves in out-lying places who were 'really living'.

"Wonderful life you chaps have," they said, "just sea fishing the whole time." It was hard to explain that we got comparatively little sea-fishing except when we were entertaining guests, and even harder not to say that if they went on losing tackle at the present alarming rate, there would be no sea-fishing after they left.

We had made a sufficient ground reconnaissance to know exactly where the richest stands were to be found. From the oblique aerial photographs the Southamptons could give us we hoped to estimate the full extent of the areas.

On our first reconnaissance we flew round the whole coastline and also covered the length of the North Island from north to south, following the saddleback ridges. Jeff gave the directions to the photographers for the different shots we needed. I went for the ride and saw the overall picture of an area in which I might spend a large part of my life working on the ground.

But what overwhelmed me at first was the beauty of the North Andaman from above. In the surrounding seas there was every shade of blue in the varying depths of water and each was variegated by the sea-bed, pink coral here and there white, or granite boulders and blotches of dark seaweed, and elsewhere seaweed the colours of cornfields waving in differing stages of ripeness.

There were greens in the water, but even more in the forests. From 500 feet up, the mangrove swamps looked like dark green oriental carpets, their growth, so tough and infuriating on the ground, reduced by distance to a beautiful deep pile. Each canopy stood out, proclaiming its dominant species by colour and texture. Most impressive were the gurjan trees which towered for light above everything else.

I sat in the open bow seat or cockpit in front of the pilot. I thought I would take my own amateur photographic record with my camera, which was loaded with film-pack.

As I took each exposure, I tore off the black screen paper, rolled it into a ball and dropped it at my feet. Then I must casually have flicked one over my shoulder into the air-stream. Perhaps I flicked more than one before I became conscious of a red light winking angrily at me.

178

I thought something must have gone wrong and we were going to crash land. I stood up and looked round at the pilot. As I stuck my head above the windscreen my helmet was snatched at and my neck wrenched. The pilot shook his fist at me and pointed at the red light on my control panel.

I dived into cover again and examined the panel. Near the 'blinking' light was what looked like the end of a speaking-tube. It was obviously not that. It undid, and inside I found a slip of paper. "Put the paper at your feet," it said. "You damn near blinded me!"

I was so contrite that I stood up again and risked decapitation in order to say "Sorry." It was not till we landed that I was told that I could have written a reply on the pad by the red light and sent it back along the tube.

The second day we made a number of special runs over the area west of Saddle Peak and over the watershed between the Kalara and Diglipor rivers. Jeff had been rather disappointed with the timber stands around Port Cornwallis Bay, so I intended to cover this main range on foot after the R.A.F. had gone back. It did not look at all inviting, the forest was terribly dense. But at least I could see pools of fresh water at frequent bends. That was valuable information.

The night before they left, the R.A.F. asked whether there were any mails which they might post for us in Singapore. I had not thought of writing to anyone; I had, indeed, been so engrossed in the day-to-day life in the Andamans that I had not given much thought to anyone outside. But now that this opportunity opened up, I found my mind filled with thoughts of Susan. I wanted to take advantage of this chance of writing to her; yet I found it very difficult to put into words what I wanted to say. Everything that I wrote sounded silly. I did not know how to write to Susan what was in my heart. Perhaps the sympathy which I thought existed between us, unspoken, was all my fancy. My letter might arrive between one date with He Man and the next. I had not the trust in my own love. I was afraid of making a fool of myself.

I had almost decided to write nothing at all, preferring the certainty of not being hurt to the possible joy that a letter might give, when I was provided with an idea from an open book lying on my camp bed. Just before I left Burma, I had received from home a copy of this book by John Still, called *Jungle Tide*. I had read it in the setting of the Andamans, and there were many things which had impressed me. More than any was the Credo which he had printed on the last page. I read it once again.

> Mountains and woods and the winds that blow over them;
> Meadows and downs, and the wild flowers that cover them;
> Rocks and ravines, and the jungles that smother them;
>   All these I love with a love that possesseth me,
>   But more than all of these I worship thee.
>
> Sea and the shore, and shells the gods squander there;
> Corals and pools, and wild things that wander there;
> Silence and cares, and the thoughts that men ponder there;
>   All these I love with a love that enchanteth me,
>   But deeper in my depths springs love for thee.

It was just what I wanted. I copied it out, but did not add another word, not even my name. I placed it in an envelope, addressed it to Susan in Rangoon and gave it casually to the pilot of one of the Southamptons. "If you can remember to post it in Singapore . . ."

The Southamptons had come up to the North Andaman as part of a reconnaissance into the activities of the Japanese mother-of-pearl fishing-boats. Licences had been issued for them in the Nicobar Andaman waters, and the Southamptons had sighted no less than twenty-one on their way up.

It was certain that these ships were poaching, the R.A.F. said. What they suspected was that they might at the same time be taking soundings. They asked us if we saw any of these fishing-boats, to board them if we could and see what they were up to.

The next morning at dawn the Southamptons left us. They were gone as suddenly as they had come. They disappeared over the Saddle Peak, and we felt very alone. The air survey had been so simple. But you can't cut and trim and transport timber by air. You can't even measure and count them from the skies, though aerial photographs, with their varying shadows, can be of enormous help in preparing estimates of yield and devising the routes to be taken on the ground.

"It seems as if the R.A.F. belong to one world," Bruno said, "where everything is quick and light and easy. And here we are, sweating away in mangrove swamps. . . ."

"And in forests filled with bamboo ticks," Jeff said.

"And with only one tin of Grape-Nuts a week," added Carl.

We saw our only Japanese fishing-boat the day after the Sunderlands departed. It was in a small bay to the north of Port Cornwallis. The crew were genuinely occupied in diving for mother-of-pearl shells, though they may easily have been taking soundings as well. We came alongside to watch. They were working two wire-mesh baskets, one on either side of their craft. Each was weighted, and a muscular young Japanese descended over and over again, filling the basket. The oysters were pitched into the hold, and at the rate they were working they would soon have had a full catch, though they almost certainly collected only a limited amount from each bed.

We tried to talk to them, but they either did not understand or pretended not to. They just went on working without taking any notice of us at all.

Their craft was a sailing-boat fitted with a small auxiliary engine for shallow-water coasting. We were amazed that they had managed to come so far from home in it. Perhaps they were innocent fishermen, wanting only to supply materials for the cheap button trade. But looking back, I wonder whether these were not the advance guard of the Japanese barbarians who during the Second World War invaded the Andamans and instituted a terror which was as savage as it was disgusting. At the time I thought only how vehement was the disgust which Nga Moh expressed for them and wondered whether it was in these boats that the illicit supplies of opium came to the convicts.

We did not think for some days about our old friends, the Andamanese. We had not seen them since Friday, and the other man had fled at the approach of the Southamptons. We assumed that when they saw the Southamptons fly away for good, they would come back. But there was no sign of that new catamaran canoe, so one morning Bruno and I went along to the beach where they camped.

Usually they came down to the water's edge to meet us and often even canoed out to join us. I thought at first they had gone, but through the binoculars Bruno saw them by the wigwam they had made. "But there are only three," he said, "and they are all daubed with something."

The one missing was Friday. The others had smeared their bodies with grey ashes and their faces and heads with a grey mud. Judging from their collection of possessions, they were packed up and about to go, with the bowl of ancestral fire and the two Johnny Walker cases filled with junk.

The old woman and the young man seemed to be stricken with a dumb grief. They were never bright at the best of times. What sparks of intelligence flickered in that dying family were in Friday and the young girl.

I thought that was why such ungovernable sorrow shook the girl. She must have known that the old man would die a natural death some time not very distant. But while he was still alive, there was a chance that he or the two of them would strike on something which would enable the family to survive. There would be a journey to the Middle Andaman or the South in search of another family of Musselmen. What she bewailed was not the death of the old man, but the end of her race and the fire in the bowl.

Bruno asked her what had happened, in his sign language, and from what she gestured it was plain what had happened. The old man had been up on a cliff near the camp, hunting wild pig, probably, and one of the Southamptons had come flying very low— perhaps that first reconnaissance of mine in which I had sat entranced at the beauty of the sea and forest—and in panic the old man had jumped off the cliff and been dashed to death on the rocks below.

182

It had happened exactly as I had feared. The clash between the outsider and the Andamanese always ended in tragedy for the Andamanese; sometimes it was through ill-will, more often it was because of the inability of the two cultures, so different, to come to terms.

We tried to console them, and Bruno did his routine to say that we would be back on the morrow.

But next day when we came there there was only the wigwam, more stinking shells and bones and the buzz of blow-flies.

On our way back I dropped overboard the letter which Athelstan Alcock had asked me to post. Perhaps it was absurd, but I had made a promise.

CHAPTER XIV

AFTER the Southamptons had departed, we spent some days working out the implications of the information we had compiled. I was the most optimistic of the party. Some years previously the Indian Forestry Department had introduced elephants into the South Islands for the extraction of timber. They were fed artificially on imported paddy, and the experiment was a failure.

The specimen fodders I had collected, with considerable assistance from Tun Gyaw, satisfied me that there was enough fodder and it was sufficiently diverse to keep them in health. Elephants are prone to digestive troubles, constipation or diarrhœa. But they seem also to have an intuitive knowledge of the medicinal value of different foods, and restore their dietary balance if left to themselves—provided, that is to say, they have the choice.

I was satisfied the Port Cornwallis area could sustain a hundred elephants without any importation of food. It was a strong argument against mechanical extractors, which would depend on imported supplies of fuel, spares and maintenance.

Jeff was not convinced that sufficient timber supplies could be delivered daily to feed the saw-mill capacity which he proposed. The sort of problem over which we wrangled was whether by carrying a light railway half a mile further up the bank of a stream we could not reduce the elephant haul and proportionately increase the daily delivery of logs.

The project envisaged the cutting of soft and hardwoods as a combined exploitation. The soft woods could be used to support the non-floating hardwoods, when rafting, and then be used in the oriental match industry. It seemed doubtful whether there were enough marketable soft woods to support the amount of hardwoods.

Our arguments, which had hitherto been good-humoured became rather testy. We had been living too closely together.

We all welcomed the idea of splitting up for a short time. On Smith Island we planned to leave the main convict party in charge of the stores. The rest of us moved south, Jeff and Bruno to do the old mill area around Stewart Sound, Carl and I with eight convicts to work north up the drainage of the Kalara River over into the Diglipor basin, crossing the Saddle Peak range at some points.

It was rather a hazardous venture. From the air the forest had looked most uninviting. On trek we might even find it impassable. In case this proved so, we arranged that Bruno should take us as far up the Kalara River as he could in *Madame X*, and should hang around there for five days, just in case we were forced to return on our tracks.

After that time he should go to Stewart Sound, join up with Jeff on the *Jarawa* and make back for Port Cornwallis, in order to be ready to pick us up at the mouth of the Diglipor River; if one can call a mouth an estuary so stuffed with mangrove swamp that a vegetable delta has been formed.

As a plan, it may seem sound enough on paper. There was one flaw in it, which we all saw and were too polite to mention. It was all very well for us to arrange a signalling system to begin in the

Port Cornwallis area on the sixth day: shots with the rifle and the shotgun. But supposing that, after we had passed the point of no return, we found that for some reason we could proceed no further, and yet we were too far from the Port Cornwallis party to communicate by shots, what then? It was a question none of us asked, because the answer to it was as obvious as it was depressing.

I took with me Nga Moh as my head convict, and told him to choose the other seven whom he wanted. Curry and rice were the easiest rations to carry, and Carl and I had the same diet as the coolies.

The trip from Port Cornwallis along the coast was without incident. Bruno forced the *Madame X* up the Kalara River to the limit of the tidal water, where all navigation was blocked by dense bamboo. There we landed, and as the *Madame X* turned and chugged away, Nga Moh ordered his route of march. Loads were distributed so that there were always two men free for cutting.

There were no signs of crocodiles this far south. We made no use of the compass, except to ensure that we were following the creek in a general northerly direction.

As the crow or the Southampton flying-boat flew, we were only about fifteen miles away from the point at the Diglipor River where we might hope to meet Bruno and Jeff. It was dense jungle, and it involved a climb of 1,500 to 2,000 feet across the Saddle Peak range. To allow a week for such a journey had seemed generous when we were on Smith Island. But now we were on the spot, I wished that I had allowed a month. The jungle was so dense that we all sat for half an hour while the cutters hacked a way through. Then we all moved on a short distance and sat down for another half-hour while the relief pair took it up.

There were signs that we were leaving the sea behind. The foliage grew paler, more luscious and luxuriant. We cut through into small open glades under towering trees and canopies which scarcely permitted light to percolate even during the leaf-fall of the hot season.

We bivouacked the first night in virgin forest, and as noticeable as any sound was the absence of the murmur of the sea, which had been in our ears for so many weeks. It was the most silent forest I had ever known and there seemed no wild animals, not even pigs.

In the stream we caught some fresh-water shrimps to flavour our rice, and we were tired early. Our convict coolies were soon asleep, aided perhaps by their opium pills. Carl and I, within touching distance of them, talked quietly on. Dense this jungle might be, I told him, but it was far freer from fear than the jungles of Burma.

Next day we made reasonable progress. The jungles were fairly open along the river-banks, and there was all the fodder required for elephants. It did not need much imagination to picture exactly how it might be. As I described it to Nga Moh, I could see his face light up. "I should like to go back, when I am free, Thakin," he said wistfully. "It was a good life."

"If I can help, I will," I promised.

It was a hot, strenuous day. For long stretches the under-growth along the stream-bank was almost impassable without cutting. Towards evening we came on an open glade well back from the stream-bed—a perfect place to camp. While the convicts were preparing the evening meal and bedding down, Carl went to bore for samples in some fine specimens of white dhup and papita. I went for a stroll by the creek, with Nga Moh following me.

I had become so used to the idea that this forest was without animal life, that I was astonished to see something move on the opposite bank. I froze. The undergrowth was a dapple of shadow and sunlight hard to break into components. I could see nothing. With my forefinger I gently beckoned Nga Moh to come up quietly. Without saying anything, I pointed gently to the spot. There was no movement there.

Then, almost like a photographic print appearing in the developing dish, I saw a pair of the most beautiful eyes watching me from that dappled verdure, unwinking, unalarmed; and then the antlers, a pair of perfect symmetry, with two delicate points and a short snag above the brow. In India, I had seen many a spotted deer, but none so lovely as this buck, nor so close and unafraid.

For a moment I wondered whether he was in balance between courage and fear and would in a moment take fright. But then he dropped his head and continued eating more peacefully than in any English park. For he was not tamed. He had never in this quiet, deserted jungle seen a human being before or any other animal of prey. His instinct was not of fear, but trust, incurious trust. He made a sound which was a cross between a sneeze and a whistle through his nostrils.

Then his small harem of does appeared from the bush

behind, glanced at us and then continued browsing. They moved down into the creek-bed, led by the stag, and drank from a pool, then they moved into the light undergrowth on our side of the bank. Their movements were full of grace and quite without fear. They were coming towards us. I wanted to put out my hand as if to call them to me, but the buck needed no calling. He led them towards us. They were both timid and inquisitive at the same time; an alert curiosity, so to speak. The buck wagged his tail, then, half turning, looked back over his shoulder, as if to say to the does, "I'm not so sure—get ready to break."

He changed his mind. He advanced again. His long neck

stretched out and the twitching nostrils of his velvet muzzle were close enough for me to touch, if I had extended my arm. I wanted to, but I knew it would be wrong.

He came closer and closer, until his muzzle touched the back of my hand, which was in front of my body. His tongue shot out and licked the salt sweat off my skin. It was an extraordinary sensation, and even more extraordinary was the buck's beginning to explore me, sniffing at my clothes.

With this endorsement, the whole family accepted both of us,

The buck and his few companions surrounded us, trying to find out what this strange new form of life might be which combined so many new and different scents.

Six hinds and a buck, but not a single faun. It was too much for Nga Moh, a Burman who could not think of adults of different sexes without immediately speculating on the offspring. (A Burman meeting a man and woman who are married immediately asks about their children.) "But where are the young ones?" he asked.

The sound of his voice was more frightening than his scent or appearance. In a flash, the whole family were away. Twenty yards away they stopped. That was their safety distance. They looked back at us. They looked around. I hoped that they would come back. But their curiosity was satisfied. They faded into the jungle as slowly as they had first appeared. We never saw another sign of them or of any other spotted deer.

"He has killed off his young bucks and is too old to breed himself," said Nga Moh in an attempt to draw me into conversation.

Perhaps they were dying out like the Andamanese. This was a vegetable kingdom. Animals held their lives on sufferance in this jungle. I wondered if the reason why the spotted deer trusted us, and why we had not the least thought of harming the spotted deer, was because all of us were animals together against a common vegetable enemy.

That thought was to proliferate in the days to come. By the third day we reached a main fork of the stream. From here on the country grew steeper. Which arm of the fork we took might be the difference between success and disaster. We did not say this to each other or even to ourselves. But we knew it, and decided to halt a day, split into two parties and explore both arms of the fork. We camped at the fork and Nga Moh came up to me and said, "Thakin, what elephant fodder!" pointing to clumps of the most succulent bamboos.

I went to sleep with that image somewhere in my mind, and it seemed to continue throughout the night. I was very tired and not certain how much was in dream and how much in waking consciousness. But there seemed to be sounds of something feeding, not the continuous noise of bamboo being pulled down, but a sharp crack every now and again of a large bamboo snapping. It was impossible to say how close. Sounds in the jungle are deceptive at night. It might have been a mile away, or perhaps only a quarter.

They had all heard it, and next morning Nga Moh was positive that it was a wild elephant. Everybody said that there were no animals bigger than wild pig and bamboo rats, and we had seen spotted deer; that of the reptilians there was an abundance of various iguanas, but no crocodiles, and we had found an ever greater abundance of crocodiles. I was more than ready to accept all that, but not wild elephants. That was too much.

With Nga Moh and three others, I was to climb the spur which was formed between the two streams, hoping to reach the top of the ridge and assess from there the best route for us to drop down in to Port Cornwallis along the Diglipor. In case I failed to find any suitable route, Carl took the left fork of the main river, noting the other tributaries on its left bank. This would provide us with an alternative route for crossing.

The ascent of the spur was easier than we had expected, though there were no game-tracks, as is usual at the confluence of two streams. No game-tracks and yet—to my astonishment, there was an elephant dropping. It was fresh; indeed, it was still warm.

Not far ahead we found the broken-down bamboos the snapping of which we had heard during the night.

We stood quite still, as one does, listening, and absolutely sure that an elephant was nearby listening to us. Then there was a noise, like someone slapping his thigh with a pair of leather gloves. There was no doubt that Nga Moh was right. An elephant, come from God knows where, was flapping its ears.

Immediately I thought: it's a tusker. A female wouldn't be alone. I loaded my rifle, as a precaution; though, after the spotted deer, it seemed impossible that he should be frightened. It would be more likely that he would come up, kneel down and carry us straightway over Saddle Peak.

My fantasy was wrong. The spotted deer had never had experience of man. Nothing had occurred to destroy their natural trust. But the elephant, as I discovered later, was one of the group which had been introduced into the South Andaman a dozen years before as a calf. He had escaped and swum the channels separating the Middle Andaman from the South and the North Andaman from the Middle. He knew us for what we were—men who could put him to work—and he broke wildly, charging up the hillside. He was one who did not forget.

At the time that we met him, he was twenty—not yet driven very hard by the desires of the flesh. It was just beginning.

It was a rather horrifying thought, as we heard him break from the ridge down towards the creek up which Carl was working, that however well he swam from island to island, he would find no female elephant in any of the hundred and forty-eight islands in whom he could implant himself. He may at this time of writing be still alive, a celibate by geography. But I saw him then as a part of the sterile animal pattern of the North Andaman, another victim of the vegetable tyranny.

We had no time or desire to follow him. The climb to the ridge would be stiff, we knew. It was made stiffer by great crags of outcrop granite, which were half hidden by trees and undergrowth.

The gurjan trees were magnificent: straight clear boles of over 100 feet to the crown. I posted two coolies in the rear, to mark our trail for the return journey. Sometimes we rested on the top of a crag and looked back on the path we had taken, blazed on the boles of trees or with the pith of slashed bamboos.

It was steep, tiring work: cutting, climbing, cutting. But at last we reached an escarpment, barefaced on its sheer cliffs, but on every ledge heavily covered with evergreen, mosses, some of which were as slippery as seaweed, lichens and ferns. For ages this escarpment had faced the drenching fury of the south-west monsoon. It was a horrible climb. From the top we could hear the roar of the breakers on the coral reefs to the west, and we were buoyed up by the thought that we should see a panorama of Port Cornwallis.

But we were then faced with a wall of forests on the main ridge. After a rest we made east along the main ridge in the direction of Saddle Peak, 2,400 feet. The eastern slope of the ridge towards Port Cornwallis was sheer precipice. I wished Carl were with me. He had climbing-irons and was expert at tree-climbing. He could have scaled one of the gurjan trees and used it as a look-out.

If we had felled one of them, it might have opened up a sufficient gap to have given us at least a limited view from which we would have been able to judge the best way down. But it was already past noon and there was no time for such a .aborious task.

We pushed on with dwindling hope towards Saddle Peak, and I was about to give the order to retreat when there was an excited cry from Nga Moh, who was slashing at bamboos and creepers furiously. I hurried forward, wondering whether he had found another elephant; and there I saw an open space where a recent cliff landslide had taken with it a patch of jungle and a few of these mighty trees. A wonderful panorama of the inland sea that was Port Cornwallis was revealed in all the colours of the rainbow. It was even more impressive than what we had seen from the air, partly because it could be surveyed at leisure and fully savoured, partly because, being on the ground ourselves, we were part of the landscape, not viewing it as another world. But beauty aside, the view was very disappointing. However much I teased my imagination, I could not identify a single feature in the landscape, not even Smith Island, which from this angle would appear as part of the mainland. Furthermore, though it was clear that the basin of the Diglipor lay below us and any way we might descend would bring us to it, there seemed no way in which we could descend without breaking our necks. It was a sheer wall of rock, in the crevices of which were enrooted trees of enormous size. There was no way down, as far we could see.

N   193

Carl and his party were already back when we reached camp. They had heard, but not seen, the elephant; and they also had climbed the ridge, several miles further to the west. The view from there had been as wonderful as ours, and they were satisfied, into the bargain, that we could drop into the Diglipor drainage next day without much difficulty. The high humour in which we all found ourselves revealed how great was the anxiety which had just fallen from us.

We moved over the divide without incident next morning, and before noon we found ourselves on the edge of an evergreen flat steppe of forest so dense that it could almost be described as impenetrable. While the coolies were hacking at it, Carl and I explored to either side to see whether we could discover a way round. But there was no circumventing it. By evening we were in the forest, but the progress was negligible in terms of the distance that lay before us. In some places, to save the fatigue of cutting, we crawled under it on hands and knees. It was so thick a dog couldn't bark in it, Nga Moh remarked.

Except that we were descending slightly, we had no sense of direction. There was no sign of any little stream to follow, just a damp mattress of leaf-mould that never saw the sun. There was no water, and we had to rely on what we had brought in our water-bottles.

The next day we sent two men back to the Kalara basin to fill the water-bottles, just in case we did not reach water in the Diglipor Basin that day. It was as well we did so. We did not cover a mile. We had passed the point of no return. Bruno by now must have moved back to Port Cornwallis. It looked as if my secret fear was being realised, that we were finding it impossible to go on when it was too late to go back. If Bruno had still been at the Kalara estuary we would certainly have gone back.

On the second day in the evergreen forest we sent back for water once more. Our spirits were ebbing, and so was our physical strength. All day long we hacked at that strangling mass of vines and creepers in relays, and by the end there was no sign that we were appreciably nearer the edge of that terrible forest, except that the ground was flatter. That made things if anything worse, as it gave us no clue to what direction we should take except by compass. It was not enough to follow a compass course such as north-east. We had to find water at all costs. It was stifling hot under three canopies of forest and undergrowth.

There was little we could discard from our rucksacks to lighten our loads. That was not the problem, anyway. Carrying our loads up after each hundred yards cutting was easy enough; it was the cutting itself which was exhausting. It was all that we could do to raise our arms. Three of the convicts dropped out, useless. Tempers became uneasy. The exercise of discipline was necessary. Voices had to command, rather than tell. Orders were not obeyed with that willingness that they had been at the outset. Going back over the ridge for water had been a coveted task; now it was disliked even more than cutting.

There being no sign of where we should find water, I kept on a general north-east bearing. We were already a day overdue. On the evening of that seventh day, Carl and I debated whether we should fire a shot, on the off chance that we were nearer the Diglipor and young Bruno than we dared to think. But we decided it was too risky. If there was no answering signal, it would depress the convicts even more, and even if there was an answer, Bruno could not make the forest any easier for us to cut through. Two more of the convicts gave up.

That evening the convicts had a little extra opium, as a result of which they slept longer and built up more strength. Carl said he did not feel affected at all, and turned over to me his brandy flask, saying that he did not need it. Mine was nearly empty.

On the eighth day we came across a clump of bamboo: the first clue that the evergreen belt might be coming to an end. We were all so thirsty that we supplemented our water ration by tapping the internodes, each of which contained an ounce or more of watery fluid. I laced mine with brandy as an evening drink, and was the only one not seized during the night with violent stomach pains and biliousness. Poor Carl was doubled up, holding his belly and groaning. I told him that he must put two fingers down his throat and vomit. He had never done this before, and shrank from the idea. But he tried it later, and felt easier.

I had seen less of Carl than of Bruno in the earlier part of the expedition, but this journey through the evergreen forest drew me very close to him. He had a wonderful way of supporting and encouraging me, without allowing the anxiety which we both felt to spread to the convicts.

On the ninth day I fired our signal—two shots—for the first time. We all stood holding our breath as we listened, waiting for an answering report. But no shot was fired in answer.

Nga Moh raised a finger and said, "But I can hear the sea." We all heard it, or said that we heard, very soft and far away, like the dimmest of hopes.

By the end of that day we were out of the worst jungle and into the woods. The nature of the country had changed from tangled creepers entwined with undergrowth to a mixed deciduous forest. The dead flatness of the ground was broken up into ridges. And then, abruptly, we came to another escarpment, from the edge of which there was a clear view of Port Cornwallis, a little nearer than before, but still frighteningly far away, across the mangrove swamps.

What to us was more disheartening than anything was this next precipice which blocked our way. We were so tired that it was almost impossible to summon up the energy to deal with this fresh obstacle.

From this commanding height I fired two more signal shots, hoping that the sound might travel further, unblanketed by trees. It seemed to make a deafening noise, echoing all over the wooded plain. But there was no answer, and after some minutes I told Nga Moh that he was to organise the convicts in making hooks and eyes of bamboos, in twenty feet lengths. Where they were to be used I did not know. Carl would go west along the escarpment and I would try the east.

We had scarcely got out of sight of the convicts who were apathetically pretending to work on the bamboos, when we heard very distantly—but quite unmistakably—the report of two shots at a minute interval. We both went hurrying back to find the sick and apparently demoralised convicts on their feet and filled with enthusiasm. Two more shots followed, and we all agreed that they were further over to the west. I replied with two shots from my own rifle, Nga Moh picking up the empty brass cartridges out of habit. But there was no answering signal from Bruno.

With hopes revived, we headed west along the escarpment for at least a mile or more. It was easier going than any we had encountered for four days. At last we found a gap down which we decided to essay a descent, using a bamboo hook-and-eye line. About twenty feet below we saw a line of green trees, marking a ravine which had been scoured by the incessant rain of successive monsoons.

It was the headwater of a waterfall, down beside which we passed with the aid of our bamboo safety-rail. We continued over enormous jagged rocks and a succession of dried-up waterfalls, whose dampness gave us hope that soon we should find water.

Carl, Nga Moh and I were so excited at the possibility that we might link up with Bruno that night that we hurried ahead, leaving the others to follow behind as best they could. The old Burmese saying that all water-courses lead to sea and civilisation did not apply in these deserted islands. But at least we were going downhill. We found stagnant pools. We found little trickles over rocks. We found running water. We entered a leafy tunnel; we had found a highway through the jungle, a stream. Later there was shingle in its bed, and it was wonderful to feel and hear it crunch beneath our boots, after the days of treading on the damp, stagnant leaf-mould of the evergreen belt.

Now and again we were halted by dense bamboo clumps and fallen trees. But there was new strength to our arms, and even the edges of the dahs seemed sharper.

Now that we were through to water, the urgency to join Bruno

197

was less. We found a good place to camp and waited for the tired, sick convicts to catch us up.

They begged me to fire two shots, but I said I would wait till dusk. I was certain we were on one of the tributaries of the Diglipor River, and I pictured Bruno sitting on *Madame X* with a loaded mauser waiting for my signal, and perhaps sipping a whisky—lucky beggar!—while he waited.

I was wrong. He fired first, two shots which were very muffled compared to what we heard on the escarpment—in fact we might have missed them if the men had not been so morose and silent, waiting for me to shoot. I fired an answer, which was acknowledged. And there, with the certainty that we were in contact, we left it for the night.

We camped on a sandy strip at a bend of the stream. We all bathed, and Carl and I shaved. There is nothing so good for morale as a close shave. Our convicts watched us with curiosity, as if they were witnessing some occult Christian rite.

We moved on next morning at dawn, convinced that it would not be very long before we joined up. Bruno's signal shots now sounded well to the east of the direction of the stream which we were following, and we discussed the possibility of leaving the sick where they were and cutting a direct route towards the sound of Bruno's fire.

"What do you think, Nga Moh?" I asked.

He shook his head. "If you want to go fast, go the old road," he said, pointing down the stream-bed.

So we followed it downwards, and it gradually grew larger as it was joined by other small tributaries and then by a wider stream. By the evening of this, the tenth day, we had hoped to see signs of tidal water. But we were disappointed. What is more, when we fired, there was no answer from Bruno. We were down in flat forest, where sound did not carry. I let Carl and Tun Gyaw go ahead on condition that they followed the downward stream. I camped with Nga Moh and the other convicts. Three of them were sullen, weary and in a state of giving in.

Yet, as leader, I felt confident for the first time since we had landed at the Kalara. We had good water. Our rations were more than enough. I felt I wanted to talk, and beckoned Nga Moh across. He came over.

"You have two empty cartridge-cases of mine," I said. It was a crime in Burma to possess empty cartridge-cases. Too often dacoits would reload them to use in stolen arms. As there were no dacoits in this jungle, my remark was intended as a joke.

"You are right, Thakin," he said, and he produced the two empty cases.

"It doesn't matter here," I said, "but in Burma now . . ."

"In my day, it was the same," Nga Moh said. "Oh yes—it was the same."

I waited, hoping that he might say something more which would explain the mystery of how he ever came to be at Port Blair. He handed me the cartridge-cases. "It is better not to have them, even here."

"What happened?" I asked.

"You do something wrong," he answered, "but what you are punished for is different."

To tell his story in his own words would be tedious. He had an instinct for narrative, but he wandered a great deal, because it had all happened so many years before. . . .

He had been Singaung in an elephant camp in the Shan States. There was a lot of gambling among his men, which he had not stopped, because he enjoyed gambling himself. One evening they had all been gambling and Nga Moh had won a little money. One of his oozies had lost a great deal, mostly to another oozie, who had been triumphant about his winnings. The loser had gone on and on, losing his future earnings as well as his past savings, becoming more and more desperate at each loss. Then suddenly, following an argument, and faced with the knowledge that his whole future was pledged away, he had caught up his dah and laid open the skull of the exultant winner.

Nga Moh realised the extent of his guilt. He had betrayed his trust. He had allowed a man to be killed through the gambling which he was supposed to suppress, or at least control. That same night, rather than face his master, he had fled the camp, hidden in the jungle, and next morning made off for Thailand—or Siam, as it was then called.

On the caravan route between Taungyi and Chiengmai, at a place called Meihongson, he met up with a gang of Burmans, who asked him to join them in going to Chiengmai to buy elephants. Nga Moh said that he would be very pleased to do so, but he had very little money. The others said that this did not matter, as they had none at all. Besides, they knew of a young Englishman who would pay for them all.

Nga Moh thought that it was unlikely that a young Englishman would give money to his new-found friends for the purchase of elephants.

His friends explained their plan. There was a young Englishman also on his way to Chiengmai to buy elephants. He had with him eight mules laden with money, under a guard of mixed police with a so-called Frenchman in command.

The leader of the Burmese gang possessed a stolen shot-gun which he would discharge close to the mules as they approached the loneliest stretch of the road. This would so alarm the mules that they would stampede and the money boxes would fall off, and all that Nga Moh and his friends had to do was to pick the money up. It could scarcely be called robbery. It was much more like finding treasure trove. The police would certainly run away at the sound of the first shot, and as for the young Englishman, he was as blind as a bat without his spectacles, and the panic would soon remove these from the bridge of his nose.

Nga Moh said that he did not picture anybody being frightened by the firing of a couple of shots. But his friends said that of course they would rush on the caravan from all sides the moment the gun went off, waving their dahs in the air and yelling blue murder. Nga Moh told me that he joined the raid for the sheer fun of it.

The attack took place soon after dawn, when mules were fresh and guards sleepy. Nga Moh was with the leader of the gang, who had the gun. He was not an experienced dacoit, but a comparison of his horoscope with those of the others proved that he was the next bravest. The dacoits acted according to plan. The leader fired off his two shots. The gang attacked from all sides, waving dahs and shouting if not blue murder as least as loud as they could. But the mules did not bolt. The guards, who were also the muleteers, took cover behind their animals. The young Englishman, with the aid of his spectacles and a revolver, shot two of the gang. The leader of the dacoits, attacked while reloading by a Gurkha with a *kukri*, shot the Gurkha dead and took to his heels. Nga Moh was about to follow when he was bayoneted in the groin by another Gurkha guard. What had been planned as a robbery without violence had degenerated into violence without robbery. Two of the dacoits had been killed and the remainder had made good their escape. Only Nga Moh had been wounded and taken prisoner. In his haversack were found two live cartridges which the head dacoit had given him as reserve ammunition. On the strength of this, he had been convicted of the murder of the guard. "It was a death, Thakin, for which I have never felt responsible," Nga Moh concluded. "And yet I know that I deserved some punishment for permitting gambling to such an extent that a man was killed."

The next morning, thinking that we should soon join Bruno, we left the three sick convicts behind. It was just as well we did. We entered the mangrove swamp at the tidal limit. It was like entering a labyrinth. The mangrove forest stretched back a mile from either bank of the rivers and two to three miles along the delta. Somewhere in the middle of it all was *Madame X* and Bruno.

Scrambling through the mangrove forest was hell enough, but, as the tide was low, there was added a further, if not hazard, at least discomfort. The mud was exposed—soft, plump, immaculate mud—which, once disturbed, gave off the foulest effluvia of marsh gas. Mussels and crabs of all colours and sizes dropped off the roots of the mangroves at our approach, greeting us with a moving barrage of stench. Flop! flop! flop! Off they fell as we disturbed them. Plop! plop! plop! Up rose the bubbles of gas as they disturbed the mud.

At high tide the mud was submerged, but so also were the roots of the lower mangrove branches, and it was far more difficult to find any foothold. It was more like trapezing across a floating forest. To have hurried and lost our tempers would have been fatal.

All day we went forward, keeping to the edge of our tributary, moving with agonising slowness. Our tributary was sufficiently broad and deep at high tide for Bruno to have travelled as far up it as we were. It was plain to us that Bruno had gone up some other tributary; and it was not long before we arrived at a confluence; but we were on the wrong bank.

Either of the two forks was navigable to *Madame X*. If we went on down-stream we might overstep Bruno if he was up the other fork. He might then return to the confluence and go up the fork which we had already come down. We decided the only thing to do was to halt at the confluence. We could go no further in our search for Bruno. It remained for Bruno to find us. We fired a number of signal shots, but could hear no answer. Then, as the tide was rising, we made a platform in the mangrove trees above high-water level and settled down to wait.

Every hour we fired off signal shots. We were very thirsty, but we hoarded the water in our bottles.

We talked over the possibilities of what could be done, supposing that Bruno did not find us. There was no possibility of building a raft in this mangrove swamp. We should have to go back beyond the tidal limit to get out of the mangrove. Thirst would drive us to do that fairly soon, anyway.

Then we began to say what we would do if we were Bruno. It was surprising how speedily we would have rescued ourselves, if we had been aboard the *Madame X*.

Then suddenly we heard the sound of a rasping hand Klaxon.

It was some way away. Later it sounded again, closer; and then closer still. Then we could hear the purring exhaust of the engines of *Madame X*, and then round the bend of the opposite fork she appeared, honking away like a river taxi looking for a fare.

We could see her through the gaps in the leaves. But could Bruno see us? We shouted and bawled. We shook the branches for all we were worth. The launch appeared to be passing, but then it swung suddenly towards us.

Until that moment I did not realise the strain under which we had been living during the last few days. I felt that I wanted to flop down as soon as possible and go to sleep. But then came Bruno's voice with some absurd bit of badinage. I forget what it was, but we answered in the same vein, and in a few minutes we were aboard, with whiskies in our hands and the fears with which we had been living had gone back into that deep recess of our consciousness where they live while we are fresh and full of hope.

Bruno heard our story and, leaving us with the whisky, he went off with Nga Moh to pick up the three convicts in the dug-out canoe which Bruno had brought in tow.

It wasn't until some hours later, when we were heading back for Smith Island, that I asked where Jeff was.

"Oh, Jeff," said Bruno. "He went back to Port Blair in the *Jarawa*. He thinks Port Cornwallis isn't a patch on the north end of the Middle Andaman as a site for a sawmill. You know, where my father had his. He's gone back to Port Blair to talk to my father. He can't see why father closed the place down." He drew a fat envelope out of pocket. "He asked me to give you this. It's all there."

"Really!" I was filled with resentment, or rather a series of resentments. What would have happened if *Madame X* had broken down on the way north? What would . . . ?

But I was beyond caring. I did not even read the letter until we were back on Smith Island and had met the friendly greeting of the other convicts.

CHAPTER XV

THERE was no point in reflecting on the disasters in which we would have been involved by Jeff's departure in the *Jarawa* if things had gone wrong. Things had not gone wrong, providentially.

I read Jeff's letter very carefully, because his decision was one which we had never discussed. I felt that it needed very sound arguments to substantiate it; or at least explain why it had been reached so suddenly.

Jeff said that when he inspected old Bruno's sawmill site on Austen Strait, he found that it had an undeniable superiority over Port Cornwallis. "I don't mean that we may not extract from the Port Cornwallis area, but if we do, we should raft it down to

Austen Strait for milling." Under those circumstances, it was natural that instead of wasting his time by returning north to Port Cornwallis, he should want to return to Port Blair to consult with Bruno's father and learn from him the reasons why he had abandoned the workings, what timber was left according to his view and whether the old man agreed with Jeff on the advantages of the site. "If there's a suitable sailing, I may go on to Rangoon for discussions with P. N. C. As far as the mill goes, there are very serious decisions to be taken and I am not prepared even to make recommendations without further consultation." He suggested now we had finished our Port Cornwallis timber survey, we should drop down to Austen Strait and cruise that area and also Interview Island. "That is, as soon as the *Jarawa* returns either with me or without."

Having read the letter through several times, I foresaw ultimate trouble with our milling engineers. But sufficient unto the day was the evil thereof. There was nothing we could do until the *Jarawa* returned, apart from making general preparations to move from Smith Island. We could with a free conscience take a holiday and explore the wonder and beauty of the place without having to 'cruise' any more forests.

It was one of the most wonderful weeks I have spent in my life— well earned, I felt, by the journey we had just made across Saddle Peak.

Minerva Bay became our favourite hunting ground. It had an open strand—none of that mangrove swamp—a sea-bed extraordinarily rich in marine wonders and a coral reef which was so near the surface at low tide that one could walk on it, provided one wore rope-soled shoes. The emphasis had to be on the word *one*. It was a dangerous sport, and the rest of us had to keep a sharp look-out from the *Madame X*.

Carl drew blood first by bagging a good-sized turtle. How he did it, we were none of us quite clear—then or afterwards. No turtle was ever captured with more luck and less science. It began with a boathook, supported later by a couple of gaffs, and it ended with a lassoo and a free-for-all getting the turtle aboard which would have capsized any boat less seaworthy. We had all read the books which said that the way to kill a turtle was to turn it on its back. But the turtle hadn't read the books, and kept turning on its front again.

When I had my spell overboard, Bruno and Carl acted as bow-spotters. I was knee-deep on a narrow reef four to six feet in width. On either side of the ledge, the water was fathoms deep, and in it lurked the shark and the octopus. I moved forward slowly, fascinated with the variety and beauty of what I saw. As I advanced, I probed with a spear, partly as protection, partly to put up anything that might be resting on the reef.

Suddenly there was a gurgle of water and the spear was snatched from my hand. It remained straight upright, quivering, and when the surface of the water grew calm again, I saw on what had previously appeared to be the level coral bed the shut shell of a giant clam (*Tridacna gigas*) with my spear gripped between its serrated edges.

I scrambled back aboard *Madame X* the moment I lost my spear. Bruno's father had told me about this huge lamellibranch, whose body could weigh twenty pounds and the shell as much as a quarter of a ton. The old man went as far as to say that the giant clam was mainly responsible for the extinction of the Andamanese. If I had stepped into it, the shell would have clamped on my ankle and held me powerless until the tide rose and drowned me—as horrifying a death as I can imagine. The horror of the death which I had just escaped determined me to capture this colossus of shell-fish. We struggled to dislodge it with boathooks and spears; but though there was a certain yielding, as if it might loose its hold upon the coral, the grip of its adductor muscles was so firm that we could not prize it loose. We tried grasping the spear, thrusting, twisting and tugging at it. But it was held so firm that we could not push it home or pull it free.

We anchored our bows to the clam and then went full astern. But it was as firm as the coral it clung to. Carl was all for going

overboard and severing the adductor muscles with a knife. But
before doing this we tried again with *Madame X*, this time from
the rear. We used a wire rope looped round the shell. It came
away with a horrible grating sensation, like that made by the
drawing of a molar. It was lucky we had it grappled with wire
rope. If it had toppled from the reef into deep water its weight
might have sunk us. We could not haul it inboard. We towed it
tied alongside and beached it on the hot sand of Smith Island. It
was only after being baked on that dry sand for two days that its
hold on life weakened and the shell opened to release the spear.
The convicts hastened its death by pouring boiling water through
the crack. It speeded death, but it did not arrest the process of
decay. Very soon the stench grew noisome. As we cut the body
away from the shell, we looked out for a pearl. It might, I suppose,
have been as big as a hen's egg.

I kept half the shell as a memento, and for many years used it on the veranda of my bungalow in Upper Burma as a drinking-bowl for my dogs. Later it became a dog-basket for an Alsatian puppy. He used to coil up in it as the coolest spot in the bungalow.

We spent three days exploring Minerva Bay. Then we transferred our attention to the unnamed bay due south of Minerva, on the mainland between Barkeley and Dundas Points. It was more exposed to the north-east breezes, and there was quite a swell each day as we crossed from Smith Island, but there was no equal to it in the area as a fishing run.

Off Barkeley Point there were patches of treacherous rocks where in a swell there was one moment a fathom of water beneath us and the next moment only a foot. On one occasion *Madame X* had such a smack on the bottom it hurt, but the skin was not broken. It was dangerous, but very exciting; because we hooked our fish almost as soon as we cast.

On the west shore of Dundas Point we discovered a depression in the coast where there was sheltered water and an underwater meadow as green and lush as those in the valleys of my native Cornwall. At low water it lay only four feet beneath the surface—a field of sea grass as fine as hair. When the tide was running, it lay flat, like long green tresses that had been combed and brushed down. I nicknamed it Godiva Bay, explaining to Carl, my only companion on this trip, the legend of how the Saxon lord's wife of Coventry rode through the streets in only her long hair to free the people of their grievous taxes and the townsfolk, not to witness her outraged modesty, stayed in their houses behind closed doors and shuttered ones, except one they called 'Peeping Tom', whom God struck blind.

I cut the engine, lest we should foul the propeller, and we drifted over this strangely lush sea-bottom, which, curiously enough, seemed quite free of animal life. One finds these pockets in nature —places, for example, in the jungle which one would expect to abound in animals and yet are deserted; and so it is with the sea.

We stood either side of the prow, prodding the grass with our

spears. It was so thick that it was rather like prodding a sorbo cushion.

Then suddenly I could feel a difference, and I jabbed down. I saw two eyes in a dome-like head through the grass and then, like an uneasy thought, the body of an octopus rose, slithered across the top of the grass for ten yards or so and then sank from view.

Carl gave a cry of surprise. Something else had risen from the place where the octopus had vanished, a sort of mermaid figure, with a pale skin, a tail like a fish but arms and hands, which paddled like a dog. That the sex was female we could see as the body turned and displayed her breasts.

She skimmed just below the surface like a young seal, then dived, turned, rolled, completely without fear, or indeed consciousness of our presence. She had a short mane on her head, which swept back with her motion.

A few gentle revolutions of the propeller brought us up to her, and at this she dived and with a wriggle was hidden, like the octopus, beneath that deep sea grass.

We began our probing again, but very gently. Whereas the octopus had provoked in us an almost blind hatred, this creature, which I realised was a dugong, aroused a tender feeling, partly because of its grace of movement, but also because of its resemblance to a human being. This was how a human being would be, I thought, who had to live underwater.

There was a grunt from Carl, who thought he had caught the dugong on his boathook. But he was mistaken, because I had caught her on mine. There was no struggle. She gave herself up sluggishly, as if indifferent whether she remained in the sea. She rose with the buoyancy of a half-filled water-drum.

Carl seized up a vicious gaff of burnished steel, the moment that he saw I had her. He was going to gaff her, but I yelled, "Put that down!" at the same time lowering the boathook to keep the dugong out of his range.

Nga Moh was on the other side of me, and I could sense he felt that the creature might be hurt. "No, Thakin, no. She is with young. It is bad luck. Bad luck, Thakin." It was the only time that I was strongly conscious of his resentment at being a convict and having to take orders from us. If we had harmed the dugong, he would never have forgiven us, but there was nothing more that he could have done.

But I had no desire to harm her. The thought of taking her from her element was impossible. I merely wanted to see what she was like at close quarters. I brought her alongside, and for the first time we had a near view, as she trod water without trying to break away. She no longer looked like a human being—though I have in my life seen some human beings who looked like her. The flipper-like, nail-less arms, the protuberant, streaming eyes, the thick lips and snout truncated for cropping sea-grass were the hideous caricature of the animal in man.

I jerked the boathook to release her, and like some huge mechanical rubber toy she slithered away, flapping her arms into the deep meadow, regaining as she disappeared her animal dignity, of which I had robbed her in thinking of her as resembling a human being. We saw no more in our underwater meadow. Indeed, we caught from Nga Moh the feeling that in hooking the dugong we had done something wrong, and by common consent we turned and ran back to Smith Island.

Perhaps it was as well we did so. That night the wind freshened to a storm—the sort of storm I feared we were going to meet when

I read the story of the *Briton* and the *Runnymede*. By dawn the roar of the breakers on the coral reefs was frightening. Any idea of our crossing to Godiva Bay was out of the question. The whole entrance to Port Cornwallis was like a wall of breakers, which looked as if it would batter into Port Cornwallis itself and yet was always smashed on the reef. The bay where we were was as quiet as ever.

"Jeff talks of rafting timber down to Austen Strait," said Bruno. "What does he do if a storm like this gets up?"

"I'm far more concerned with what the *Jarawa* will do, if she's on the way back, which she ought to be," I answered.

It was three days before we could cross the harbour back to Godiva Bay. There was still no sign of the *Jarawa*, and we decided to land on Dundas Point so that Carl could climb on an enormous gurjan tree which stood out like a sentinel. From the top, he could see for miles.

Carl had the most modern, but very simple, equipment. Before the convicts had cleared the dense undergrowth from the base of the tree, Carl was up and away. He was soon out of sight above the canopy given by the surrounding trees. We stood back and watched till through a gap he appeared again, still climbing easily. At last he reached the massive crown and disappeared from view. We could hear his voice, but all meaning was lost in what Bruno called 'that Nordic mutter'. He seemed to be hacking away with his tomahawk, and some small branches and chips fell. We thought that he must be trying to improve his view.

Then the noise of the tomahawk stopped and we heard Carl shouting to us to look out below.

We stood still further out, and something crashed to earth—his axe, a climbing iron or something. Tun Gyaw ran forward to pick it up and then leapt to one side as something else fell, narrowly missing him.

We waited until we were sure that Carl was himself descending and there was nothing more to fall.

I was looking up admiring the agility with which Carl was

coming down, when I noticed Tun Gyaw standing close to me with something he wanted to show. It looked like a chunk of tree-bark, until he handed it to me.

On first scrutiny, I thought it was a honeycomb. But it was something far more astonishing: a home-made brick of dirty red clay as hard as the day it had been fired. The second object was a half-brick similarly covered in bark.

Carl, now back on terra firma, explained that as he stood in the main fork of the tree, at least ninety feet up, he felt that he was standing on something strange and, looking down, found these bricks. "There were no more," he said apologetically, as though we might expect him to find a complete building up there.

It was obvious what had happened. The gurjan tree as a young sapling had grown up through the debris of masonry and had carried up this brick and a half in the cleft of the fork, embodying them deeper and deeper in the body of the tree as they were hoisted aloft over a century.

Carl had seen no sign of the *Jarawa*, so we turned our attention to the ground at our feet. There was nothing in the patch that had been cleared but earth and leaf-mould. But Nga Moh turned the convicts on to clearing more ground, and we soon found, once the dense undergrowth of twisted cane and creeper was cleared, that the ground below was uneven.

Then we made the exciting discovery that a certain shrub seemed to run for about twenty yards in a straight line as if it had been planted. But this was wrong. The shrubs were growing along the line of a brick wall. Perhaps they had been able to establish themselves on the crumbling wall, before anything else.

There was a tremendous number of bricks. But we only found the line of this single wall.

There was a small mound, which we thought might have been a kitchen midden. We dug into it expecting to find shells, but the only yield was some fragments of English earthenware pottery. Some of it was roughly patterned in blue. It was old, but none of us knew enough to say how old.

We spent the whole day clearing and digging; but the only other discovery that we made was a skull, which we all handled in a knowing way and made the basis of different theories. Bruno thought it belonged to an Andamanese. Carl was sure it was a woman's. I thought it had sat on the shoulders of a Regimental Sergeant-Major. It had that sort of look about it.

We sat up late that night arguing who had built what on Dundas Point. For a time we favoured the possibility that the *Briton* and *Runnymede* had really been wrecked on Dundas Point and not on the Archipelago. But that could not be true, because Portman had seen the remains of the *Briton* on John Lawrence Island in Ritchie's Archipelago at the turn of the century.

There were three other reported shipwrecks in the neighbourhood of the North Andaman, but none of them seemed to have touched Port Cornwallis area or lingered long enough for building. In fact there was only one recorded occupation large enough and long enough to make bricks and to build, and that was during the settlement at Port Cornwallis in the eighteenth century. The old buildings on Chatham Island impressed Dr. Mouat sixty years later with their solidity. But there was no mention in any books which I have managed to acquire of any building on Dundas Point.

I am sure that just as we, in our anxiety about the *Jarawa*, had made for Dundas Point, so the original settlers on Chatham Island had felt the need for a look-out post in precisely the same spot. It could have served several purposes: to guard against a surprise attack by Malay pirates, to keep a look-out for relief ships or vessels in distress and perhaps provide some primitive form of lighthouse, signalling to incoming ships by smoke or flame.

We agreed that this was probably what had happened, and we decided to go back next day to see what else we could unearth. The convicts accompanied us excitedly, because they had also talked it over during the night and arrived at the conclusion that a vast quantity of treasure was buried there.

"It doesn't matter which of us is right, provided that it keeps us busy till the *Jarawa* arrives," Bruno said; "that is, if the *Jarawa* is going to arrive."

We excavated for three days, and on the second day we laid bare a massive great wall of heavy stonework that must have been built under a master stonemason. But we did not find any gold. Nor had anything important been left behind except this skull. Bruno's theory was that when they evacuated Port Cornwallis, one of them lost his head and it was too late to go back for it.

When we told him not to be facetious, he answered, "Then perhaps you've got an explanation of what happened to the rest of the skeleton."

We thoroughly explored the rocks and coast nearby for any clues. Perhaps there were anchors or chains? No, there was nothing of that sort. But there was something which went straight not only to my heart but also to Nga Moh's. It meant nothing to Bruno, Carl or the convicts, as they had never worked in a timber forest. It was a great teak log, trimmed and sawn, wedged between two boulders. It was from Burma. It had all the signs of Burmese workmanship—hammer-marking and holes at either end for elephant dragging. It might have followed me all the way from one of my own forests in Burma. After all these weeks of forest in the raw, of unfellable gurjan and impenetrable mangrove, such a trim, processed, obedient log went to my heart. It was like a messenger come to say, "You can never do anything with this overgrown island group. Come back to Burma and forget about that dream of being the Tsar of the Andaman Forests. If you ever persuaded anyone to give you the management, the monsoons would take it away from you."

The weather had settled again to blue skies and calm seas. But there was no sign of the *Jarawa*, until the evening of the thirteenth day, when she came in gaily with the Serang at the wheel. I could see his fez, but I could not see Jeff. He had gone to the Rangoon, and that was the last I should see of him on this trip.

There was another letter which I expected, with the advice I could have written myself. "You've got a month, Bill. Go down

to Austen Strait. . . . We want to know more about the areas surrounding the Barkeley group . . . and Interview Island . . . that
might be very rich."

I knew that Jeff had made up his mind that the project had too
many hazards. Perhaps he was right. Certainly he would put his
points across to P. N. C. in Rangoon, who would then kill the
scheme in the kindest way. But meanwhile there was a month to
kill, according to schedule. I could come to no harm cruising the
forests of Interview and other Islands.

We had consumed a great deal of our stores. But even so we
reckoned it would take two journeys to ship all we needed in the
Jarawa, Madame X and the dug-out canoes. The convicts were
heartbroken. There were two standards on Smith Island. What
we threw away as junk was the rarest of the treasure trove to the
convicts. There was a whole stack of corrugated-iron sheet, which
even to us was valuable but we had no room for. There were
dozens of empty drums and cases of all descriptions. Strung on
wire ropes from between the trees was still a parade of Swedish
biscuits in soldered air-tight tins the size of tea-chests. The
bamboo rats would have to wait till the wire broke, unless they
learnt to walk a tight rope; or the Andamanese came back.

We had not seen the Andamanese since the death of the old
man. But we were sure that they were close and had watched
every move of ours. We talked to the convicts of coming back.
But of course we knew that we wouldn't, and the thought of this
Oyster Age family feasting on Ryvita after we left, was almost the
only thing which kept my food down on the boisterous trip from
Smith Island to Austen Strait.

Looking back, I date this as the end of my being a young man.
I had always lived in the present and the immediate future. But I
no longer believed in the importance of anything which we did at
Austen Strait or Interview Island. All that we had already done in
the Andamans had been a waste of time, at some times arduous, at
others delightful, but always useless.

215

CHAPTER XVI

THE old Manager's bungalow was on Bonington Island, and with the aid of an advance party of convicts Bruno had cleaned it up and made it look in comparison with Smith Island almost civilised.

Our first task was to inspect the abandoned workings on Austen Strait, and very depressing it was. An American logging engineer had visited the site for Bruno's father and produced a series of calculations arrived at by the Mental Yardstick method, on the basis of which modern mechanical methods were to be used throughout. None of this old fashioned nonsense about elephants, no Sir!

The result was this battlefield strewn with deserted logs and rusty derelict equipment. Every forester feels a pang when a giant tree is brought crashing to the ground. But there is nothing which hurts him more than to see logs which these great trees have yielded left abandoned to rot instead of being taken to the sawmills.

There they were, logs of all kinds and sizes, scattered like corpses on the hillside, stranded, water-logged or floating slimy in the tideway. How depressing, compared to the virgin forests of Port Cornwallis!

Our biggest task was to cruise Interview Island, which lay opposite the western entrance of Austen Strait, the passage dividing North from Middle Andaman. Fifteen miles long, three to four miles wide, most of Interview was a flat plateau between fifty and 150 feet above sea level. The stream-beds were shallow and the supply of water only seasonal. The west side, exposed to the Indian Ocean, was fringed with coral reefs. The eastern or landward side possessed in Interview Passage a deep sheltered harbour.

From the old mill at Bonington Island through Austen Strait to Interview was eighteen miles. It must have been a place of rare beauty until it was wrecked by the miscalculations of the logging experts' mental yardstick. Already the jungle was swallowing up the debris. Soon it would be hidden from view.

As I was declaiming against the incurable folly of trying to extract this timber mechanically, Bruno said, "If you were going to use elephants, where would you water them during the dry season?"

Bruno had put his finger on the weak spot. The timber on Interview Island was far better than any I had seen on North Andaman. But for the dry season the elephants would have to be moved to forests on a different island, and that would raise difficulties which, though not insuperable, were enough to shatter my hopes.

One evening as we were returning to Stewart Sound we saw a sight familiar to all who have shot duck in India. Flight after flight of what looked like teal were flying very high to the west. My first thought was not what sort of teal were they, but where had they come from and where were they going? One thing was certain, they had come from fresh water and were making for it; to judge from the number of flights, there must have been a large expanse of fresh water. It might be the answer to the question Bruno had asked me, where should I water my elephants?

That night we discussed the possible solutions. We were pretty sure that there was no lake on North Andaman. We would have seen it from one of the Southamptons. There was nothing marked on the map which gave us the slightest clue, but from the direction in which the birds had been flying it appeared most likely that they were making for North Reef Island. At any rate, we decided to make this the beginning of our search.

It was not a pleasant run even for the *Jarawa* from the western mouth of Austen Strait to North Reef Island, and we received a good pounding. We approached it about noon on the following day. There was no high ground; it appeared flat and forest-clad. Owing to the open sea trip, we brought only the *Jarawa*. We had to be very careful to avoid coral reefs. We made for a strip of sandy beach where the jungle came close to the shore, as on our beach in Smith Island. We were looking for somewhere where we could bring the *Jarawa* right alongside. Bruno was at the controls, while I stood in the bow sounding and keeping a look-out. There was no sign of teal.

We got into a deep-water lagoon inside a reef. It was dead calm and we were able to move right up to the edge of the sandy beach, where there were three fathoms of water. Our plan was for our small party to land ashore and the Serang to stand off and anchor till we needed him.

I held a small line in my hand, telling Bruno to give her easy ahead till I jumped, and then immediately full astern.

The sand was a very pure white and at a steep incline. I waited until I was within leaping distance and then, shouting, "Now!" I jumped into what I realised even while I was in mid-air was not sand but the softest of coral powder, into which I sank down and down till it was above my head and upstretched arms. I had only experienced such an extreme of terror before in nightmare. I screamed and with a flaying of my arms beat my way blinded towards the water, anxious for the moment only to get out of that deep, thin dust that in a matter of seconds would clog my lungs.

But the moment I was out of the coral dust and found myself in deep water I realised I was not out of trouble. A shark might take me while I was still blinded, and I struck out, eyes closed, hit my hand against something, and I felt my wrist grasped, and Bruno shouted, "Hang on, I'm backing off further."

As the launch backed out of the cloud of dust which hung over the shore, Carl pulled me aboard.

If the moments which had just passed had been among the most terrifying in my life, then those that followed were among the funniest. As I slowly regained my sight and cleared my lungs, I saw that the *Jarawa* and crew had been magically transformed. The Serang and his Indian crew had been metamorphosed into fakirs, dusted with white wood-ash. The decks and deck-house appeared as if they had been dusted with snow. As for myself, I had escaped with everything except my dignity. Carl, Bruno and the crew roared with laughter at me in a way I thought was absurd until I realised I looked even worse than they did.

There was no talk of renewing the landing at this point. We were on the eastern and sheltered side of the island, and we passed slowly up the lagoon, washing ourselves down with buckets of water. Though we expected this snow-white powder to mix into a loathsome paste, it washed off our bodies and decks as easily as it had settled. It must, we decided, have been piled up ashore as a result of a gale.

We soon found a bank clear of coral dust and landed without mishap. Having watched the *Jarawa* successfully anchor offshore, we cut across the sickle-shaped island.

Two hundred yards after we had entered the jungle, we came to a fringe of tall grasses of a type we had seen previously on the banks of creeks above the tidal limit. There was also a patch of muddy swamp.

Our next surprise was a noise as if a tropical thunderstorm had broken, though the sky was cloudless. We looked at one another, wildly conjecturing what would be revealed as the source of this strange sound. But the noise faded away without our seeing anything.

The cause of the noise was soon apparent, for over us came the greatest mass of teal that I have ever seen in my life. It was not merely a flight. There were tens of thousands of them. They literally darkened the sky.

A wisp of them passed at lightning speed, and I dropped one with my right barrel, missing with my left. The mass broke and formed itself into several separate flights or flocks, as if they were about to migrate to some other islands, perhaps the Cocos. These flights went off one by one, rising higher and higher as they strung out across the sky like necklaces of onyx.

Nga Moh was examining the bird I had dropped. It was like no teal I had seen before and I warned him not to pluck any feathers. It might prove the only one which I could collect for identification.[1]

Now that we were sure that there was a swamp or lake harbouring the teal, we moved inland eagerly. For some way we had to wade ankle deep through brackish water among tall reeds. Nga Moh, who was ahead of me, suddenly exclaimed "Ingyi!"—a lake. He parted the reeds and there was a large stretch of water, looking rather like an extinct volcanic crater, nearly full to the brim. There was not a sign of any bird or other living creature.

I knew that the teal would return later, and we agreed to wait and see. Carl and Bruno went one end of the lake with four of the convicts, while I went the other end with Nga Moh. We found a dry patch leading to the water's edge. There was cover, and Nga Moh tied up a sheaf of reeds on which I sat. It made a perfect stand, and I motioned Nga Moh to stay silent.

For a time neither of us spoke. Each was busy with his thoughts,

[1] *The Andaman Teal*—scientific name, *Nettionalbigulare*. Mainly dark mottled brown, ring of white feathers round the eye, white throat, black bar in wing. Bill slatey with black nail. Feeds by night in swamp of fresh or tidal water; rests in trees or reeds by day. Does not dive, or very rarely.

and I knew the thoughts of Nga Moh were turned to Port Blair and of this half liberty which he had enjoyed with us.

"Do you think you will come back, Thakin?" he asked in a low voice.

"I don't know," I answered. "It is not for me to say." Nga Moh's silence, eloquent of misery, spoke also for the other four dozen. "I promise you I will try," I added, "and if I do, you will be my Chaungoke."

"If you are not back here," he said, "may I come to work for you in Burma when I finish my sentence next year? I have no other friends, not even Burmans." He knelt in the 'shiko' position with his hands before his face. "You are my father."

"I promise I shall give you work," I said. I was deeply stirred by what he said. Even if in all other respects this Andaman excursion was proved to be a failure, it had enabled me to prove Tun Gyaw and meet in Nga Moh a man whom a long prison sentence had not demoralised.

Nga Moh pointed to the sky. They were coming back, myriads of them, and from all points of the compass; diving in formation, passing each other at various heights, but all converging on that mirror of fresh water, as though it was a magnet drawing them.

I decided to let almost all of them alight. This was a sight I had never seen. It seemed impossible that the lake could accommodate them. I ducked as a wisp passed over my head so close that their wings seemed to ruffle my hair. They spotted us, and tails dropped as they shot upwards and away. Perhaps they were scouts for one of the flights; but the teal were coming in so thick now that they could not have warned all of them.

I whispered to Nga Moh to keep his eyes looking downwards, and I did the same myself. I knew that, high as they were, they could see our eyes if we looked up. I wondered how many of them were aware that I had already killed one of their number or knew that a gun meant death for them. They had probably never been shot at before. This was their haven, their quiet asylum where they could feed and breed in absolute peace.

Bending down, Nga Moh opened up the semi-webfoot of the shot bird. He inserted his finger to show that the foot could grip. It could not only swim, it could also roost.

The first flight dived to the water's surface, skimmed just above it for the length of the lake and soared steeply up again over the trees, probably spotting Carl and Bruno. Wave after wave followed suit, each with its whirr of wings. This 'fly-past' continued for over half an hour and then suddenly they were all gone, the sky above was clear and I thought that this detailed examination of the lake had led them all to discover our presence.

Then silently a new and smaller flight planed in and landed in the centre of the lake, well out of range. In a moment myriads of them appeared from tree-top level, hovering over the water, dropping in flat to alight, all flapping and chattering. The lake grew mottled brown with them. Thousands of others alighted on the tree-tops like starlings, scrambling over each other and flapping awkwardly to find a foothold.

Those that alighted on the trees above us rose and took flight again, and those in the water too close to where we were, flapped towards the centre. They were really alarmed by us, but had to settle somewhere. I could have 'browned' a bag of them with two shots had I been thinking only of a teal supper. How they would taste was another matter. The bill of the one Nga Moh held was a slaty green, an indication that their flesh would taste muddy.

Finally they settled. I stood up. They seemed too tired to take off again. Then I shouted.

It was as if the lake itself was erupting. They rose in a mass, flapping the water with their wings as they took off in fright, their legs hanging down like jammed under-carriages.

I 'browned' them a right and a left. About a dozen dropped round us before I could reload. Nga Moh retrieved them faster than a springer spaniel, while I took several more shots at individual birds, before they all left. Two or three birds had been winged and were swimming away from shore. I hesitated whether I should kill them outright.

As I hesitated, I heard Nga Moh shout. I looked round and saw Nga Moh chasing something and yelling at the top of his voice. I could not see what it was he was chasing for a moment. Then I saw that it was a huge iguana, at least five feet in length. The iguana was making off with one of our teal in its mouth. I could not fire, as I should have hit Nga Moh.

At that moment another iguana came from behind me, snatched up another dead teal and was off, screened this time by the reeds.

"Come here," I shouted to him. "If you don't they'll get you too!"

He rejoined me, at the same time grinning and cursing these thieves of iguanas. "And look at them!" he shouted. He pointed out across the lake, where the birds I had winged were being pursued by three iguanas swimming like young crocodile. The teal jinked and turned to avoid capture. They did not attempt to dive, as most teal would. But it would have been useless. The iguanas were as agile as otters.

One by one the iguanas retrieved the wounded teal and carried them off, keeping beyond my range. My image of this lake being a little asylum brutally violated by us humans had to be revised. They were all round, these iguanas. They must have lived on teal, as the crocodiles at Port Cornwallis lived on wild pig. I went on shooting till my gun was hot and my cartridges finished. Though the sport was good, I lost a great proportion of my bag to these thieves of iguanas. For many years I wondered if an iguana could not have been tamed as a water retriever when hunting for lost duck and teal.

Even so, I had twenty couple by the time I joined the others; I shot two iguanas for the birds' sake, and I felt glad that we were not permanent additions to their already harassed lives.

It was almost dark when we passed through Stewart Sound. Flanked on either bank by dense mangrove swamp, this passage was like a winding canal with a good depth of water at high tide. At its western end there were some scattered islands, one of which especially blocked the view. Rounding it, we expected to see twinkling ahead of us some light from the old bungalow.

Instead we saw to our astonishment a 5,000-ton ship anchored near Bonington Island, well off shore, the *Shah Jehan*, which just three months previously had brought us from Rangoon to Port Blair. Her small promenade deck was flood-lit and the portholes were all aglow with the reflections twinkling on the water.

She was anchored about half a mile beyond our pier. Her presence mystified us. I went into the wheelhouse and asked the Serang, "Does she often call here?"

"She used to when the mill was working, to drop supplies and machinery. But she hasn't called here for years."

There was only one possible explanation. Jeff must have arranged for her to make a special call to drop him off.

The Serang said that she was probably bound for Calcutta, between which port and Port Blair this was not far out of course.

As I went back to the others, I was met by Nga Moh. He looked old and worried. "What is it, Thakin?" he asked.

"*Shah Jehan* with Jeff Thakin returned. That's all."

He shook his head. "I think it is to take us back."

I did not try to cheer him, because I knew no more than he. When I joined the others, they seemed as depressed as Nga Moh, and for some unknown reason I shared it. Contact with civilisation, the bright lights, iced drinks, a meal in a saloon raised no excitement; for my part this was not entirely due to the lowering effect produced by thought of the canary-loving captain of the *Shah Jehan*. We were far happier the way we were; and that way, we realised, looking round at one another, was far more like a gang of Malay pirates than a group of eager timber-cruisers.

It was almost dark by the time that we approached the jetty, but we could see a figure silhouetted against the sky. A ship's motor-launch had just cast off and was heading back to the *Shah Jehan*. An unmistakable and recognised voice hailed me, "Any whisky left, Bill. This is a damn fine reception." It was Mac.

At that moment I scrambled up the old pier and the siren of

the *Shah Jehan* sounded her departure, drowning all other noise.

Mac quickly explained that the *Shah Jehan* had dropped him as a favour and was now away to Calcutta. It was typical, I thought, of that surly canary-breeder that he should not wait to ask us aboard for what might be called a civilised meal if it did not have to be shared with him. But none of us resented that so much as the fact that he had not stopped long enough to take off any mail. Given the chance I might have dropped a note to Susan.

"I suppose he didn't think it worth while," Mac said. "I told him I'd come out to help you pack up."

How he intended to do that he did not say. But his authority was already recognised by my servants, who had gathered on the pier. To them he was the Burra Sahib Engineer, the Big White Chief. He had come, clearly, to replace Jeff; and equally clearly the reason why Jeff needed to be replaced was that on the engineering side they wanted to outgun me. I knew I could at least reason with Jeff; but Mac had the advantage that he knew what was going on in the Rangoon Office, and he wasn't going to tell me until or unless it paid him to.

"How's P. N. C.?" I asked.

"P. N. C.?" he said. "Oh fine! Fine!"

"He didn't send any message?"

"He asked me to give you his salaams," Mac said.

"And his views on what Jeff had to say?"

He smiled. "He's reckoning on me to interpret those, I'd daresay."

I waited for him to continue, but he said no more. It was not that we disliked one another as people. It was just that he was an engineer who thought in terms of machines and I was an elephant manager who thought of fodders and perennial water.

"Anyway, you'll be pretty busy packing up," Mac said. "I've arranged for the *Surmai* to come up in a week's time and take your chain gang back to Port Blair. We'll stay on for a further week, and then S.S. *Maharajah* will call and take us straight back to Rangoon."

NO LONGER *MY* EXPEDITION

"And what did you propose to do with the *Jarawa* and *Madame X*?" Mac seemed to have forgotten little details like this; the sort of trouble it was going to cause in Port Blair when the convicts found that we weren't going back with them, the agreement that Bruno and Carl should come to Rangoon for conference.

"I think it would be best if the chain-gang go back to Port Blair under the impression that they are the advance guard," Mac said. "Bruno and Carl can take the *Jarawa* and *Madame X* back to Port Blair when we're finished with them, and then come on to Rangoon in the next boat." He looked round us all. "What do you chaps say to that? Does it make sense?"

"Of course it makes sense," I said in a voice which implied that it didn't. But it did in fact make sense. There was nothing I could object to in what Mac said except that it disabused me of the illusion which P. N. C. had been careful to foster, that this was *my* expedition.

From now on what Mac said went. I had a hunch I was not going to like what Mac said.

CHAPTER XVII

WHEN they heard that they were soon to return to Port Blair, the convicts became sullen. They showed no willingness to pack up, and I was afraid that I should have trouble before S.Y. *Surmai* arrived. Now was the time that they would attempt an escape, if they intended to. We redoubled our precautions on immobilising the boats. I had another long talk with Nga Moh, emphasising that my recommendations to the prison governor would have a great influence on the remission of their sentences and promising once again that if we implemented the scheme, we should depend on convict labour. It would be tragic if the scheme was turned down on the ground of the unreliability of convict labour, as it certainly would be if there was trouble.

Nga Moh asked me to call the convicts together and tell them myself. I did so. I did not tell them that we were not coming back to Port Blair, but I did nothing to disabuse them of that idea. I gave Nga Moh a plentiful ration of opium for the journey back and then I sank the football, now sadly depleted, by stuffing a stone into the case and tossing it overboard after dark.

The dreaded evening arrived when the S.Y. *Surmai* came into view and steamed into Stewart Sound anchoring alongside the old pier. The same policeman arrived and he had brought with him an armed guard. I had seen many prisoners under guard during the war and the rebellion, but never were my heart-strings so torn as seeing 'my own men' trooping aboard the *Surmai*, and as they did so sinking back into that sheep-like lethargy from which they had escaped during the time they were with us. They were as good and honest and reliable as any crowd of free men that I had employed, and the thought of their being taken back to the boredom and harsh discipline of that penal settlement made me resolved if I possibly could to convince the powers-that-were that our timber scheme was sound.

Whilst Carl and I had been 'packing up' the convicts and preparing reports and conduct sheets for the prison authorities, Bruno had been entertaining Mac by running him round the various islands in the Stewart Sound area.

We had a week before S.S. *Maharajah* was due and I had one further task to perform. I wanted to inspect a camp of elephants working padauk timber for Bruno's father. It was the farthest north that elephants had worked in the Andamans, a day's run down the east coast from Stewart Sound. I proposed that we should go down one day and come back the next. I was particularly anxious that Mac should see elephants at work in the area, as a practical demonstration of what could be done.

Bruno had visited this camp with his father during the previous cold weather. He said that the entrance to the creek was very treacherous and they had made a previous arrangement to be brought in from the open sea by raft. There was no time for us to give them previous notice, and we had to chance that we should be able to attract the attention of those ashore.

Mac resented the idea of coming. "The trouble about you, Bill," he said, "is you haven't seen an elephant for so long you're feeling homesick." I was determined to see the elephants myself.

"You stay at Stewart Sound if you like," I said, "but I must have the *Jarawa* and Bruno. And Carl must see an elephant camp, anyway."

Very reluctantly Mac agreed to come along. He wasn't an elephant man, but in some ways that made his opinion all the more important, if I could only impress him with elephant extraction.

We reached the mouth of the creek in the early evening. We anchored half a mile off shore, well outside the breakers. We could see the entrance, but there was no sign of life. The only indication that anyone was there was a line of tall bamboo stakes fixed to mark the channel to the creek mouth. During the hot season the elephants pushed small rafts of logs from the creek mouth out to sea, where the logs were transferred on to barges and towed to the sawmill.

There was a camp of eight elephants with about fifteen Indians who had been brought over from India at the same time as the elephants, working there. We blew the *Jarawa*'s klaxon continually in the hope of attracting someone's attention; but without any success. It was not surprising, since the roar of the breakers between us and the shore was deafening.

"They'll never hear and you'll never land across those breakers," Mac said. "It'd be madness to try."

Bruno and I said nothing. With high tide the following morning we knew the picture would change, so we settled for the night. We put Mac on to fishing to keep him quiet, and with enormous pride he caught his first shark.

Next day at high tide the seething mass of breakers disappeared. In their place were long, unbroken rollers galloping one after another right over the sand-bar to the mouth of the creek and racing up it. There was still no sign of any interest in us from the shore. There was nothing for it except to attempt a landing in a catamaran canoe. Bruno essayed it, with one of the *Jarawa* crew who was an expert canoeist. The intention was to contact the elephant men and get them to bring out a raft, if one was ready.

The moment they let go our stern, they were whipped away on the current. They rode the first roller dangerously, beam on. They disappeared into the trough, but the next roller straightened them out. They followed the line of stakes, using the paddles, it seemed, only for direction. The rollers gave them all the impetus they needed, the tide running so swiftly up the creek that it looked almost as if there was some vacuum sucking the catamaran shorewards.

Hazardous as it looked, the journey was soon over and without mishap. There was an hour before high tide, and in half that time the two were back with what must have been the full complement of Indians, waving and signalling us to come ashore.

"What do they expect us to do?" Mac asked. "Swim?"

Mac was looking at the rollers very thoughtfully. "I believe they're right," he said. "If we came in at a good pace, we could make it, following the line of those stakes."

"It's a hell of a risk," I said.

"I thought you wanted to see those damned elephants," Mac said.

I could have thought of no better way of ensuring that he went ashore than by suggesting that it was dangerous. It wasn't a moment before Skipper Mac had shouted to the Serang to start up the diesels and to Carl to weigh the anchor.

We moved direct out to sea as if we were going to leave Bruno behind, then we circled and came back on a line heading direct for the creek. The Serang stood on a small box affair at the wheel for a commanding view. Mac was at the engine controls. Carl and I stood on the deck gripping the top of the wheelhouse.

Mac opened the throttle full out. It was like heading for the first jump of a point-to-point, but in this race the fences were also mobile. We had to go faster than the waves. If a following wave overtook us, we should end up broached to on a beam sea. That was a danger as great as grounding on the bar.

We jumped the first, and for a moment the propellers were clear out of the water. They raced with a screeching roar, as if they were going to shear off. Then we were in again, riding on the second with a fearful pitch, making a heavy sea break across the stern as if followed us. We still kept right direction, and as we crossed the bar, she seemed to flatten out or plane like an aircraft about to land. We entered the mass of broken water, and what we had anticipated would be the worst stretch, was in fact the easiest.

I was watching the Serang's face, and just as I expected it to relax, it grew taut. The *Jarawa* suddenly pitched forward into deep water beyond the bar. I felt as if the launch was being sucked under and would sink on an even keel, the flat water rising higher and higher over the decking; then suddenly she rose, bobbing up like a great cork. For the first time during the trip, I saw the Serang smile, exposing a mouthful of teeth red with betel nut. I don't know why he's smiling, I thought; we're in; but how the hell do we get out?

But that was a future worry. Within an hour we were watching elephants at work and I was cursing myself for my folly in bringing Mac. The elephants were small, compared to any I had handled in the Burma forests. They were well up to weight, but they were suffering from being worked and bathed in tidal waters. Their skins were rough, scaly and a dull grey. Their feet and toe-nails were soft and pale through constant working in stagnant mangrove swamp-mud.

They were not self-supporting in fodders. They grazed a certain amount from the surrounding jungle, but after a few months everything within a mile of the camp had been eaten out. Even the largest girth trees had been so stripped of bark at about waist high that they had died. Some species had been so gouged into by the tusks and tushes that they had fallen. It was more than probable that the elephants had deliberately felled them to get at the higher leaves.

They weren't allowed to forage any distance from camp. Instead they were given a liberal ration of unhusked paddy-rice, a basket a day, or about thirty pounds weight. All their feeding supplies had been dumped from rafts six months previously, before the break of the monsoon. From these supplies the elephant men pounded their own ration of rice, and I suspected that they did not give the elephants their full rations, because they wanted to hold sufficient paddy grain in store in case for some reason they were not relieved on time. They lived a miserable existence.

The grain for the elephants was boiled in a huge iron cauldron with a liberal addition of salt and then placed on bamboo mats, each animal with its own plate. We watched their feeding, and there was terrible wastage. For every mouthful which the elephant sucked into its trunk and shot back into its throat behind its tongue to chew, it shot another to either side to keep the flies off. Paddy grains ricocheted off their flanks like grapeshot from an eight-bore shot-gun. To stand behind a feeding elephant was to risk being blinded. There was a plague of flies on account of the filth in the camp.

The timber they were extracting was valuable red padauk. To reduce the circular dead weight in dragging from stump to tidal creek, each log was roughly adzed to squares at stump. Being dead-weight green timber, it was very heavy going. It would have been simple to lighten the elephants' work by laying rollers, made with little trouble from the greasy mangrove roots nearby. Instead the mahouts shortened the length of the drag-chains or traces so that by brute force the butt end of the log was raised. A spreader was fixed between the traces to ease the pressure of the chain on the elephant's hind legs. But there was not an elephant without a raw wound on either flank.

It was not for me to criticise how Bruno's father allowed his elephant camp to be run, but it depressed me beyond words. Furthermore, it was a shocking example to place before Mac, confirming him in every prejudice he had against elephant extraction. He felt about these methods as I would have done if he had shown me a huge winding drum, hauling in and skidding timber with twisted ropes and no grease or oil.

From stump to creek the elephants had to drag only about a mile through flat jungle. Yet the market value of the padauk had been more than halved in many cases by short cross-cutting by saw or hacking by axe.

The Indian mahouts were living far worse than our convicts had been. They had not the simplest medical supplies. Their skins were as dry and grey as their elephants. We spent some time doctoring mud sores and doing what we could to improve the conditions of the men who had to remain for another two months, before they were relieved. They had already done nine months. It was altogether a sad camp; the men and animals were lethargic and the standard of work far below anything in the forests of Burma.

Carl was particularly interested in watching a raft of padauk squares being made up ready to be floated to offshore. For every padauk square, two soft-wood logs were lashed on either side to give it buoyancy. He expressed great concern that tidal water would stain the matchwood logs green.

We examined the soft-wood logs in the water. Apart from stain, they were spoiled by wood-borers, chiefly the tidal teredo. They were useless for any market. To satisfy Carl we had one of these logs recovered from the water by an elephant and placed over a saw-pit. Two Indian sawyers ripped it down the centre from end to end. Little effort was needed. The sound the rip-teeth made was more like that made in cutting soft slate than wood. When it fell apart, it looked like Gruyère cheese. It was riddled with a honeycomb of different-shaped holes, harbouring a great variety of marine life, sea-worms, coloured winkles and even small fish. This log had been in the water only a month. There was no need even to look at Carl's face. For him the last three months had been an utter waste of time. He hadn't even found the volume of timber for matchwood supplies. The soft-wood timbers for the large-scale match factories of India would not come from these forests.

I felt very depressed. Carl's report was obviously going to be negative, and I had completely failed to convince Mac of the advantages of elephant extraction. I decided on one last attempt. "I'd like you to see the elephants doing their off-shore log punting," I said. "If nothing else, it ought to amuse you."

The oozies made a small raft, consisting of two heavy padauk squares lashed to two buoyant logs of papita softwood. This was done at the head of the creek and pushed down by oozies wading and swimming until they reached the sea. There two elephants took over, with riders in position. The elephants took the raft into deeper water, until they were swimming, pushing it with their heads.

Bruno had ordered the oozies to take the raft over the bar to a place approximately where we had anchored the *Jarawa*. I told Mac he would have to imagine there was a barge on which the raft might be loaded.

The whole camp turned out to watch, because this off-shore rafting was normally done only during the calm weather of the hot season. The waves were too big for it to be easily done at this time, and I was frightened that the oozies might be washed off, until I saw that they were gripping rope surcingles.

The elephants swam with a dog-paddle action, bobbing in the sea like enormous corks. One would push it angrily over the crest of a wave; then the raft would spin in the cross-currents of the broken water, with first one elephant butting it and then the

other, as if between them were dribbling a water-polo ball out to sea.

The raft rode the waves and the elephants crashed through them, disappearing completely beneath the crest and coming into view again in the troughs. They were as confident as if they were going through a routine in a circus; and watching Mac's face, I could see that he was, if not impressed, at least delighted with the performance. Whether he imagined there was a barge did not matter. Having reached the place where a barge ought to have been, the elephants considered their work done. They gave it a final shove, and without apparently a command they turned and, sitting in the water, using their rumps as surf-boards, came riding back on the waves, with their tails sticking out like rudders. It was a wonderful piece of animal clowning, and when we had stopped laughing, I said to Mac, "Have you got a machine that could do anything like that?"

"That's easy," Mac said. "I'd build a timber pier with a light railway, and instead of having to hoist the logs on to barges with a crane, I'd roll them aboard with far less trouble."

"Could you make a folding pier?" Bruno asked.

"Why should I want a folding pier?" Mac asked.

"To fold it in at the first storm," Bruno said. "Otherwise you'd have to build another one."

"Anyway, none of these direct sea-entry creeks would yield more than a thousand tons of timber," I said. "In a few years with your piers, you'd have this looking like the south coast from Brighton to Bournemouth."

But nothing could prove Mac wrong. "If there's no timber, there's no need for elephants to work it," he said.

We went back to the *Jarawa*, where Bruno cooked us a meal, before which we had many drinks. We were very cramped in our sleeping quarters, and that contributed to the shortness of our tempers. The main quarrel was one which had been brewing from the moment Mac had met us on the jetty at Bonington Island; it was a quarrel about modern engineering extraction and elephant animal extraction. Mac poured contempt on the elephant.

"What is it?" he asked, "except an outsize machine, running on a very expensive fuel of unhusked rice, subject to innumerable breakdowns through attacks of wind, pus, worms or sex, taking twenty years to manufacture, another five or so to train and needing constant attendance. The elephant is all very well, my dear chap, standing on a tub in a circus or giving rides to schoolchildren in a zoo. But as a machine, the elephant went out with Hannibal."

"As a means of extracting timber from this sort of jungle," I answered, "these wretched machines of yours have never even started. Your machines have no intelligence, no versatility, no power to stand up to assaults of this climate without great care and frequent maintenance. For every machine you need another in spare parts. This elephant camp is merely an example of how *not* to run one. Those convicts under Nga Moh and Tun Gyaw could do a far, far better job. But can you see them operating your machines? Can you imagine training them even in the elementary details of maintenance? Bruno's father isn't using elephants because he's too old-fashioned to think of using machines," I went on. "He's tried machines and he's failed! If you want to see just how he's failed, the next thing we do when we get back north is to take you over to Interview Island. You're sarcastic about this method. But if you want to see the total failure of your own wonderful system, you can see it on Interview."

That very briefly was our argument, lasting the whole evening and late into the night, acrimonious on both sides, though the more so on mine because I was the more deeply committed to some sort of forestry scheme in the Andamans. Mac could afford to be dispassionate because he had invested none of his life in the research. He did not seem to realise that one can't do the sort of trip that Carl and I had done across the Saddle Peak without getting implicated. The only justification for doing it would be if we produced a positive result.

We went to bed that night with nothing decided. The debate was still on; but next morning it was postponed while we concentrated on re-crossing the bar. We had anchored some distance up the creek, as there was ample water even at low tide. We ran the diesels for some time before starting to get them really ticking over. Mac said that we should find it easier to run out against the flood-tide than we had found it to run in. He said this with the same confidence with which he talked about the merits of mechanical extraction; I hoped with more justification.

The Indians came to watch us from the mouth of the creek. The excitement threw us together again as friends. This time we were going full ahead into the breakers, and it was plain from the beginning that Mac was right. We crossed without any difficulty and were at sea. We waved to the Indians, and they turned back to their work. I was very grateful that there was no special triumph in Mac's look.

On the run back to Stewart Sound, I learnt two things which Mac had not been prepared to tell me before. The first was that when the S.S. *Maharajah* called to pick us up, personages concerned in the financial and forest sides of our project would be aboard. "The idea is that we should have the whole thing discussed before we reached Rangoon," Mac said. The second, which I only heard of quite incidentally, was that, at any rate as far as Mac was concerned, the whole of the Andaman extraction project would stand or fall by whether we could supply to its full full capacity a second-hand sawmill which was redundant in Moulmein. This sawmill had a far larger capacity than anything which I had ever envisaged, and the problem of feeding it would amount to approximately two hundred log tons a day, whatever the season. Storage was impossible. Matchwoods would deteriorate by immersion, and hard woods would harden to iron woods.

"Dammit," I said. "You're putting the cart before the horse. There is no calculation of timber supplies as yet. That's why I was sent up here. Given the amount of timber, I could reckon the number of elephants needed to bring it from the stumps to the coast shores, and the number of elephants I have must not, I insist, exceed the local fodder available."

On the basis of what timber I could get to the coast, the rafting experts could then calculate the time it would take to reach the mill and the best means of doing it. On the basis of these calculations one could reckon the size of the sawmill needed. To hell with Moulmein and its second-hand sawmills!

But that wasn't the way Mac worked. Given reams of paper, a slide-rule and an unlimited supply of noughts, Mac could settle anything.

"Let's say you need a hundred and fifty elephants," Mac would say, "what personnel would be needed for that?"

238

I would hesitate. "Let's say very roughly five hundred to cover saw fellers and so on . . ."

"Call it seven fifty," Mac said. "The mill would need another two hundred, I reckon. A hundred, say, for rafting. That's one thousand and fifty. Call it fifteen hundred, to be on the safe side. What European forest staff would you need?"

Again I would hesitate.

"Say something, man! A dozen? Two dozen?"

I'd suggest that six might be quite enough.

"Don't be such a B.F.," Mac would say. At this moment an entirely new line of thought would sidetrack him. "Of course, health! That's going to be one of your biggest jobs here. Got to have a damned good hospital. Two, three doctors. And couple of ravishing Burmese nurses. Nothing like a pretty girl to rally the old will to live, eh?"

A fresh sheet of paper for every new subject mentioned, with a guess at the cost to the nearest lakh of rupees. This wild compilation of fantasy figures seemed to me a prodigious waste of time; but not to Mac.

"Now we're getting somewhere," he would say, finishing his whisky. "This bottle's empty. Don't forget it's all on the firm, you know." And another bottle of whisky would arrive, which came out of our pores almost as fast as it went down our throats.

It went on every night, with Mac riding his hobby-horses for all he was worth. "Of course, communication," he said. "Communication is all important. We've got to have all-the-year-round communication, foul weather and fair. A weekly service between Rangoon and here, right through the south-west monsoons."

"You could never do that," I'd say, thinking of the *Briton* and the *Runnymede* and the typhoons that blew.

"Just wouldn't I?" Mac asked. "As it happens, launch design is a hobby of mine, and I flatter myself I have the very thing—a cruiser launch."

He produced the blueprint. It was unrolled and placed on the camp table and anchored at the top by two pressure lamps and at the bottom by a bottle of whisky and a bottle of gin. Even Carl and Bruno, excluded from our highly technical discussion of the rival merits of elephants and machines, were called in to admire this blueprint, which was perfect to the last detail. Mac explained it all to us as if it was already on the stocks. He had thought of everything, even down to a special sick bay for the accommodation of European casualties. "Sure to be a lot of sickness, malaria and so on, to start with." He helped himself to a three-finger peg of whisky and braced his shoulders. "Of course she'll cost a tidy bit to build; but she'll be worth it. Don't want any of these second-hand jobs."

"What would you say?" Bruno asked timidly.

"Wouldn't do it under a couple of lakhs," Mac said.

I poured myself a four-finger peg of whisky. "I do so agree with you about getting things new, Mac," I said. "It's just a waste of time picking something up second-hand and mucking everything up trying to gear the operation to it."

"Don't you get me wrong," Mac said; "that sawmill's the best gift I've seen for years."

Next day I took him to Interview Island and showed him the chaos caused by trying to supply by mechanical methods a sawmill which, compared to the bargain in Moulmein, was a toy affair more suitable for a child's nursery. All day I hammered at him, and I think that before we left Interview Island I had made some impression; or rather the sight of tangled masses of rusted hawsers and ropes, twisted and buckled light rails, decayed and rotten old barges, all being submerged in the tide of the jungle, put my arguments more eloquently than I ever could myself. If mechanical extraction had failed on flat, heavily-timbered Interview Island, how could it ever succeed in the precipitous interior of North Andaman?

That night Mac suggested we should bury the hatchet. "There'll be an armoury of big shots aboard the *Maharajah*," he said, "and we've got to preserve a United Front."

"I thought we should just have to report to P. N. C.," I said.

"Good Lord, no!" Mac said. "This is policy on the highest level. The Indian Government Forestry Department is responsible for the Andamans. And believe you me, there's going to be quite a tussle about royalties, from all I hear."

Just before noon next day, our servants spotted the hull of a big steamer on the horizon and we went down to the jetty, ready to take the *Jarawa* out to the S.S. *Maharajah* as soon as she dropped anchor.

"Nice timing," Mac said. "I wonder what's on the menu for lunch."

Through the binoculars we watched the big black steamer growing larger. I think that Carl and Bruno, and perhaps even Mac, felt a pang, as I did, at the thought the time had come to leave these islands which were so beautiful and so rich in surprises.

The Serang started up the engines of the *Jarawa*. He had put on his best alpaca coat with the polished buttons and his bright red fez. He was as trim as he had appeared that first evening I had seen him in the harbour at Port Blair. I looked at the others, who had not changed or even shaved, and I realised that I must look as ruffianly a pirate as they did. But it was too late now. We went aboard the *Jarawa*, as the S.S. *Maharajah* gave us the signal on her siren. We sat on the hatch and none of us said anything, until Carl, who had the binoculars, whistled and said, "Quite a lot of passengers."

There were four big shots, two of them from the Bombay office of Bombine, one a forest expert and the other financial. Mac knew them of old and I had met them both before. If they were shocked by our appearance, they did not show it. The other two looked a trifle surprised, and I felt that I ought to wipe my hand on the seat of my trousers before shaking hands. The first was a very senior official from the Government Forest Department. The fourth man was a Swede, the Indian matchwood representative. He knew Carl, and in a moment they were laughing and chattering away in Swedish as freely as if they had had half a dozen cocktails, while we of the British contingent were humming and hawing as if we had been reluctantly brought together at a vicarage tea-party.

A steward appeared, beating a gong for All Passengers Ashore as if we were on a trans-Atlantic liner. I leapt up and shook Carl and Bruno cheerfully goodbye and a good voyage back to Port Blair. We went to the head of the gangway and waved goodbye to them, as the *Jarawa* romped its way back to the jetty. Then I turned to the Swedish matchwood expert. "What was Carl talking to you about?" I asked. "I bet it wasn't matchwood."

"No," he said in perfect English. "He was telling me about the Andaman Lido you are going to start in Port Cornwallis."

It was a fancy that we had evolved after Jeff had left us, when our thoughts had turned away from timber to enjoyment; what a wonderful playground the North Andaman would make for those who were sick and tired of hill-stations like Simla, a resort which was not developed. Its whole charm would be that it remained undeveloped, reverting back at the end of each season to its primitive condition.

Very willingly I took up the tale of our adventures where Carl had left off, telling him about the turtle and the teal, finding the dugong and the spotted deer in the forest.

I had come on board, keyed up by Mac for high-powered conferences, but for the first night we only discussed in a light-hearted way the Lido idea. The Swedish Match King appealed to me every now and again to support this wonderful scheme, which could make all our fortunes and enlarge the happiness of the world. "You mustn't cut down those trees," he said. "It would spoil everything."

Next morning we got down to our first conference. There proved to be no need for Mac and me to conceal our differences. The problems with which we had been concerned were ignored. What did it matter whether there was enough timber to be extracted or how the extraction was done? No, the important point was how much the Indian Forestry Department could make out of the project.

Their representative stuck out for a high royalty per ton, pointing out the enormous expense involved in setting up an organisation to see that the Bombine and the Matchwood Interests didn't get into mischief; while the other three argued that the expense of extracting, milling, transporting and marketing the timber was so enormous that the Indian Government really ought to pay them to take the stuff away. I remained respectfully dumb for some time, though sorely tempted to say that it might be worthwhile our paying the Forestry Department not to set up an organisation, which would only set up the sort of frictions we had had during the Burmese rebellion.

"Then we've got to consider the Health Services," he said. "That's a very big item."

"I didn't have a single case of sickness with my convicts," I said.

"You didn't?" he said. "To what do you attribute that?"

"I took a football with me," I answered.

"Of course I am all in favour of sport," he said, smiling bleakly. "But we shouldn't exaggerate it as a preventive medicine. Ha! ha!"

They then turned to the question of the labour force. He expressed his pleasure that the convicts had proved amenable to discipline.

"They proved amenable to lack of discipline," I answered. "I could not guarantee any results if they were under guard. So there is no need to include the salaries of prison officers in your budget."

"But you'll have to recruit the bulk of your labour from outside," said one of the Bombine men. "The Andamans aren't very popular with your Burmans."

"I could recruit all the labour I need from the Karen Hills. There wouldn't be any difficulty about that."

"Perhaps not from your point of view," he said. "But we must remember that it is necessary to have Government Settlement Officers to oversee any labour camps you set up."

"Well, let's leave that one till later," the Bombine representatives said.

So it went on during the whole voyage to Rangoon. It was the old wrangle between Government and Trade, which we had experienced so bitterly before the rebellion. Mac and I with our private differences were relegated to the background. Elephants and fodders, fresh water supplies, sawmill sites and estimated volumes of timber were as unimportant for the purpose of these discussions as giant clams and bricks in trees.

CHAPTER XVIII

Many who have spent their lives in India maintain that its loveliest sight is the lights of Bombay seen from astern. Anyone who has ever visited Rangoon must agree that one of the loveliest sights in the world is the view of the sun catching the gold-leafed dome of the Shwe Dagon Pagoda at mid-day, as one stands in the bows of an approaching ship. It excited me even more now than when I had first seen it, because Burma had accumulated such a variety of associations.

I felt not that I had been to the Black Islands, but as I might if I had been on a three months tour in the forest. The Andamans to me were Burma across the water.

But what was I to find waiting for me? What of Molly Mia and Susan? How had Archie made out while I was away? What of the fifty transfer elephants coming from Siam?

I thought it was conceivable, though by no means certain, that Susan and Molly Mia might be on the quayside. But in this I was disappointed. But there was He Man, slightly larger than life, as usual, waving away, with a grin all over his face. "She wasn't able to come," he said, springing aboard from dock to deck rail without waiting for any gangway. "But she sent a note."

It was marked Urgent. I opened it and read.

Molly Mia sends apologies not meeting you, but we are delayed a day in Mandalay. Have booked same ship as you home leave! Susan.

I read it through twice, "I didn't know that I'd booked a ship for home leave," I said.

"I did it for you," He Man said. "Sailing in June. Give you time to settle the Siamese transfers in and then off you go." He burst out laughing. "Funny thing, though. Susan *thinks* she's booked in the same ship. But she hasn't. She's got the *wrong one*."

He roared with laughter at this gargantuan jest, typical of the unpracticality of all women; and the next morning, when Susan and Molly Mia arrived, we corrected the error of the bookings, which, according to Susan, was due to He Man getting the dates wrong.

I asked Susan whether she had got my letter from Singapore, and she smiled and said "Yes." We left it at that. Though nothing more was said, there was an understanding between us.

Meanwhile I wrote my report on the Andaman project, confining myself, according to instruction, to a plan for elephant extraction, basing my calculations on an elephant force which could live on the land all the year round. It took a week, and during that time I had not a single argument with Mac over second-hand sawmills or first-hand cruiser launches. The Andamans were receding into memory, and I was eager to get up-country and settle the Siamese elephant transfers.

In Rangoon I read the three monthly reports or diaries which Archie had sent in. They were competently and confidently written. I had no doubt that he had done a first-class job. Everything that he told me when we met confirmed this impression. He had sketch-mapped the whole area, plotting camps in parties of seven elephants, each with a liberal grazing range without overlaps. There was plenty of fodder and water in each area, and there was very little more to be done until the recruited oozies arrived.

My old Chaungoke, U San Din, had reported to me that he had finished recruiting his oozies. He had covered hundreds of square miles, and though he was not sure how experienced his oozies were, he was convinced that they all knew how to ride. He arranged for a rendezvous with Archie and myself so that we could assemble well in advance of the elephants and get the oozies used to working together. The men had been given a month's wages in advance with instructions when and where to report; and of seventy of them, sixty-eight arrived on time. The pay of riders was twenty-five rupees a month (about £2) for tuskers, twenty rupees for females and thirty rupees for dangerous tuskers, of whom there were five so described. Each of the dangerous animals was guarded by a spearman, as a protection to the rider.

There were seven camps of seven elephants each. A Tawgaung, Sinôke or headman had to be chosen for each group. San Din had already picked three of them. The remaining four we allowed the oozies to choose for themselves. They were the best judges of whom they would like to serve under. Our only stipulation was that each could write a letter in Burmese and prepare a pay-sheet.

After they had been chosen, Archie had them up and said, "One of your elephants is supposedly dead, and you must write me a letter explaining how it died." Archie was to correct the test. After all, he would have to read their letters, if ever they had to write one in earnest.

I was surprised at the ease with which Archie read them. "Your logging clerk must have put in nearly as much tuition as Ma Kywai," I said.

It was the first time I had mentioned Ma Kywai. I don't think Archie welcomed it. "How's she getting on?"

"I haven't seen her for quite a time," he said. "In fact, I think it's quite likely we shan't see one another again."

"I'm very glad," I said.

247

"Oh, she's delightful," he said. "But I just cannot stand that mother of hers."

"Oh, she's been bothering you, has she?" I asked.

"Yes, she came along to suggest how helpful Ma Kywai would be as a camp-follower. I got rid of her. Yet one evening who should turn up in my camp but Ma Kywai, though I thought I'd made it quite plain that our little affair was finished."

"What did she come for?" I asked. "More iodine or money?"

"I don't know. She said she was very exhausted when she arrived, and she stayed the night—as a matter of fact she stayed two nights; then I told her to run along home and gave her some money, and that was that."

"Well, that's all right, then?"

"I'm not so certain," Archie said. "She is no longer the innocent kid I knew in Mehaw. But her goitre is cured, anyway."

I was not interested in these romantic post-mortems. As long as Archie had finished with Ma Kywai, that was all that mattered as far as I was concerned.

Once we had appointed the Tawgaungs, we ignored individual oozies and concentrated on getting to know these headmen. The most outstanding was a young man called San Hla. He was very good looking and his fairness of complexion suggested Shan blood. He wrote a very good legible Burmese script. It was as good as old Kyan Thoung's was bad. This old man, another selected Tawgaung, had written as his test a graphic description of two of his tuskers fighting until one was killed. His script suffered from his excitement and, as Archie said, one couldn't be sure whether he was trying to write or to draw what had happened. We wanted to fail him, but San Din was so emphatic about his age and experience of elephants that we let him remain.

These oozies came from widely separated districts; never more than three were from any one village. Yet within a week we had between us constructed a new community with a quite distinct corporate personality, with Archie at their head.

Archie had won respect not merely in virtue of his position. There was a story which every newcomer was told by Archie's own travelling oozies.

They had found a Samba stag which had been killed by a tiger in a creek-bed. There was no tree within two hundred yards which could be used to support a platform from which Archie could shoot the tiger when it came back to feed. Not to be beaten, Archie had a six-foot-deep pit dug in the shingle, and an hour before sunset he got into the pit and had an elephant place heavy logs over him, leaving only a nine-inch aperture all round, from which he could shoot. He gave orders for the elephants to be brought next morning at dawn to roll the logs away and release him.

Two hours later a shot was heard, and when the oozies and elephant came the next morning, it was some time before they could get an elephant to approach the hole in the shingle. Within twenty yards of the hide a tiger lay dead, and no elephant dared to go near. Even if Archie had been far less experienced than he now was, this story would carry him a long way.

Everything was now in readiness for the arrival of the transfers. The hot season was really on us. The heavy leaf fall of the deciduous trees was over. It was swelteringly hot. Archie had chosen the site of the rendezvous camp well. It had been a village, though it was now deserted. There were a dozen huge tamarind trees, which gave a wide and welcome shade. The only hut was the newly erected go-down to store the rice. Alongside was a wide, dry creek, with just a trickle of water down the main channel and a stretch of shingle ideal for parading this large batch of elephants.

I had of course full details of the elephants in advance: their names, their registered numbers, their descriptions, age and measurements, their sex, their distinguishing features, such as scars. A forest assistant in Siam had made all the details and a Siamese clerk, no draughtsman, had drawn a sketch of each animal to indicate distinguishing features. Archie looked at this gallery

Q 249

of mammoths, mastodons and other apparently extinct animals and said, "I thought they were sending us *elephants*."

Among these elephants there was a high proportion of tuskers, one in every four. Our forward scouts arrived back with reports of the expected date of arrival. For this last march old U San Din went out to meet them and lead them into camp. For half an hour before they arrived we could hear the music of their combined bells, the sound carrying through the jungle with an extraordinary penetration. From the first sound, the newly recruited oozies were lined up on the bank to see the arrival of the elephants that were to be their care.

They came up the creek, Old U San Din and two of the Siamese
leaders in the van, and behind them a magnificent tusker. On one
foot he wore a fetter, attacked to which was a heavy chain slung
across his withers. He was on musth. A rider was on his neck, and
on either side was a spearman with a vicious-looking spear. He
was halted opposite where we stood on the bank, as if on parade.

Behind came the main body in Indian file. Nearly all the Shan
and Siamese oozies wore short black bombees, loose-fitting trousers
like pyjamas. As they were stripped to the waist, they looked as if

they all belonged to a regiment which had succeeded in giving them only half a uniform. But they were a wonderful sight all the same. Every fourth or fifth elephant had a gleaming pair of tusks.

Archie was speechless with pride. Never in my service had I seen such a parade of magnificent animals. They were stockier than the Burmese elephants, the reason being, it is said, that in North Siam there are fewer areas of elephant grass. In kaing grass an elephant's back is exposed to the sun, and sunlight promotes growth, it is believed. Their condition was superb, in spite of having been almost a year on the march.

I walked down the line of animals, followed by Archie, U San Din and the Siamese headman. I remembered my first batch of elephants when old Willie had said, "The four on the right are yours, and God help you if you don't look after them," and before I knew where I was one had died on my hands of old age.

I gave the order to disperse and, standing with Archie looking after them, I said, "There are fifty of the finest elephants in Burma. They're yours, and God help you if you can't look after them."

The handing over of the elephants by the old oozies to the new took a little time. But the Burman left to himself is a master at working things out, and we did not interfere, unless we were asked. The Shans and Siamese explained the peculiarities of their particular animals, effected the introduction between each elephant and the oozie taking over. They were anxious to go home after this year-long journey. I signed a receipt for the animals. Each man was given an advance against the expenses of his journey and a statement of the wages he was to be paid when he reached Chiengmai in Upper Siam. They were allowed two months in which to make the return journey. It was our policy not to pay the men off in Burma. If we had done so, there would have been gambling, perhaps murder, perhaps dacoity on the way home. Kept short of money, they would stick together and make a good time on the return journey.

Great was my relief when I saw them depart. My home leave was one step closer. I returned immediately to my headquarters, where my relief was to join me. Archie remained and made a round of his new camps to see them settled in. He was then to join me at headquarters, with the other forest assistant staff who were to come in for a rest and leave, while the forest-working elephants had their hot-weather-season rest.

On my march to headquarters, I thought over my plans. The way Archie had looked after his two Great Danes so impressed me that I decided to ask him to look after Molly Mia for me also while I was on leave. It was a great relief to know that she would be well cared for.

At headquarters there was a letter from Bruno thanking me for what I had done for him. He had been offered an appointment on the Bombine forest staff, as I expected, and, with some imagination, they had given him three months leave in England so that he could join the firm in the usual way. He was leaving immediately.

Amongst my official mail was a letter enclosing copies of correspondence which had passed between Rangoon Office and the Rangoon Police authorities, concerning a certain ex-convict by name Nga Moh. This man had arrived in Rangoon and alleged that he had worked for me in the North Andaman and been recommended for an early discharge on the strength of this. On reporting to the police in Rangoon, he had produced a document which he alleged was written by me and which guaranteed his employment. The Rangoon Police informed the Rangoon Head Office that they would raise no objection to the man being employed by the Bombine, provided that it was understood that wherever he was employed, he would still be under Police Observation and must report once a month to the nearest Police Headquarters.

The covering letter from Rangoon Head Office left it open for me to repudiate any connection I might have had with this ex-convict, implying that the unwisdom of issuing such a guarantee of work was something which they regarded as inadvisable. Anyway, let me think the matter over very carefully before undertaking a commitment which I might have made rather hastily in the Andamans. It bristled with caution.

I wrote back saying that I readily accepted responsibility, that I could certainly find a job for him and that he was going to be invaluable, if the Andaman project went ahead.

In due course Nga Moh arrived. He had seen a barber since I saw him last; his ragged old mandarin moustache had been trimmed and brushed. He wore a new coat and putso. I felt proud of him, as I introduced him personally to my local District Superintendent of Police. I remembered that scene on the shores of the lake on North Reef Island while we were waiting for the teal to come back. I gave my guarantee that Nga Moh should be near enough to report monthly at this particular police station. The policeman was a personal friend and I told him, "This man has served his time. I want you, if you can, to let him make good." I repeated it in Burmese so that Nga Moh should understand.

It was only on his account that I regretted going on leave. If not, I should have made him a personal 'tour servant'. I felt desperately sorry for him. He had a royal welcome from my servants, especially Joseph and Aung Net. He seemed happy, and I thought he was going to settle down.

But when he heard that I was going on leave to England, he clung to me as if he was a stranger in a new land instead of someone returning to his people after a long absence. How could he start a new life, when my servants knew all about him and they would gossip? Couldn't I find him some job in the jungle? I promised I would arrange something. I sounded my relief, but he was not enthusiastic. It was twenty-one years since the old man had worked with elephants. There was no sense in trying to find him a mount. Then I hit on the solution of making him rice storeman for the new transfer elephants. He was absolutely reliable, no one would know about him, it would be easy for him to report at Police Headquarters and Archie would not get flustered with an ex-convict, whom I had often talked about since my return.

So one morning with the mail-runners off went Nga Moh, a sad, forlorn figure. In letting him go I had no fears about dishonesty in the rice issues. My only qualm was whether twenty-one years at Port Blair had made it impossible for him ever to readjust himself to freedom in Burma.

Archie arrived at headquarters in due course and joined in the annual 'beat-up' in the large communal hostel called the Chummery. After a week of what was called 'relaxation' he staggered back into the jungle to recover himself. "I feel a different man," he said, yawning. "Well, so long. And it really is going to be long this time, with you on Home Leave."

But he was wrong. He never reached his elephant camps. On his last march out he was dacoited. He sent me a message to say he was staying in camp until he received instructions from me. Next morning I left for tour again with the Superintendent of Police. What we both were worried about was not that five thousand rupees had been stolen, but that Archie's shot-gun had been taken. That was far more serious.

We did not hear the full story until we reached Archie's camp. The only witness was a young oozie named Po Loo, who had been the rider of the hindmost of Archie's travelling elephants, when moving in Indian file. This particular animal carried in its pannier two specie boxes full of silver and Archie's shot-gun in a leather case. Archie, with his rifle, and also his servants were all ahead of the elephants. There was no one behind Po Loo.

While he was crossing a small creek, Po Loo saw a white cotton shirt lying on the river bank. Thinking someone ahead had dropped it by mistake, Po Loo dismounted and was just picking it up, when he heard a voice order him to put his hands up. He looked up and there, not fifteen yards away, was a dacoit with a gun, who said, "If you try to call for help, I'll shoot you!"

The dacoit had covered the lower part of his face with a towel, and Po Loo did not recognise him as anyone he knew. The man waited, until the other elephants and their oozies were out of hearing. Then he told Po Loo to make his elephant 'sit'.

Po Loo made the elephant sit and then, being still threatened with the gun, he unloaded the specie boxes and shot-gun.

The dacoit held him up for a further quarter of an hour. Then he told Po Loo that he could mount his elephant and give the alarm.

Between one and two hours later, Archie and a party of his men returned to the scene of the crime. The open specie boxes had been robbed of their notes, but there was a thousand rupees in silver left in each box. They were too heavy for the dacoit to carry. The boxes had not been broken open. They were fastened with large brass padlocks and the thief had possesssed duplicate keys. Nearby was the empty guncase; and most ironical of all, the home-made dummy gun with which the 'armed' dacoit had held up the young oozie.

The fact that the dacoit had keys of the specie boxes indicated that it was an 'inside' job. The handsome young Shan Tawgaung, San Hla, immediately fell under suspicion, because he had deserted his camp and was missing from the day preceding the dacoity.

As ill luck would have it, the nearest inhabited place to the scene of dacoity was the rice go-down where Nga Moh was acting as caretaker. "There is an extraordinary similarity between this dacoity and the other one your convict friend was mixed up in," said the Superintendent of Police. "We have all the old case-papers and I think I'll have a talk with Nga Moh."

Nga Moh had no alibi. He was entirely on his own, except when he issued rice, and he had issued no rice on that day. He might not be guilty, as Archie observed, but he was far easier to arrest than San Hla.

Inquiries about San Hla revealed very little. He had followed U San Din up to my headquarters, while I was away in the Andamans. He told U San Din that he knew that elephant men were needed. He came from the Shan States. He had obviously worked with elephants before, but he had never worked with any of Archie's other oozies. There was nothing in police records that could be pinned on San Hla.

Archie went back to headquarters to replenish his money-boxes. A mere dacoity could not hold up the payment of oozies' wages. I stayed in the jungle waiting for him, refusing on his behalf an offer of police protection. He would have to live with the threat of dacoity for the rest of his forest life, and the sooner he learned to travel without breaking standing orders the better. "When carrying money, your personal servants form the vanguard and you form the rearguard," I said. "Observe that rule and you won't be dacoited—not often, anyway."

When I returned to my headquarters I went round to see the Superintendent and protested against Nga Moh's detention. There wasn't a shred of evidence against him and it was just a case of Give a dog a bad name. Nga Moh was bitter, when I saw him. He said he would prefer to be in the Andamans. There they were used to convicts. Here they would give you no second chance.

I nagged the Superintendent for a week, at the end of which time he agreed to release him, provided I posted him somewhere closer in, where he could be checked daily by a headman. I agreed and sent him as assistant storeman to the go-down at Mehaw, the village where Tun Gyaw had had his fateful gamble and Archie had tried to cure goitre.

Nga Moh was most terribly distressed when he left by river steamer for Mehaw. "What can I do, Thakin, to clear myself?"

"You could find who did it," I suggested. "Clean your ears out; there are many things that the police do not know, but the people in the village know."

There was no harm in setting a thief to catch a thief.

In a week he was back to see me. "There is a girl in Mehaw called Ma Kywai," he said.

"Her mother is a widow," I said.

"She used to take pleasure with Thakin Galay. You know that?"

"That was long ago," I said. "That is all over. Before I left for the Andamans it was all over."

"While you were in the Andamans, she went to Thakin Galay three times. Was it then all over?"

"She went once and he turned her away," I answered. "I know this."

"But in the village she says that she went three times," said Nga Moh. "She says this openly, but there is something else which she does not talk of openly. Five days after the dacoity a strange woman came to stay at the house of Ma Kywai's mother. She stayed for three days, but no one know who she was."

"Would you have me tell the police this?" I asked.

He was vehement. "You must say nothing to the police, or more suspicion will fall on my head. I beg you to come to Mehaw and see the village headman."

I did not like acting the private sleuth, but, after all, I had put him up to it in the first place. Before going to Mehaw I wrote an urgent note to Archie. "Ma Kywai asserts she went to your camp three times. You say once. Can you fix the exact date she was with you? This is important."

I went to see the headman as soon as I arrived in Mehaw. Ma Kywai had certainly been to see the Thakin Galay on three occasions, he said. He gave me the three dates, as he remembered them by other incidents.

"Do you know anything about the strange woman who stayed with them here?" I asked.

"Yes, an aunt," said the headman. "As a woman and a relation, she wasn't registered."

"Did you see her?"

He shook his head.

"Did anyone see her?"

"Would anyone want to see anyone's aunt?" the headman asked, with devastating logic.

"That might be the reason for calling whoever it was, an aunt," I said. "You'd better find out quietly whether anybody saw or spoke to 'her'."

I sent word back immediately to the police to join me in Mehaw. My suspicions were aroused. There was something very suspicious about this 'aunt' of Ma Kywai's.

"Where did this aunt come from?" asked the Superintendent of Police.

"From Kadû in the Upper Shweli River, of course," Ma Kywai's mother said again.

Kadû bordered on the Shan States and U San Din was immediately summoned and rushed there in the company of the Police Superintendent.

There he at once identified San Hla, living as a wealthy young Shan who had recently made money trading in jade-mines. San Hla was immediately arrested on suspicion, and in his house were found numbers of the notes identifiable as stolen from Archie. But there was no sign of the stolen gun.

The Superintendent let it drop that if he could not find the shot-gun, Ma Kywai and her mother would certainly have to be arrested. A beautiful girl, he said. It would be a pity if she should suffer.

San Hla confessed that before he arrived at Mehaw, he had hidden the shot-gun inside a large nyaung tree. At Ma Kywai's house he had dressed in the clothes of a woman, an unforgivable crime for a Buddhist, something only the meanest of criminals would do.

Archie got back his gun, but the breech was so rusted that it would not open and the barrels were pitted beyond recovery. "That was my father's gun," he said. "The old man would have been absolutely livid to see it like this!"

By the time that San Hla came up for trial, the police had combed their files and discovered beyond doubt that he was also Hgnet Pyaw, alias Soe Bone, wanted for murder during the rebellion. There was no doubt that before very long he would be an inmate of the Port Blair retreat.

I thought that Nga Moh would be pleased. But he came to me to complain with disgust of the inefficiency of the police.

"These things are not true, Thakin. That young man, San Hla, they talk as if he was the aunt or uncle of Ma Kywai. All the world knows he was her lover. When she said that she had been to see the Thakin Galay she had been of course to see San Hla. He told her to visit the Thakin Galay and steal his keys to make impressions. Ma Kywai's real uncle is a clever blacksmith and the last time that she went to see San Hla, she was taking him the copies of the keys." He was indignant. "And why do they not take me into the police force, who have helped them?"

"Nga Moh," I said. "We have had enough of the truth to bring San Hla to justice. A witness must speak the truth, the whole truth and nothing but the truth. But it is enough for the police to tell enough of the truth to bring justice. If they did what you wish, they would have to expose the little love affair folly of the Thakin Galay with Ma Kywai. What is the need of that, when he has learnt his lesson? They are grateful to you for your part, but if you want to make a new life here in Burma, it is better that we should not talk of these things. A thief who catches a thief is not loved by others."

He looked up stroking his old mandarin moustache.

"You have been good, Thakin," he said. "Grant me a last favour."

"I will grant you anything I can, Nga Moh. We have seen many good things together." I thought of those good things, the way the convicts became free men away from their guards, and assured of their opium, the queer afternoon by the teal lake, but most of all that evening when we saw the spotted deer and he came up fearless with his does, because the jungle threatened him and his, more than any human being, until a voice spoke. "What is it you want?" I asked.

The old man with a gesture of his hand took Burma in and held it between us. "It is not as when I was a boy. Perhaps if I was growing up now . . . But I belong to the Andamans now. When you go to your country, send me back to Port Blair—I can work there. Here I listen for the sound of the sea. And perhaps you will come to the Andamans again."

I took him to Rangoon with me. That sinister phrase they used of the Andamans, 'The Isles of No Return', had another less ominous meaning. Convicts did not come back, because they did not want to. The Andamans were in a sense Isles of Acceptance.

But they were not Isles of Acceptance as far as the Bombine were concerned. "The figures estimated for the cost were astronomical," said the report.

I saw the last of the Andamans, when I was homeward bound with Susan on a Bibby liner. I had been trying to explain to her, and incidentally to myself, the confusion of feelings in which I had found myself during the past months. There had been the rebellion during which all that had been fine and beautiful and invigorating in my life in the Burmese forests had been threatened with extinction. The trust which had been the basis of working with the oozies had been shot through with suspicion, and I had wondered if it could ever be re-established. This was what had made the fight with Tun Gyaw such a disturbing experience. And this was what had made the Andaman adventure so immensely rewarding: to discover that among a gang of convicts sentenced for crimes of violence the spirit of trust could work like a leaven and bring them back to common humanity.